D0122900

MECHANICS·
MERCANTILE
LIBRARY.

The Pioneer Woman

The Pioneer Woman

Black Heels to Tractor Wheels

A Love Story

Ree Drummond

MECHANICS' INSTITUTE LIBRARY
57 Post Street
San Francisco, CA 94104
(415) 393-0101

WILLIAM MORROW
An Imprint of HarperCollins*Publishers*

THE PIONEER WOMAN. Copyright © 2011 by Ree Drummond. All rights reserved. Printed in the United States of America. No part of this book may be used or reproduced in any manner whatsoever without written permission except in the case of brief quotations embodied in critical articles and reviews. For information address HarperCollins Publishers, 10 East 53rd Street, New York, NY 10022.

HarperCollins books may be purchased for educational, business, or sales promotional use. For information please write: Special Markets Department, HarperCollins Publishers, 10 East 53rd Street, New York, NY 10022.

FIRST EDITION

Designed by Lisa Stokes

Library of Congress Cataloging-in-Publication Data
Drummond, Ree.
  The pioneer woman : black heels to tractor wheels—a love story / Ree Drummond. — 1st ed.
    p. cm.
  ISBN 978-0-06-199716-7
1. Drummond, Ree. 2. Oklahoma—Biography. I. Title.
  CT275.D8764A3 2011
  976.6′054092—dc22
  [B]
                                                                      2010038872

11 12 13 14 15 OV/RRD 10 9 8 7 6 5 4 3 2 1

92
D795

MAY 2 6 2011

For my children . . . Mama loves you.
For my husband . . . Mama loves you, too.

MAY 2 6 2011

CONTENTS

INTRODUCTION

*O*NE DAY a few years ago, I began jotting down the story of how I met and married my husband. I got as far as the middle of the first chapter, then abruptly stopped writing, stuck it in a drawer, and went on to other things. Sometime later, after waking up with an uncharacteristic case of writer's block, I pulled the roughly written story out of the drawer. A regular blogger, I was brain-dead that day, and while I was certain few people would find my love story interesting, I wanted to give the readers of my site something new. I said a couple of Hail Marys, hoped they wouldn't hate it, and posted it on my website.

To my surprise, readers responded . . . and asked for another chapter. I wrote it that same night. A second chapter led to a third, and then a fourth. Encouraged by readers of ThePioneerWoman.com, I began posting regular, weekly installments of my real-life online serial love story, complete with romantic tension and cliffhangers at the end of each episode. It became an integral part of my writing routine for over eighteen months, and my friends and readers were there with me every step of the way. I loved the entire experience. I loved going back . . . and remembering.

By the end of that time frame, I'd written over forty installments and had only gotten as far as our wedding day. I decided to end the online version at that point, then immediately began writing the next part of the story, which continues through our first year of marriage.

This book is the complete, combined story—both the rip-roaring romance novel–style saga that I posted on my website (with some new material), which begins the night I met my husband and ends when we leave for our honeymoon, and a new section, which documents the early days of our life as a married couple.

I hope you love the story.

I hope it makes you smile.

I hope it reminds you of the reasons you fell in love in the first place.

And if you haven't yet found love, I hope it shows you that love often can come to find you instead . . . probably when you least expect it.

Part One

Chapter One
ONCE UPON A TIME IN THE MIDWEST

FORGET THIS, I said to myself as I lay sprawled on the bed in which I grew up. In my Oklahoma hometown on a self-imposed pit stop, I was mired in a papery swamp of study guides, marked-up drafts of my résumé, listings of available Chicago apartments, and a J.Crew catalog, from which I'd just ordered a $495 wool gabardine winter coat in olive, not chocolate, because I'm a redhead, and because Chicago, I reminded myself, is a tad more nippy than Los Angeles, which I'd just left weeks earlier. I'd been at it all week—searching, editing, shopping, ordering—and I was worn smooth out, my eyes watery from reading, my middle finger pruney from licking and flipping through pages, my favorite fuzzy socks dingy and rank from languishing on my feet for two days straight. I needed a break.

I decided to head down to the J-Bar, a local dive where some of my friends were meeting for a Christmas break drink. I'd begged out earlier in the evening, but by now that glass of chardonnay seemed not only appealing but necessary. *Mandatory.* But I was a disheveled mess, the downside of not leaving one's bedroom for over forty-eight hours. Not that I had anyone to impress, anyway. It was my hometown, after all, the place that had raised me, and though relatively picturesque and affluent, it wasn't exactly the kind of town that required getting dressed to the nines to go out for wine.

With this in mind, I washed my face, threw on some black mascara—an absolute must for any fair-skinned redhead with light eyes—and released my hair from its tired ponytail. Throwing on a faded light-blue turtleneck and my favorite holey jeans, I dabbed some Carmex on my lips and blew out the door. Fifteen minutes later, I was in the company of my old friends and the chardonnay, feeling the kind of mellow buzz that comes not only from your first couple of sips of the night but also from the familiar contentment of being with people who've known you forever.

That's when I saw him—the cowboy—across the room. He was tall, strong, and mysterious, sipping bottled beer and wearing jeans and, I noticed, cowboy boots. And his *hair.* The stallion's hair was very short and silvery gray—much too gray for how young his face said he was, but just gray enough to send me through the roof with all sorts of fantasies of Cary Grant in *North by Northwest.* Gracious, but he was a vision, this Marlboro Man–esque, rugged character across the room. After a few minutes of staring, I inhaled deeply, then stood up. I needed to see his hands.

I casually meandered to the section of the bar where he stood. Not wanting to appear obvious, I grabbed four cherries from the sectioned condiment tray and placed them on a paper napkin as I caught a glimpse of his hands. They were big and strong. Bingo.

Within minutes, we were talking.

He was a fourth-generation cattle rancher whose property was over an hour away from this cultured, corporate hometown of mine. His great-great-grandfather had emigrated from Scotland in the late 1800s and gradually made his way to the middle of the country, where he'd met and married a local gal and become a successful merchant. His sons would be the first in the family to purchase land and run cattle at the turn of the century, and their descendants would eventually establish themselves as cattle ranchers throughout the region.

Of course, I knew none of this as I stood before him in the bar that night, shuffling my Donald Pliner spiked boots and looking nervously around the room. Looking down. Looking at my friends. Trying my best

not to look too gazingly into his icy blue-green eyes or, worse, drool all over him. Besides, I had other things to do that night: study, continue refining my résumé, polish all of my beloved black pumps, apply a rejuvenating masque, maybe watch my VHS tape of *West Side Story* for the 3,944th time. But before I knew it an hour had passed, then two. We talked into the night, the room blurring around us as it had done at the dance in *West Side Story* when Tony and Maria first saw each other across a crowd of people. *Tonight, tonight, it all began tonight.* My friends giggled and sipped wine at the table where I'd abandoned them earlier in the night, oblivious to the fact that their redheaded amiga had just been struck by a lightning bolt.

Before I could internally break into the second chorus of song, my version of Tony—this mysterious cowboy—announced abruptly that he had to go. *Go?* I thought. *Go where? There's no place on earth but this smoky bar* . . . . But there was for him: he and his brother had plans to cook Christmas turkeys for some needy folks in his small town. *Mmmm. He's nice, too,* I thought as a pang stabbed my insides.

"Bye," he said with a gentle smile. And with that, his delicious boots walked right out of the J-Bar, his dark blue Wranglers cloaking a body that I was sure had to have been chiseled out of granite. My lungs felt tight, and I still smelled his scent through the bar smoke in the air. I didn't even know his name. I prayed it wasn't Billy Bob.

I was sure he'd call the next morning at, say, 9:34. It was a relatively small community; he could find me if he wanted to. But he didn't. Nor did he call at 11:13 or 2:49 or at any other time that day, or week, or month. Throughout that time, if I ever allowed myself to remember his eyes, his biceps, his smoldering, quiet manner, which was so drastically unlike those of all the silly city boys I'd bothered with over the past few years, a salty wave of disappointment would wash over me. But it didn't really matter anyway, I'd tell myself. I was headed to Chicago. To a new city. To a new life. I had zero business getting attached to anyone around there, let alone some Wrangler -wearing cowboy with salt-and-pepper hair. Cowboys ride horses, after all, and they wear bandanas around their necks and pee outside and whittle. They name their children Dolly and Travis and listen to country music.

Talk about my polar opposite.

*S*IX MONTHS earlier, I sat with J over sushi, telling him I was leaving Los Angeles. "I'm just going home for a pit stop," I told him. He took a nervous bite of sea urchin.

I'd been in L.A. for years and had spent four of them with him. Since blowing into the city as a college freshman, I'd spent my time in the sprawling city, breathing in all the culinary, retail, and urban pleasures the city had to offer. Having come from the relative calm of the Midwest, I was an absolute kid in a candy shop in Los Angeles. My four years at USC had been marked not just by classes, exams, and essays, but by celebrity sightings, delicious cuisine, and boys. I'd experienced it all—partying on the Sunset Strip, running into Sean and Madonna at a movie, kissing James Garner in an elevator, and surviving the aftermath of the Rodney King verdict. And strangely, suddenly, as I sat at the sushi bar with J that night, I knew I'd had enough.

Not with Los Angeles. With J.

The sweet Southern California boy sitting before me had no idea any American land existed east of the Mojave Desert. We'd been joined at the hip since college, and now, four years later, I was announcing in between mouthfuls of cucumber rolls and tamago that I was leaving Los Angeles and heading home instead of following him to San Francisco, where he'd accepted a new engineering job the week earlier. He'd taken the job because it was a great opportunity, and because he assumed I'd move there with him; this seemed the logical next step for a couple who'd dated four years. Initially, I thought I'd go, too. But somehow, in the week after he'd taken the job, my better sense had shaken me violently by the shoulders.

I didn't want to stay in California. I didn't want to stay with J. I wanted

out of there; I wanted to leave. It had been building for a while, starting with a tiny ache, for life as I'd known it before, and culminating—once J accepted his new job—in a full-blown resolve that I wanted to head back to the Midwest. Chicago probably. It would be closer to home—one short plane ride away rather than two, sometimes three legs and an entire day of travel. I'd be closer to friends, closer to family.

I'd be in a climate more suited to my complexion.

Most important, I'd be away from the chokehold of what I'd realized was a textbook dead-end relationship. If I didn't leave now, it would only get harder.

"I'm not going," I told him. "It just doesn't feel right to me." The onslaught of one-liners commenced.

"I just can't follow you up there like this."

"I have to learn to stand on my own two feet."

"I just don't know what I'm doing here anymore."

The pathetic clichés spewed from my mouth as thick as the wasabi paste I stirred into my soy sauce. I hated the way I sounded.

"I'm just going home for a while . . . to clear the cobwebs," I continued.

"But you'll be right back, right?" J asked. He took a healthy shot of sake.

J.

He'd never quite gotten it.

A FEW WEEKS later I walked through the front door of my parents' house, my normally fair and freckled skin a forced golden brown from walking to and from my car in L.A. for the last several years. Throwing down my California bags in the foyer, I darted upstairs and plopped facedown onto the bed of my youth. I fell asleep almost immediately and hardly left the solace of my 300-thread-count faded peach sheets for a week. My beloved family dog Puggy Sue cuddled up next to me and didn't move for days, her soft velvet ears the perfect security blanket for my confused, in-limbo heart.

My brother Mike sat with me sometimes, too. Eighteen months my senior, he had nothing better to do. His developmental disabilities allowed him to be perfectly content patting my head, telling me how pretty I was, and sharing with me whether he'd had biscuits and gravy or a *"ch-ch-ch-cheese omblett"* for breakfast that morning. I'd take it all in as if I were listening to the State of the Union address. It was just so good to be home. Eventually Mike would ask me to give him a ride to Fire Station no. 3, his regular hangout, and I'd tell him no, I was way too busy. Then he'd leave in a huff and I'd go back to sleep for a while. It was glorious.

I'd wake up occasionally, long enough to thumb through the hilariously dated magazines on my bedside table—one *Seventeen* magazine had Phoebe Cates on the cover—and work on my cuticles and just lie there and stare at my taupe floral wallpaper, mentally rearranging all the delicate white flowers, as I'd always done as a little girl.

I cried sometimes, too. The truth was, I'd given J so, so much. As strong and self-assured as I'd always wanted to believe I was, I'd somehow pathetically allowed myself to become uncomfortably dependent on him in California. I was ashamed I'd allowed myself to settle into that groove— that deep ditch of insecurity and fear into which so many young women are doomed to plunge at least once in their lives. Once . . . if they're lucky. I also cried as a response to the sheer relief I felt, as if 80,000 pounds of compressed emotional air had been released from my gut. I exhaled for days and days; it kept coming out in a steady, hissy stream. I cried because I'd left J, not the other way around, which really would have sucked.

I cried because he was cute, and he'd become a habit.

I cried because I missed him.

To KILL time, I began having dinner with my grandmother, Ga-Ga, and her small circle of close friends in their small town twenty miles away. They had a standing Tuesday-night dinner date at the Ideal Café, and had invited me to tag along. My first dinner with Ga-Ga, Ruthie, Delphia, and Dorothy turned out to be grueling and brutal; I ordered vegetarian side dishes of mashed potatoes and canned green beans and watched the ladies eat horrible things like liver and onions, chicken fried steak, and meat loaf as they talked about the upcoming banquet at the church, how much the Retired Teachers' bake sale had raised, and how much the neighborhood kids had grown. Then they'd all split two pieces of pie—always rhubarb and lemon meringue—while I ordered another Diet Coke and looked restlessly at my watch. I couldn't believe how important they considered all of this to be. Didn't they know how small their town was? How large Los Angeles was? Didn't they know there was a whole world out there? Didn't they ever get bored? I loved Ga-Ga so much, but her small-town scene was almost too much for me to take. I was meant for larger things than these.

Much larger things.

When their pie was finally finished, we'd all bid one another farewell, and I'd go home and get in bed for two more days.

Finally, one morning a couple of weeks later, I sprang out of bed and never looked back. What did I have to mope about? I had a little money in the bank and no real expenses, thanks to my new cushy, rent-free digs in my parents' home on the golf course. I could take my time planning for Chicago. And J, my constant companion for the past 1,460 days (give or take an hour), was nowhere in sight. It didn't take long before the reality of my youth hit home and I began to realize, in all my midtwenties freedom, that I was a free agent.

Even if J didn't quite know it yet.

*T*RACY, a hunky blond attorney from my hometown, was my first voyage into Post-J Dating. We had four dates and laughed the whole time, but he was way too old—nearly *thirty*—and probably found me flighty. After Tracy came Jack, a British assistant tennis pro at the country club. He was gorgeous and I loved his accent, but at two years my junior, he was *way* too young. Next came an old boyfriend from church camp who lived in a faraway town and heard I was back in Oklahoma. Sweet, but a no-go for the long term. A couple of other miscellaneous, unremarkable dinner dates followed.

That's when I met Mr. B., a man sixteen years my senior and a three handicap, and not a half-bad kisser.

That's basically the extent of what Mr. B. and I did together—kissed. Tracy had sprung for a couple of movies and a dinner or two. Jack and I had taken a couple of walks with his dog. But Mr. B. and I just sat around and smooched. It was all his idea. It was as if he'd never heard of the concept before me, and my lips were in a constant state of chap. It was great, though; there were no strings, no risks, no great rewards. But after a month, I was frankly tired of having to buy so much lip balm, so I delicately broke things off. He called me crying the next night, telling me he'd just added me as the sole beneficiary on his life insurance policy. Sometime during the course of the month, Mr. B. had decided that I was The One, the answer to all of his never-married prayers. He'd figured we'd wind up getting married, he said, and he just couldn't believe I was breaking up with him when we were so clearly perfect for each other. He'd already begun planning our marriage, apparently, right down to the reception menu and the middle name of our redheaded, blue-eyed, fair-skinned third-born child. He wasn't wasting any time.

Mr. B. carried on and on and cried—blubbered—for two whole hours. And as I listened, trying my best to be gentle and compassionate, I actually found myself missing J, who never was much the kissing type or the demonstrator-of-love-and-affection type but on the other hand wasn't prone to making illogical, ridiculous plans and breaking down in tears.

This, in turn, made me miss city life and start getting serious about Chicago. As eager as I'd been to flee L.A., I knew, based on my brief time at home that an urban environment was really where I belonged. I missed the conveniences, the coffee shops on every corner, and the book-stores open till midnight. I missed the take-out food galore and the little makeup shops and the Korean nail salons where ladies would eagerly swarm me and rub my shoulders in five-minute intervals until I ran out of money.

I missed the anonymity—the ability to run to the market without run-ning into my third-grade teacher.

I missed the nightlife—the knowledge that if I wanted to, there was always an occasion to get dressed up and head out for dinner and drinks.

I missed the restaurants—the Asian, the Thai, the Italian, the Indian. I was already tired of mashed potatoes and canned green beans.

I missed the culture—the security that comes from being on the tour-ing schedule of the major Broadway musicals.

I missed the shopping—the funky boutiques, the eclectic shops, the browsing.

I missed the city. I needed to get on the ball.

That's when Kev called. *Kev.* My first love, my first obsession with any-thing that wasn't related to Billy Idol or Duran Duran. We'd dated in high school and had remained in deep, abiding, you-were-mine-first love, off and on, for the previous eight years. We'd been involved with other people during that time, of course, but Kev had always, always been there. He'd been mine, after all, before he'd been anyone else's. And I'd been his. And seeing his name on caller ID the evening I broke things off with Mr. B. was like lifeblood being pumped into my veins.

Kev—what a brilliant idea! He'd just graduated from law school and was most likely trying to decide where he was going next. Yes, of course. *Kev.* Finally. We were adults now, and we were familiar, comfortable, and free. The possibilities rushed wildly into my imagination, and within seconds it all became perfectly clear to me: Kev and I, together, could be the perfect solution. I already knew everything there was to know about him; there'd be no nasty secrets hiding under the surface, and we wouldn't even have to go through that nettlesome flirtation/courting stage, an appealing prospect given the dates I'd had. Rather than starting all over, Kev and I could just pick up where we'd left off; I could be packed within two days and join him in whatever big-city locale he'd picked: Chicago, Philadelphia, D.C. I didn't care. I had to get away from Mr. B.'s lips. And his life insurance policy.

"Hey . . . it's Kev," the voice on the other end of the line said. He sounded exactly the same.

"Kev!" I said, with a combination of excitement, anticipation, nostalgia, and hope.

"Hey, guess what?" he said. My imagination ran wild: *He's gotten a job and wants me to come with him. Go ahead, Kev. I'm ready. And the answer is a resounding yes.*

"I'm getting married," Kev said. My knees went weak.

The next day, I began making plans for Chicago.

A month later, I met the cowboy in the smoky bar and he turned my soul to mush. In the four months that followed, I would continue to make preparations to move. While I'd occasionally find myself haunted by the rugged Marlboro Man character I'd met in the J-Bar that Christmas, I continued to tell myself it was a good thing he'd never called. I didn't need anything derailing my resolve to get back to civilization.

Back where normal people lived.

I DECIDED TO stick close to home through my oldest brother Doug's wedding that April and leave for Chicago a couple of weeks later. I'd always intended for my time at home to be a pit stop, anyway; before too long, Chicago would be my new home. I'd always loved it there—the pulse, the climate, the cute Catholic boys. Moving there seemed such a natural fit, and it would be a great step toward my separating permanently from J, who was technically still in the picture, albeit two thousand miles away.

J and I had not officially broken up. I'd been away from California for months—we'd even visited each other at our respective locations here and there. But in the weeks leading up to my brother's wedding, I'd been distancing myself. The more time I spent away from him, the more I realized just how much of our relationship had been based on my dependence on him during my years in Los Angeles. He was from Orange County, born and bred in Newport Beach, and in J (his parents, too), I'd found a cozy, secure home so far away from my own. I had a place to go on weekends, when the USC campus was a ghost town; I had a family that was always glad to see me when I visited; I'd found a place that was familiar. Comfortable. Easy.

It was around this time that J began calling and pressuring me to move back to California—something I knew wasn't going to happen, though I hadn't yet mustered up the courage to tell him for good. Chicago would provide that opportunity; I just had to hold out a little longer before I'd break the news I was going. J wanted to be together again, wanted to make it work, wanted to work toward getting married. *Work toward getting married.* There was something about the use of the word *work* in that context that just didn't seem to fit. But J kept at it; he wanted things back to the way they'd been. Back when I was in California. Back when I was all his.

But I was over J. My eclectic assortment of dates over the previous few months had only served to cement that I wasn't at all ready to settle down, and that any passion I'd felt for J during the first year or so of our relationship had long since been replaced by a need for stability during my time in Los Angeles—a city which, in between all the parties and the shopping and the all-night glitz, can sometimes be a terribly lonely place.

The week before my brother's wedding, I decided it was time. Too cowardly and lacking in eloquence to adequately explain over the phone, I penned a long, drippy letter to J, effectively uninviting him to our family wedding, which he'd made plans to attend, and euphemizing all the reasons I thought we should end things for good. To my surprise, he agreed not to come to the wedding but eerily avoided talking further about our relationship. "You can just come here in a few weeks," he said. I wasn't sure if he realized what my letter had said. But that had been my relationship with J: Clear communication had never been our strong suit.

The weekend of my brother's wedding, I wound up in the company of Walrus, my brother's best friend from Connecticut. Bespectacled and affectionate, he turned out to be just the fun diversion I needed that weekend, and my sister Betsy wept and wailed and gnashed her teeth that she was only a freshman in college and too young to date a twenty-seven-year-old. Walrus was as cute as it gets, and we were like peas and carrots, sitting together at the rehearsal dinner and joking around at the party afterward. We stayed up late that night, talking and sipping beer and not doing anything either of us would regret. During the ceremony itself, Walrus smiled and winked at me. I smiled back, mostly because I was feeling free and giddy about Chicago. About my freedom. About my future.

Walrus had been just what the doctor ordered, if only for that weekend. He was the perfect date, kissing me good night after the reception and saying, "See you at the next wedding." So when all the festivities were over, my brother and his new wife left for Hawaii, and my phone rang late Sunday afternoon, I was sure it had to be Walrus, calling from the airport to say a quick good-bye, and maybe go on and on about what a great time he'd had with me all weekend.

"Hello?" I answered the phone.

"Hello . . . Ree?" The strong male voice on the other end said.

"Hey, Walrus!" I shrieked enthusiastically. There was a long, silent pause.

"Walrus?" I repeated.

The deep voice began again. "You might not remember me—we met at the J-Bar last Christmas?"

It was the Marlboro Man.

Chapter Two

YOUNG HEARTS AFIRE

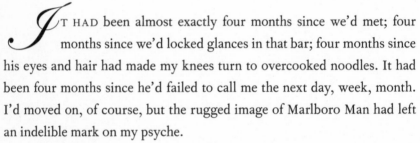

*I*T HAD been almost exactly four months since we'd met; four months since we'd locked glances in that bar; four months since his eyes and hair had made my knees turn to overcooked noodles. It had been four months since he'd failed to call me the next day, week, month. I'd moved on, of course, but the rugged image of Marlboro Man had left an indelible mark on my psyche.

But I'd just begun my Chicago planning before I'd met him that night and had continued the next day. And now, at the end of April, I was just about set to go.

"Oh, hi," I said nonchalantly. I was leaving soon. I didn't need this guy.

"How've you been?" he continued. Yikes. That voice. It was gravelly and deep and whispery and dreamy all at the same time. I didn't know until that moment that it had already set up permanent residence in my bones. My marrow remembered that voice.

"Good," I replied, focusing my efforts on appearing casual, confident, and strong. "I'm just gearing up to move to Chicago, actually."

"No kidding?" he said. "When are you going?"

"Just a couple of weeks," I replied.

"Oh . . ." He paused. "Well . . . would you like to go out to dinner this week?"

This was always the awkward part. I could never imagine being a guy.

"Um, sure," I said, not really seeing the point of going out with him, but also knowing it was going to be next to impossible for me to turn down a date with the first and only cowboy I'd ever been attracted to. "I'm pretty free all this week, so—"

"How 'bout tomorrow night?" he cut in. "I'll pick you up around seven."

He didn't know it at the time, but that single take-charge moment, his instantaneous transformation from a shy, quiet cowboy to this confident, commanding presence on the phone, affected me very profoundly. My interest was officially ablaze.

I OPENED THE front door of my parents' house the next evening. His starched blue denim shirt caught my eye only seconds before his equally blue eyes did.

"Hello," he said, smiling.

Those eyes. They were fixed on mine, and mine on his, for more seconds than is customary at the very beginning of a first date. My knees—the knees that had turned to rubber bands that night four months earlier in a temporary fit of illogical lust—were once again as firm as cooked spaghetti.

"Hello," I answered. I was wearing sleek black pants, a violet V-necked sweater, and spiked black boots—a glaring contrast to the natural, faded denim ensemble he'd chosen. Fashionwise, we were hilariously mismatched. I could sense that he noticed this, too, as my skinny heels obnoxiously clomped along the pavement of my parents' driveway.

We talked through dinner; if I ate, I wasn't aware of it. We talked about my childhood on the golf course; about his upbringing in the country. About my dad, the doctor; about his dad, the rancher. About my life-long commitment to ballet; about his lifelong passion for football. About my brother Mike; about his older brother, Todd, who had died when he was a teenager. About Los Angeles and celebrities; cows and agriculture. By the end of the evening, I had no idea what exactly I'd even said. All I knew was, I was riding in a Ford F250 diesel pickup with a cowboy—and there was nowhere else on earth I wanted to be.

He walked me to the door—the same one to which I'd been escorted many times before by pimply high school boys and a few miscellaneous suitors along the way. But this time was different. *Bigger.* I felt it. I wondered for a moment if he felt it, too.

That's when the spike heel of my boot caught itself on a small patch of crumbling mortar on my parents' redbrick sidewalk. In an instant, I saw my life and any ounce of pride remaining in my soul pass before my eyes as my body lurched forward. I was going to bite it for sure—and right in front of the Marlboro Man. I was an idiot, I told myself, a dork, a klutz of the highest order. I wanted desperately to snap my fingers and magically wind up in Chicago, where I belonged, but my hands were too busy darting in front of my torso, hoping to brace my body from the fall.

But someone caught me. Was it an angel? In a way. It was Marlboro Man, whose tough upbringing on a working cattle ranch had produced the quick reflexes necessary to save me, his uncoordinated date, from certain wipeout. Once the danger was over, I laughed from nervous embarrassment. Marlboro Man chuckled gently. He was still holding my arms, in the same strong cowboy grip he'd used to rescue me moments earlier. Where were my knees? They were no longer part of my anatomy.

I looked at Marlboro Man. He wasn't chuckling anymore. He was standing right in front of me . . . and he was still holding my arms.

I'D ALWAYS been boy crazy. From the high school lifeguards at the pool when I was a little girl to the Izod-wearing caddies that traipsed the golf course, cute boys were simply one of my favorite things. By my midtwenties, I'd met and enthusiastically dated practically every category of cute boy under the sun. There was Kev the Irish Catholic; Skipper the Edgy; Shane the Hood; Collin the Playful; J the Surfer; Mr. B. the Unstable; and many others in between. I'd gone on dates with every flavor of cute boy under the sun.

Except for one. Cowboy. I'd never even spoken to a cowboy, let alone ever known one personally, let alone ever dated one, and certainly, absolutely, positively never kissed one—until that night on my parents' front porch, a mere couple of weeks before I was set to begin my new life in Chicago. After valiantly rescuing me from falling flat on my face just moments earlier, this cowboy, this western movie character standing in front of me, was at this very moment, with one strong, romantic, mind-numbingly perfect kiss, inserting the category of "Cowboy" into my dating repertoire forever.

The kiss. *I'll remember this kiss till my very last breath,* I thought to myself. *I'll remember every detail. Strong, calloused hands gripping my upper arms. Five o'clock shadow rubbing gently against my chin. Faint smell of boot leather in the air. Starched denim shirt against my palms, which have gradually found their way around his trim, chiseled waist....*

I don't know how long we stood there in the first embrace of our lives together. But I do know that when that kiss was over, my life as I'd always imagined it was over, too.

I just didn't know it yet.

*H*E CALLED the next morning at seven. I was sound asleep, still dreaming about the kiss that had rocked my existence the night before. Marlboro Man, on the other hand, had been up since five and, he would explain, had waited two hours before calling me, since he reckoned I probably wasn't the get-up-early type. And I wasn't. I'd never seen any practical reason for any normal person to get out of bed before 8:00 A.M., and besides that, the kiss had been pretty darn earth shattering. I needed to sleep that thing off.

"Good morning," he said. I gasped. That voice. There it was again.

"Oh, hi!" I replied, shooting out of bed and trying to act like I'd been up for hours doing step aerobics and trimming my mom's azalea bushes. And hiking.

"You asleep?" he asked.

"Nope, nope, not at all!" I replied. "Not one bit." My voice was thick and scratchy.

"You were asleep, weren't you?" I guess he knew a late sleeper when he heard one.

"No, I wasn't—I get up really early," I said. "I'm a real morning person." I concealed a deep, total-body yawn.

"That's strange—your voice sounds like you were still asleep," Marlboro Man persisted. He wasn't letting me off the hook.

"Oh . . . well . . . it's just that I haven't talked to anyone yet today, plus I've kind of been fighting a little sinus trouble," I said. That was attractive. "But I've been up for quite a while."

"Yeah? What have you been doing?" he asked. He was enjoying this.

"Oh, you know. Stuff." Stuff. Good one, Ree.

"Really? Like, what kind of stuff?" he asked. I heard him chuckle softly, the same way he'd chuckled when he'd caught me the night before. That chuckle could quiet stormy waters. Bring about world peace.

"Oh, just stuff. Early morning stuff. Stuff I do when I get up really early in the morning. . . ." I tried again to sound convincing.

"Well," he said, "I don't want to keep you from your 'early morning stuff.' I just wanted to tell you . . . I wanted to tell you I had a really good time last night."

"You did?" I replied, picking sleepy sand from the corner of my right eye.

"I did," he said.

I smiled, closing my eyes. What was happening to me? This cowboy—this sexy cowboy who'd suddenly galloped into my life, who'd instantly plunged me into some kind of vintage romance novel—had called me within hours of kissing me on my doorstep, just to tell me he'd had a good time.

"Me, too," was all I could say. Boy, was I on a roll. *You know, stuff,* and *Me, too,* all in the same conversation. This guy was sure to be floored by my eloquence. I was so smitten, I couldn't even formulate coherent words.

I was in trouble.

*W*E HAD a second date that night, then a third, and then a fourth. And after each date, my new romance novel protagonist called me, just to seal the date with a sweet word.

For date five, he invited me to his house on the ranch. We were clearly on some kind of a roll, and now he wanted me to see where he lived. I was in no position to say no.

Since I knew his ranch was somewhat remote and likely didn't have many restaurants nearby, I offered to bring groceries and cook him dinner. I agonized for hours over what I could possibly cook for this strapping new man in my life; clearly, no mediocre cuisine would do. I reviewed all the dishes in my sophisticated, city-girl arsenal, many of which I'd picked up during my years in Los Angeles. I finally settled on a non-vegetarian winner: Linguine with Clam Sauce—a favorite from our family vacations in Hilton Head.

I made the delicious, aromatic masterpiece of butter, garlic, clams, lemon, wine, and cream in Marlboro Man's kitchen in the country, which was lined with old pine cabinetry. And as I stood there, sipping some of the leftover white wine and admiring the fruits of my culinary labor, I was utterly confident it would be a hit.

I had no idea who I was dealing with. I had no idea that this fourth-generation cattle rancher *doesn't eat minced-up little clams*, let alone minced-up little clams bathed in wine and cream and tossed with long, unwieldy noodles that are difficult to negotiate.

Still, he ate it. And lucky for him, his phone rang when he was more than halfway through our meal together. He'd been expecting an important call, he said, and excused himself for a good ten minutes. I didn't want him to go away hungry—big, strong rancher and all—so when I sensed he was close to getting off the phone, I took his plate to the stove and heaped another steaming pile of fishy noodles onto his plate. And when Marlboro Man returned to the table he smiled politely, sat down, and polished off over half of his second helping before finally pushing away from the table and announcing, "Boy, am I stuffed!"

I didn't realize at the time just how romantic a gesture that had been.

Later that night, after I'd arrived back home, I smiled when my phone began to ring. I'd grown accustomed to hearing his voice.

"Hey," the voice on the other end of the phone said. But the voice was different. It wasn't the least bit gravelly.

"We need to talk," he said.

It was J.

Chapter Three

REBEL'S RETURN

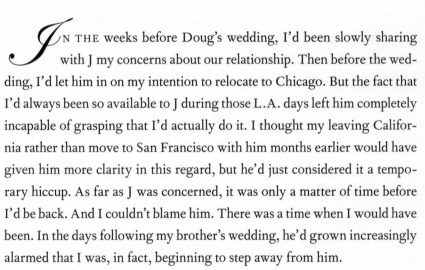

*I*N THE weeks before Doug's wedding, I'd been slowly sharing with J my concerns about our relationship. Then before the wedding, I'd let him in on my intention to relocate to Chicago. But the fact that I'd always been so available to J during those L.A. days left him completely incapable of grasping that I'd actually do it. I thought my leaving California rather than move to San Francisco with him months earlier would have given him more clarity in this regard, but he'd just considered it a temporary hiccup. As far as J was concerned, it was only a matter of time before I'd be back. And I couldn't blame him. There was a time when I would have been. In the days following my brother's wedding, he'd grown increasingly alarmed that I was, in fact, beginning to step away from him.

He absolutely couldn't believe it.

Meanwhile, I'd been busy spending every single evening with Marlboro Man, my new hot cowboy romance, getting more and more swept off my pedicured feet with each passing day. I'd hardly thought of J once that whole week. Naive on my part, but that's what Marlboro Man did to me: took away my ability to reason.

"I'm coming there tomorrow," J continued, an uncomfortable edge to his voice.

Oh no. What?

"You're coming *here* tomorrow?" I asked him. "Why?" My voice was cold. I didn't like the way I sounded.

"What do you mean, 'Why?'" he asked. "I need to talk to you, Ree."

"Well, we're talking now . . . ," I replied. "Let's just talk now." (And hurry, please, because Marlboro Man might call in a sec.)

"It might take a while," he said.

I looked at my watch. "I thought we'd kind of figured everything out," I said. "I thought you understood the state of things."

"The 'state of things'?" J bit back. "What the hell are you talking about?" This conversation was headed south, fast.

"I don't know what else there is to talk about," I replied. "I told you . . . I just think we need to move on."

"Well, I don't buy that," he shot back. "And I'm coming so we can talk about it."

"Wait a second," I said. "Don't I get a vote here?"

"No, actually you don't," he continued. "I don't think you really know what you're doing."

I was sleepy, I was giddy, and I was high on the scent of Marlboro Man's cologne, and I wasn't going to let J buzz-kill me out of it. "J," I said, mustering up every ounce of directness I could find, "don't come. There'd be no reason for you to come." I asked him to call me the next day if he wanted, and we said good-bye.

I took a deep breath, feeling wistful and wishing there was some way that relationships, if they had to end, could always end mutually and amicably—not with at least one of the parties feeling hurt and rejected. Then I fell asleep and dreamed the dreams I'd wanted to dream, about Marlboro Man and his boots and his lips and his strong, impossibly masculine embrace. And when my phone rang at seven the next morning, I was never more glad to hear Marlboro Man's voice on the other end. We made plans for that evening, and I gave nary a thought to the fact that California J had just announced the day before that he would be flying to Oklahoma to see me. Somehow, I thought my saying "don't come" would be sufficient. Now I realize just how formidable someone in the throes of a new love is, whether they're a cheating spouse or a defiant teenager or a flighty city girl in the arms of a cowboy; at that point, I was simply so drunk on the excitement Marlboro Man had brought me, nothing J said—not even "I'm coming tomorrow"—had truly registered.

*D*ENIAL. IT'S a powerful animal.

The only thing on my mind the next morning was my date that night with Marlboro Man. It had become my new hobby, my new vocation, my interest in life. Marlboro Man had invited me to his ranch; he said he'd cook dinner this time. I didn't much care what the plans were; I just wanted to see him again. Spend time in his presence. Get to know more about him, to kiss him good night for an hour. Or two. That was the only thing on my mind when I pulled out of my parents' driveway that morning to run a few errands.

When my car suddenly shook from a series of unsettling bumps, I knew something dire had happened. To my horror, when I looked in my rearview mirror, I saw that I'd run over Puggy Sue. Puggy Sue, my fat, prognathic canine who'd settled into my arms the day I'd returned from California and had become, in effect, my child during my time at home, was now lying on my parents' street, squealing, writhing, and unable to move her hind legs.

Hearing Puggy's yelps from inside the house, my mom darted outside, scooped her up, and immediately rushed her to the vet's office. Within thirty minutes, she called to tell me the news to which I'd already started resigning myself: Puggy Sue, my little package of fawn-colored love, was dead.

I spent the next several hours in a fetal position, reeling over the sudden death of Puggy. My brother Mike came over as soon as he heard the news and consoled me for over an hour, affectionately stroking my hair and saying, "It's ok-k-k-kay . . . you c-c-c-can get another pug," which only made me cry harder.

But when my phone rang around midafternoon, I shot out of bed, ordering Mike not to say a word. Then I took a deep breath, shook off my tears, and said, cheerfully, "Hello?"

It was Marlboro Man, calling to remind me of the complicated directions to his house on the ranch and asking what time I'd be arriving later, as he was growing more impatient by the minute—something, I reflected, that J had never said to me in all the years we'd been together. My stomach fell to the floor and my throat felt tight as I tried to talk to my new man as if nothing was wrong. When I hung up, Mike said, "Wh-wh-wh-who was dat?" I sniffed, wiped my nose, and told him it was a guy.

"Who?" Mike said.

"Some cowboy," I said. "I'm going to his house tonight."

"Ooooooh, c-c-c-can I come?" He had a devilish grin on his face.

I told him no, and scram, because I'm getting in the shower. Mike left in a huff.

As I blow-dried my hair in preparation for my date that night, I tried to take my mind off Puggy Sue by planning my wardrobe for the evening: Anne Klein jeans, charcoal gray ribbed turtleneck, and my signature spiky black boots. Perfect for a night at a cowboy's house on the ranch. Before putting on my makeup, I scurried to the kitchen and removed two of the spoons I kept in the freezer at all times. I laid them on my eyes to reduce the swelling—a trick I'd learned from a Brooke Shields book in the mid-1980s. I didn't want to look like someone who'd just spent the day sobbing over a dead family pet.

I began the hour-long drive to his ranch. Marlboro Man had picked me up and driven me home the night before, but I didn't have the heart to ask that of him again, and besides, I loved the drive. The slow transition from residential streets to unpaved county roads both calmed me down and excited me, probably because the man I was growing more crazy about every day was at the end of that unpaved county road. I wasn't sure how long I—or my wimpy tires—could keep this up.

My Toyota had just crossed the line from my county to his when the jarring ring of my analog car phone sounded. It must be Marlboro Man, I figured, checking on my whereabouts.

"Hello?" I picked up, dripping with romantic expectation.

"Hi," said the voice. It was J.

"Oh, hi," I said. I felt my chest fall in disappointment.

"I'm at the airport," he said.

Deep breath. Look at the prairie. Could this day get any worse? Exhale. "You're at the airport?" I asked.

"I told you I was coming," he said.

"J, no . . . seriously . . . ," I pleaded. This might just do me in. "I told you I didn't think it was a good idea."

"And I told you I was coming anyway," he countered.

I answered as clearly and plainly as I could. "Don't get on the plane, J. Don't come. I mean . . . do you understand what I'm saying? I'm asking you not to come."

"I'm at *your* airport," he said. "I'm already here!"

I pulled over on the shoulder of the two-lane highway and pinched the bridge of my nose between my thumb and index finger, squinting my eyes and trying with all my might to rewind to the part where I picked up my phone so I could convince myself I hadn't. "You're here?" I asked. "You're kidding, right?"

"No, I'm not kidding," J said. "I'm here. I need to see you."

I sat there on the quiet shoulder, stunned and deflated at the same time. This wasn't what I'd planned for that evening.

"J . . ." I paused and thought. "I don't know what to say. I mean, I asked you not to come. I told you it was not a good idea for you to come." I thought about Puggy Sue. Her soft, velvety ears.

"Where are you?" he asked.

"I'm . . . on my way to see a friend," I replied. *Please don't ask me any details*.

"Well, I think you need to change your plans, don't you?" he asked.

It was a valid question. And sitting there on the side of the highway, watching the sun set in front of me, I had no idea what I should do. On the one hand, I'd been very clear, as clear as I could have been, with J the day before. *Don't come;* I didn't think I'd left any ambiguity. On the other hand, J—a really decent guy under less intense circumstances—had been important to me for a long time and had, after all, traveled 1,800 miles to talk to me in person. Still, I wondered what good could possibly come from my going to see him. We could hardly get through a simple phone conversation without hitting total gridlock; how much better could that possibly be in person, particularly since I was 100 percent sure the relationship, from my perspective, was over? Plus, I'd run over Puggy Sue that day; I just didn't have much emotional fortitude left.

And besides . . . Marlboro Man was waiting for me.

With that, I pulled off the shoulder of the highway and continued driving west toward the ranch. "J, I'm not coming," I said. The pause on the other end of the line seemed endless. And the subsequent click from J hanging up on me was so quiet, it was almost deafening.

Chapter Four

A WOMAN CALLED HYSTERICAL

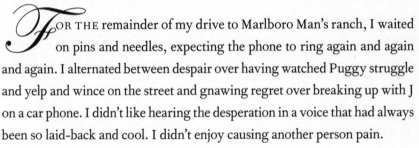

OR THE remainder of my drive to Marlboro Man's ranch, I waited on pins and needles, expecting the phone to ring again and again and again. I alternated between despair over having watched Puggy struggle and yelp and wince on the street and gnawing regret over breaking up with J on a car phone. I didn't like hearing the desperation in a voice that had always been so laid-back and cool. I didn't enjoy causing another person pain.

I'd deliberately gone about the breakup process slowly, compassionately, gently—taking great care not to hurt the one person who'd meant the most to me during all my years in California. But driving down that lonely highway, I realized the hard way that there was no such thing as gradually breaking someone's heart, no matter how much you think prolonging the process might help. There was always going to have to be The Moment—that instant in which the *break* in *breakup* actually executes, when the knife finally plunges into the gut, when all the plans and hopes that have ever gone in a relationship finally die a violent, bloody death. When the real pain begins.

Was I wrong, I wondered, not to turn around and give J an hour? Or two? But what could possibly come of the face-to-face meeting? Tears? Pleading? A proposal, God forbid? Anything was possible at that point, and I wasn't up for any of it. Right or wrong, I just knew I had to keep driving west toward Marlboro Man. My life with J was over.

MECHANICS' INSTITUTE LIBRARY
57 Post Street
San Francisco, CA 94104
(415) 393-0101

My phone remained dead silent until I pulled into the graveled driveway at Marlboro Man's house. Checking my eye makeup in the rearview mirror, I swallowed hard, trying to force away the grapefruit-size lump that had taken up residence in my throat. Then I thought of Puggy again. *Dear Lord,* I thought, *I loved that dog. She doesn't belong in the ground, she belongs on my lap. And her ears belong between my fingers. I loved those velvety ears.*

Then I saw the figure standing outside my car door: it was Marlboro Man, who'd come outside to greet me. His jeans were clean, his shirt tucked in and starched. I couldn't yet see his face, though, which was what I wanted most. Getting out of the car, I smiled and looked up, squinting. The western sunset was a backdrop behind his sculpted frame. It was such a beautiful sight, a stark contrast to all the ugliness that had surrounded me that day. He shut the car door behind me and moved in for a hug, which provided all the emotional fuel I needed to continue breathing. Finally, in that instant, I felt like things would be okay.

I smiled and acted cheerful, following him into the kitchen and not at all letting on that my day had sucked about as badly as a day could have sucked. I'd never been one to wear my feelings on my sleeve, and I sure wasn't going to let them splay out on what was merely my sixth date with the sexiest, most masculine man I'd ever met. But I knew I was a goner when Marlboro Man looked at me and asked, "You okay?"

You know when you're not okay, but then someone asks you if you're okay, and you say you're okay and act like you're okay, but then you start realizing you're not okay? Then you feel your nose start to tingle and your throat start to swell and your chin start to quiver and you tell yourself, *In the name of all that is good and holy, do not do this. Do not do this* . . . but you're powerless to stop it? And you try to blink it away and you finally think you've just about got it under control?

But then the cowboy standing in front of you smiles gently and says, "You sure?"

Those two simple words opened up the Floodgates of Hell. I smiled and laughed, embarrassed, even as two big, thick tears rolled down both my cheeks. Then I laughed again and blew a nice, clear explosion of snot from my nose. Of all the things that had happened that day, that single moment might have been the worst.

"Oh my gosh, I can't believe I'm doing this," I insisted as another pair of tears spilled out. I scrambled around the kitchen counter and found a paper towel, using it to dab the salty wetness on my face and the copious slime under my nose. "I am so, so sorry." I inhaled deeply, my chest beginning to contract and convulse. This was an ugly cry. I was absolutely horrified.

"Hey . . . what's wrong?" Marlboro Man asked. Bless his heart, he had to have been as uncomfortable as I was. He'd grown up on a cattle ranch, after all, with two brothers, *no* sisters, and a mother who was likely as lacking in histrionics as I wished I was at that moment. He led a quiet life out here on the ranch, isolated from the drama of city life. Judging from what he'd told me so far, he hadn't invited many women over to his house for dinner. And now he had one blubbering uncontrollably in his kitchen. *I'd better hurry up and enjoy this evening*, I told myself. *He won't be inviting me to any more dinners after this*. I blew my nose on the paper towel. I wanted to go hide in the bathroom.

Then he took my arm, in a much softer grip than the one he'd used on our first date when he'd kept me from biting the dust. "No, c'mon," he said, pulling me closer to him and securing his arms around my waist. I died a thousand deaths as he whispered softly, "What's wrong?"

What could I possibly say? *Oh, nothing, it's just that I've been slowly breaking up with my boyfriend from California and I uninvited him to my brother's wedding last week and I thought everything was fine and then he called last night after I got home from cooking you that Linguine with Clam Sauce you loved so much and he said he was flying here today and I told him not to because there really wasn't anything else we could possibly talk about and I thought he understood and while I was driving out here just now he called me and it just so happens he's at the airport right now but I decided not to go because I didn't want to have a big emotional drama* (you mean like the one you're playing out in Marlboro Man's kitchen right now?) *and I'm finding myself vacillating between sadness over the end of our four-year relationship, regret over not going to see him in person, and confusion over how to feel about my upcoming move to Chicago. And where that will leave you and me, you big hunk of burning love.*

"I ran over my dog today!" I blubbered and collapsed into another heap of impossible-to-corral tears. Marlboro Man was embracing me tightly now, knowing full well that his arms were the only offering he had for me at that moment. My face was buried in his neck and I continued to laugh, belting out an occasional "I'm sorry" between my sobs, hoping in vain that the laughter would eventually prevail. I wanted to continue, to tell him about J, to give him the complete story behind my unexpected outburst. But "I ran over my dog" was all I could muster. It was the easier thing to explain. Marlboro Man could understand that, wrap his brain around it. But the uninvited surfer newly-ex-boyfriend dangling at the airport? It was a little more information than I had the strength to share that night.

He continued holding me in his kitchen until my chest stopped heaving and the wellspring of snot began to dry. I opened my eyes and found I was in a different country altogether, The Land of His Embrace. It was a peaceful, restful, safe place.

Marlboro Man gave me one last comforting hug before our bodies finally separated, and he casually leaned against the counter. "Hey, if it makes you feel any better," he said, "I've run over so many damn dogs out here, I can't even begin to count them."

It was a much-needed—if unlikely—moment of perspective for me.

WE SHARED a Marlboro Man–prepared meal of rib eye steaks, baked potatoes, and corn. I'd been a vegetarian for seven

years before returning home to Oklahoma and hadn't touched a speck of
beef to my lips in ages, which made my first bite of the rib eye that much
more life-altering. The stress of the day had melted away in Marlboro Man's
arms, and now that same man had just rescued me forever from a life without beef. Whatever happened between the cowboy and me, I told myself, I
never wanted to be without steak again.

We did the dishes and talked—about the cattle business, about my job
back in L.A., about his local small town, about family. Then we adjourned
to the sofa to watch an action movie, pausing occasionally to remind each
other once again of the reason God invented lips. Curiously, though, while
sexy and smoldering, Marlboro Man kept his heavy breathing to a minimum. This surprised me. He was not only masculine and manly, he lived
in the middle of nowhere—one might expect that because of the dearth of
women within a twenty-mile range, he'd be more susceptible than most to
getting lost in a heated moment. But he wasn't. He was a gentleman through
and through—a sizzling specimen of a gentleman who was singlehandedly
introducing me to a whole new universe of animal attraction, but a gentleman, nonetheless. And though my mercury was rising rapidly, his didn't
seem to be in any hurry.

He walked me to my car as the final credits rolled, offering to follow me
all the way home if I wanted. "Oh, no," I said. "I can get home, no problem." I'd lived in L.A. for years; it's not like driving alone at night bothered
me. I started my car and watched him walk back toward his front door,
admiring every last thing about him. He turned around and waved, and as
he walked inside I felt, more than ever, that I was in big trouble. What was I
doing? Why was I here? I was getting ready to move to Chicago—home of
the Cubs and Michigan Avenue and the Elevated Train. Why had I allowed
myself to stick my toe in this water?

And why did the water have to feel so, so good?

I pulled out of Marlboro Man's gravel driveway and turned right,
onto the dirt road. Taking in a deep breath and preparing myself for the

quiet drive ahead, my thoughts turned suddenly to J. God only knew where he was at that point. I wouldn't have known if he'd tried to call all evening; in the mid-1990s there was no "missed call" feature on car phones. Neither would I have known whether J had made a surprise visit to my parents' house with a chain saw or an ax, as they'd left town that evening for a trip . . . but then, J never really was the chain saw type.

Winding around the dusty county road in the pitch-black of night, I found myself equal parts content and unsettled—a strange combination brought on by the events of the day—and I began thinking about my move to Chicago and my plans to pursue law school. Was this the right choice? Was it a fit? Or was it just a neat and tidy plan, something concrete and objective? The easy road? An escape from creativity? An escape from risk?

The loud ring of my car phone disrupted my introspection. Startled, I picked up the phone, certain it would be J calling from the airport after, probably, persistently calling all night. *Another phone confrontation.* But at least this time I'd be ready. I'd just had a four-hour dose of Marlboro Man. I could handle anything.

"Hello?" I said, readying myself.

"Hey, you," the voice said. The voice. That voice. The one that had infiltrated my dreams.

It was Marlboro Man, calling to say he missed me, a mere five minutes after I'd pulled away from his house. And his words weren't scripted or canned, like the obligatory roses sent after a date. They were impulsive, spur-of-the-moment—the words of a man who'd had a thought and acted on it within seconds. A man who, in his busy life on the ranch, had neither the time nor the inclination to wait to call a girl or play it cool. A man who liked a woman and called her just as she left his house, simply to tell her he wished she hadn't.

"I miss you, too," I said, though words like that were difficult for me. I'd conditioned myself to steer clear of them after so many years with J, whose phlegmatic nature had bled over into almost every other aspect of his life. He was not affectionate, and in the four-plus years I'd known him, I couldn't recall one time he'd called me after a date to say he missed me. Even after I'd left California months earlier, his calls had come every three or four days, sometimes less frequently than that. And while I'd never considered myself a needy sort of gal, the complete dearth of verbal affirmation from J had eventually become paradoxically loud.

I hung up the phone after saying good night to Marlboro Man, this isolated cowboy who hadn't had the slightest problem picking up the phone to say "I miss you." I shuddered at the thought of how long I'd gone without it. And judging from the electrical charges searing through every cell of my body, I realized just how fundamental a human need it really is.

It was as fundamental a human need, I would learn, as having a sense of direction in the dark. I suddenly realized I was lost on the long dirt road, more lost than I'd ever been before. The more twists and turns I took in my attempt to find my bearings, the worse my situation became. It was almost midnight, and it was cold, and each intersection looked like the same one repeating over and over. I found myself struck with an illogical and indescribable panic—the kind that causes you to truly believe you'll never, ever escape from where you are, even though you almost always will. As I drove, I remembered every horror movie I'd ever watched that had taken place in a rural setting. *Children of the Corn*. The children of the corn were lurking out there in the tall grass, I just knew it. *Friday the 13th*. Sure, it had taken place at a summer camp, but the same thing could happen on a cattle ranch. And *The Texas Chain Saw Massacre*? Oh no. I was dead. Leatherface was coming—or even worse, his freaky, emaciated, misanthropic brother.

I kept driving for a while, then stopped on the side of the road. Shining my brights on the road in front of me, I watched out for Leatherface while dialing Marlboro Man on my car phone. My pulse was rapid out of sheer terror and embarrassment; my face was hot. Lost and helpless on a county road the same night I'd emotionally decompensated in his kitchen—this was not exactly the image I was dying to project to this new man in my life. But I had no other option, short of continuing to drive aimlessly down one generic road after another or parking on the side of the road and going to sleep, which really wasn't an option at all, considering Norman Bates was likely wandering around the area. With Ted Bundy. And Charles Manson. And Grendel.

Marlboro Man answered, "Hello?" He must have been almost asleep.

"Um . . . um . . . hi," I said, squinting in shame.

"Hey there," he replied.

"This is Ree," I said. I just wanted to make sure he knew.

"Yeah . . . I know," he said.

"Um, funniest thing happened," I continued, my hands in a death grip on the steering wheel. "Seems I got a little turned around and I'm kinda sorta maybe perhaps a little tiny bit lost."

He chuckled. "Where are you?"

"Um, well, that's just it," I replied, looking around the utter darkness for any ounce of remaining pride. "I don't really know."

Marlboro Man assumed control, telling me to drive until I found an intersection, then read him the numbers on the small green county road signs, numbers that meant absolutely nothing to me, considering I'd never even heard the term "county road" before, but that would help Marlboro Man pinpoint exactly where on earth I was. "Okay, here we go," I called out. "It says, um . . . CR 4521."

"Hang tight," he said. "I'll be right there."

Marlboro Man *was* right there, in less than five minutes. Once I determined the white pickup pulling beside my car was his and not that of Jason Voorhees, I rolled down my window. Marlboro Man did the same and said, with a huge smile, "Having trouble?" He was enjoying this, in the exact same way he'd enjoyed waking me from a sound sleep when he'd called at seven a few days earlier. I was having no trouble establishing myself as the clueless pansy-ass of our rapidly developing relationship.

"Follow me," he said. I did. *I'll follow you anywhere,* I thought as I drove in the dust trail behind his pickup. Within minutes we were back at the highway and I heaved a sigh of relief that I was going to survive. Humiliated and wanting to get out of his hair, I intended to give him a nice, simple wave and drive away in shame. Instead, I saw Marlboro Man walking toward my car. Staring at his Wranglers, I rolled down my window again so I could hear what he had to say.

He didn't say anything at all. He opened my car door, pulled me out of the car, and kissed me as I'd never been kissed before.

And there we were. Making out wildly at the intersection of a county road and a rural highway, dust particles in the air mixing with the glow of my headlights to create a cattle ranch version of London fog.

It would have made the perfect cover of a romance novel had it not been for the fact that my car phone, suddenly, began ringing loudly.

OUR PHONE'S ringing," Marlboro Man said, his mouth a mere centimeter from mine. I kept my eyes closed and pulled him tighter, if that was even possible, trying to drown out the clanging cymbal of the car phone by stirring up even more passion between us. It was a beautiful moment; the dark, rural setting had made it so easy to pretend we were in another time and place, in another world. Aside from the ringing of the phone and the headlights from our vehicles, we could have been any two people in the whole history of time.

But the ringing wasn't going away, and ignoring it became impossible. "Who is that?" Marlboro Man asked. "It's a little late, isn't it?" His strong embrace loosened just enough for me to notice.

It was a little late, yes—just after midnight. Way too late for a mom or a brother or most casual friends.

It was also too late for J. We'd been together so long, and he'd never felt compelled to assert his love and affection like this before—only now, when he realized I was out the door, when he saw that my mind was made up, was he finally mustering up the wherewithal to make his true feelings known. And, of course, it had to be now, when I was standing in the arms of a man I was falling more in love with every day. It was way too late for J. Too late for anyone except Marlboro Man.

Finally the ringing stopped, hallelujah, and the kissing resumed. Marlboro Man's grip tightened, and I was swept away, once again, to that other time and place. Then the ringing began again, and I was thrown back into reality.

"Do you need to get that?" he asked.

I wanted to answer. I wanted to explain that in all our great conversations over the previous week, I'd managed to omit the fact that I was fresh out—barely out—of a four-year relationship. That I'd been slowly breaking it off over the past few weeks and that it had come to a head in the past day or two. That he was at the airport two hours from here, wanting to see me in person. That I'd refused him . . . because the only thing on my mind was coming here.

How do you talk to a new love about an old one, especially so early in a relationship? If I'd brought it up earlier in the week, spilled the whole story about J and me, it might have appeared I was being way too open way too soon. Plus, when I was with Marlboro Man, right or wrong, J hardly crossed my mind. I was too busy staring at Marlboro Man's eyes. Memorizing his muscles. Breathing in his masculinity. Getting drunk on its vapors.

But now, standing in the dark and feeling so close to him, I wished I'd told Marlboro Man the whole story. Because as uncomfortable as the truth was, the incessant after-midnight phone calls were worse. For all Marlboro Man knew, it was my next date for the evening—or worse, my sugar daddy, Rocco, wanting to know where I was. The phone calls would have sounded much better if I'd provided more context before they arrived with a vengeance. "Sounds like you need to go," he said as reality swept away the beautiful mist. He was right. As little as he knew about the phone calls that kept coming, he knew they were something that had to be dealt with.

What could I possibly say? *Oh, it's just my ex-boyfriend . . . no big deal* sounded trite and clichéd. And it *was* a big deal—if not to me, then certainly to J. But spilling the whole tale about J flying to see me against my wishes was more drama than I cared to insert into this love scene, especially after my breakdown in Marlboro Man's kitchen earlier in the evening. But silence wasn't appealing, either, as it would have just looked sketchy. I could have lied and said it was my brother Mike, calling for a ride to the fire station. But Mike wouldn't have been up that late. And besides, I didn't want to have to explain why my adult brother would even want to hang out at fire stations. My hands were tied.

So I chose the middle ground. "Yep," I agreed. "I'd better go. Old boyfriend. Sorry." My mouth could form no words beyond that.

I expected a sudden change in atmosphere, absolutely certain the words *old boyfriend* would cause a drastic drop in ambient temperature and Marlboro Man would simply say good-bye, get in his pickup, and drive away. And he would have had good reason. After all, he really hadn't known me very long. Beyond some good conversation and a few fiery kisses, he didn't know much about me. It would have been easy for him to put up his guard and step back until he had a little time to assess the situation.

Instead, he wrapped his solid arms around my waist and picked me up off the ground, healing the awkward moment with a warm, reassuring hug. Then, touching his forehead to mine, he said, simply, "Good night."

I climbed back into my car just in time to watch Marlboro Man drive away. Pulling out onto the highway, I took a deep breath and sighed . . . then I picked up my still-ringing phone. It was J, calling from a depressing airport hotel to say he was crushed, and that he'd brought a ring—and a marriage proposal—with him.

I'd suspected this. He'd been so urgent about wanting to see me when he arrived earlier that day, I knew he must have had a concrete objective in mind. In that sense, I was glad I hadn't given in to his requests for me to come to the airport to see him in person. It would have been terrible: an awkward hug, limited eye contact, the presentation of the Last-Ditch Diamond, the uncomfortable silence, the inevitable no, the tears, humiliation, and pain.

"I'm sorry," I said after spending the next forty-five minutes listening to J say everything he wanted to say. "I really am. I hate that today happened like it did."

"I just wanted to see you," J replied. "I think you would have changed your mind."

"Why do you think that?" I asked.

"I think once you saw the ring, you would have realized everything we could have had together."

I didn't say what I was thinking. That, in fact, I would have seen the ring for what it was: a tangible, albeit expensive, symbol of the panic J felt at the prospect of facing change. We'd been so comfortable with each other for so long. I'd always been so available to him, so easy for him to be with—losing me would mean the end of that source of comfort.

"I'm sorry, J," I repeated. It was simply all I could say. He hung up without responding.

My phone didn't ring the rest of the night. When I arrived back at my parents' house, I fell onto my bed, collapsing in an exhausted heap. Staring at my dark ceiling, I twiddled my hair and found myself, strangely, unable to sleep. Thoughts raced through my mind—of my beloved Puggy Sue—that she wouldn't be greeting me with a playful bark the next morning. Of J—that he was hurting. Of our relationship, which was finally, after so many years, over for good. Of Chicago and all I had left to do to prepare for my move.

Of Marlboro Man . . .
Marlboro Man . . .
Marlboro Man . . .

I awoke early the next morning to the sound of my phone ringing. My phone had rung so much over the past twenty-four hours, I wasn't sure whether to welcome it or run screaming from my bedroom. Groggy, eyes closed, I felt around in the dark until my hand found the receiver. Rubbing my eyes in an effort to awaken myself, I said, softly and with great trepidation, "Hello?"

"You're not asleep, are you?" Marlboro Man said with his signature chuckle.

I opened my eyes and smiled.

Chapter Five
BEGONE, DESTINY!

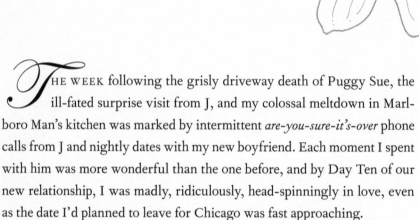

THE WEEK following the grisly driveway death of Puggy Sue, the ill-fated surprise visit from J, and my colossal meltdown in Marlboro Man's kitchen was marked by intermittent *are-you-sure-it's-over* phone calls from J and nightly dates with my new boyfriend. Each moment I spent with him was more wonderful than the one before, and by Day Ten of our new relationship, I was madly, ridiculously, head-spinningly in love, even as the date I'd planned to leave for Chicago was fast approaching.

Chicago had been months in the making, and suddenly I found myself avoiding the subject like the plague. Had I lost my mind? Taken leave of my senses? Whenever I allowed myself to enter into the realm of thinking about it, I felt a terrible, uncomfortable tug. I felt guilty, like I was playing hooky or cheating on myself. Suddenly, a cowboy comes along and I can think of nothing but him. I needed only to hear his voice on the other end of the line, saying good morning or saying good night or teasing me for sleeping past six and chuckling that chuckle that made everything go weak . . . and Chicago—the entire state of Illinois, for that matter—would simply flitter out of my mind, along with any other lucid thought I ever tried to have in his presence. I was doomed.

Around town I'd field the occasional question about the status of my migration. And I'd always give the same answer: *Yep, I'm headed there in a couple of weeks. I'm just tying up some loose ends.* What I didn't tell them was that the loose ends were rapidly, nightly, winding their way around my waist and my shoulders and my heart. Logically I knew I couldn't possibly allow this new man to derail me from where I really wanted to go in life. But it would take a little more time for me to work up the gumption to put the brakes on our ever-increasing momentum. I simply wasn't finished kissing him yet.

After a few more dates in my town, Marlboro Man invited me, once again, to his house on the ranch. Taking into account how much he'd loved the first meal I'd fixed for him, I confidently offered, "I'll make you dinner again!" Since I'd gone the seafood route before, I decided to honor his ranching heritage by preparing a beef dish. After scouring my formerly vegetarian brain for any beef dishes I remembered eating over the previous twenty-five years, I finally thought of my mom's Marinated Flank Steak, which had remained in my culinary memory even through all the tofu and seaweed I'd consumed in California.

To make it, you marinate a flank steak in a mixture of soy sauce, sesame oil, minced garlic, fresh ginger, and red wine for twenty-four hours, then grill it quickly to sear the outside. The flavor—with its decidedly Asian edge—is totally out of this world; combined with the tenderness of the rare flank steak, it's a real feast for the palate. To accompany the flank steak, I decided to prepare Tagliarini Quattro Formaggi—my favorite pasta dish from Intermezzo in West Hollywood. Made with angel hair pasta and a delectable mix of Parmesan, Romano, Fontina, and goat cheese, it had been my drug of choice in the L.A. years.

I bought all the ingredients and headed to Marlboro Man's house, choosing to ignore the fact that Marinated Flank Steak actually needs to marinate. Plus, I didn't know how to operate a grill—Los Angeles County apartment buildings had ordinances against them—so I decided to cook it under the broiler. Having not been a meat eater for years and years, I'd forgotten about the vital importance of not overcooking steak; I just assumed steak was like chicken and simply needed all the pink cooked out of it. I broiled the beautiful, flavorful flank steak to a fine leather.

With all my focus on destroying the main course, I wound up over-cooking the angel hair noodles by a good five minutes, so when I stirred in all the cheeses I'd so carefully grated by hand, my Tagliarini Quattro Formaggi resembled a soupy pan of watery cheese grits. *How bad could it possibly be?* I asked myself as I poured it into garlic-rubbed bowls just like they did at Intermezzo. I figured Marlboro Man wouldn't notice. I watched as he dutifully ate my dinner, unaware that, as I later learned, throughout the meal he seriously considered calling one of the cowboys and asking them to start a prairie fire so he'd have an excuse to leave.

It was a beautiful spring night, and we adjourned to the porch after dinner and sat side by side on two patio chairs. Taking my hand in his, Marlboro Man propped his cowboy boots on the porch railing and rested his head against the chair. It was quiet. Cattle were mooing in the distance, and an occasional coyote would howl.

Suddenly, inexplicably, in the black of this impossibly starry night, with no action movie or other distractions playing in the background, I began thinking about Chicago. *I should be packing,* I thought. *But I'm not. I'm here. With this man. In this place.*

During my months back home, I'd realized more than ever how much I'd missed living in a city: the culture, the anonymity, the action, the pace. It had made me feel happy and alive and whole. That I was even sitting on a cowboy's porch at this point in my life was strange enough; that I actually felt comfortable, at peace, and at home there was surreal.

I felt a chill, the air getting crisper by the minute. I shivered notice-ably, unable to keep my teeth from chattering. Still holding my hand, Marl-boro Man pulled me toward him until I was sitting on his lap. Enveloping my upper body in his arms, he hugged me tightly as my head rested on his strong shoulder. "Mmmm . . . ," he said, even as the same sound came from my own mouth. It was so warm, so perfect, such a fit. We stayed that

way forever, kissing occasionally, then retreating back to the "Mmmm . . ." position in each other's arms. We didn't speak, and the cool night air was so still, it was intoxicating.

With no sounds save for the thumping of my own heart inside my chest, I was left to swim around in my thoughts. *I've got to get going. This will only get harder. I don't belong here. I belong in the city. God, his arms feel good. What am I doing here? I need to get that apartment before it goes. I'm calling in the morning. This has been wonderful, but it isn't reality. It isn't smart. I love the smell of his shirt. I'll miss the smell of his shirt. I'll miss this. I'll miss him. . . .*

I was half asleep—tipsy on his musky fumes—when I felt Marlboro Man gently nuzzle his face toward my ear. Taking a deep breath, he exhaled, his chest falling—the words *I love you* escaping from his mouth so quietly, I wasn't sure whether I'd dreamed it.

I'D KNOWN him just ten days, and it had just left his mouth in an unexpected whisper. It had been purely instinctive, it seemed—something entirely unplanned. He clearly hadn't planned to say those words to me that night; that wasn't the way he operated. He was a man who had a thought and acted on it immediately, as evidenced by his sweet, whispery phone calls right after our dates. He spent no time at all calculating moves; he had better things to do with his time. When we held each other on that chilly spring night and his feelings had come rushing to the surface, he'd felt no need to slap a filter over his mouth. It had come out in a breath: *I love you*. It was as if he had to say it, in the same way air has to escape a person's lungs. It was involuntary. Necessary. Natural.

But as beautiful and warm a moment as it was, I froze on the spot. Once I realized it had been real—that he'd actually said the words—it seemed too late to respond; the window had closed, the shutters had clapped shut. I responded in the only way my cowardice would allow: by holding him tighter, burying my face deeper into his neck, feeling equal parts stupid and awkward. *What is your problem?* I asked myself. I was in the midst of what was possibly the most romantic, emotionally charged moment of my life, in the embrace of a man who embodied not only everything I'd ever understood about the textbook definition of lust, but everything I'd ever dreamed about in a man. He was a specimen—tall, strong, masculine, quiet. But it was much more than that. He was honest. Real. And affectionate and accessible, quite unlike J and most of the men I'd casually dated since I'd returned home from Los Angeles months earlier. I was in a foreign land. I didn't know what to do.

I love you. He'd said it. And I knew his words had been sincere. I knew, because I felt it, too, even though I couldn't say it. Marlboro Man continued to hold me tightly on that patio chair, undeterred by my silence, likely resting easily in the knowledge that at least he'd been able to say what he felt.

"I'd better go home," I whispered, suddenly feeling pulled away by some imaginary force. Marlboro Man nodded, helping me to my feet. Holding hands, we walked around his house to my car, where we stopped for a final hug and a kiss or two. Or eight. "Thanks for having me over," I managed.

Man, I was smooth.

"Any time," he replied, locking his arms around my waist during the final kiss. This was the stuff that dreams were made of. I was glad my eyes were closed, because they were rolled all the way into the back of my head. It wouldn't have been an attractive sight.

He opened the door to my car, and I climbed inside. As I backed out of his driveway, he walked toward his front door and turned around, giving me his characteristic wave in his characteristic Wranglers. Driving away, I felt strange, flushed, tingly. Burdened. Confused. Tortured. Thirty minutes into my drive home, he called. I'd almost grown to need it.

"Hey," he said. His voice. Help me.

"Oh, hi," I replied, pretending to be surprised. Even though I wasn't.

"Hey, I . . . ," Marlboro Man began. "I really don't want you to go."

I giggled. How cute. "Well . . . I'm already halfway home!" I replied, a playful lilt to my voice.

A long pause followed.

Then, his voice serious, he continued, "That's not what I'm talking about."

H E MEANT business; I could hear it in his voice.

Marlboro Man was talking about Chicago, about my imminent move. I'd told him my plans the first time we'd ever spoken on the phone, and he'd mentioned it once or twice during our two wonderful weeks together. But the more time we'd spent together, the less it had come up. Leaving was the last thing I wanted to talk about while I was with him.

I couldn't respond. I had no idea what to say.

"You there?" Marlboro Man asked.

"Yeah," I said. "I'm here." That was all I could manage.

"Well . . . I just wanted to say good night," he said quietly.

"I'm glad you did," I replied. I was an idiot.

"Good night," he whispered.

"Good night."

I woke up the next morning with puffy, swollen eyes. I'd slept like a rock, having dreamed about Marlboro Man all night long. They'd been vivid dreams, crazy dreams, dreams of us talking and playing chess and shooting each other with Silly String. He'd already become such a permanent fixture in my consciousness, I dreamed about him nightly . . . effortlessly.

We went to dinner that night and ordered steak and talked our usual dreamy talk, intentionally avoiding the larger, looming subject. When he brought me home, it was late, and the air was so perfect that I was unaware of the temperature. We stood outside my parents' house, the same place we'd stood two weeks earlier, before the Linguine with Clam Sauce and J's surprise visit; before the overcooked flank steak and my realization that I was hopelessly in love. The same place I'd almost wiped out on the sidewalk; the same place he'd kissed me for the first time and set my heart afire.

Marlboro Man moved in for the kill. We stood there and kissed as if it was our last chance ever. Then we hugged tightly, burying our faces in each other's necks.

"What are you trying to do to me?" I asked rhetorically.

He chuckled and touched his forehead to mine. "What do you mean?"

Of course, I wasn't able to answer.

Marlboro Man took my hand.

Then he took the reins. "So, what about Chicago?"

I hugged him tighter. "Ugh," I groaned. "I don't know."

"Well . . . when are you going?" He hugged me tighter. "*Are* you going?"

I hugged him even tighter, wondering how long we could keep this up and continue breathing. "I . . . I . . . ugh, I don't know," I said. Ms. Eloquence again. "I just don't know."

He reached behind my head, cradling it in his hands. "Don't . . . ," he whispered in my ear. He wasn't beating around the bush.

Don't. What did that mean? How did this work? It was too early for plans, too early for promises. Way too early for a lasting commitment from either of us. Too early for anything but a plaintive, emotional appeal: *Don't. Don't go. Don't leave. Don't let it end. Don't move to Chicago.*

I didn't know what to say. We'd been together every single day for the past two weeks. I'd fallen completely and unexpectedly in love with a cowboy. I'd ended a long-term relationship. I'd eaten beef. And I'd begun rethinking my months-long plans to move to Chicago. I was a little speechless.

We kissed one more time, and when our lips finally parted, he said, softly, "Good night."

"Good night," I answered as I opened the door and went inside.

I walked into my bedroom, eyeing the mound of boxes and suitcases that sat by the door, and plopped down on my bed. Sleep eluded me that night. What if I just postponed my move to Chicago by, say, a month or so? Postponed, not canceled. A month surely wouldn't hurt, would it? By then, I reasoned, I'd surely have him out of my system; I'd surely have gotten my fill. A month would give me all the time I needed to wrap up this whole silly business.

I laughed out loud. Getting my fill of Marlboro Man? I couldn't go five minutes after he dropped me off at night before smelling my shirt, searching for more of his scent. How much worse would my affliction be a month from now? Shaking my head in frustration, I stood up, walked to my closet, and began removing more clothes from their hangers. I folded sweaters and jackets and pajamas with one thing pulsating through my mind: no man— least of all some country bumpkin—was going to derail my move to the big city. And as I folded and placed each item in the open cardboard boxes by my door, I tried with all my might to beat back destiny with both hands.

I had no idea how futile my efforts would be.

Chapter Six
INTO THE FLAMING BARN

H E WASN'T a country bumpkin. He was poised, gentlemanly, intelligent. And he was no mere man—at least no man the likes of whom I'd ever known. He was different. Strikingly different.

Marlboro Man was introspective and quiet, but not insecure. The product of an upbringing that involved early mornings of hard work and calm, still evenings miles away from civilization, he'd learned at an early age to be content with silence. I, on the other hand, was seemingly allergic to the quiet. Talking had always been what I did best—with all the wide-open airspace we, as humans, had been given, I saw no need to waste it. And as a middle child, I simply had a lot to say to the world.

I'd finally met my match with Marlboro Man. It had taken all of five seconds for his quiet manner to zap me that night we'd first met over four months earlier, and the more I'd been around it over the previous two weeks, the more certain I'd become convinced that this type of man—if not this man specifically—had to be my perfect match. In the short time I'd been with him, I'd seen clear examples of just how complementary our differences were. Where I'd once been quick to fill an empty conversational void with vapid words, I now began to rein it in when I was with him, stopping long enough for the silence between us to work its magic. Where he'd never learned to properly twirl a forkful of linguine around in a large tablespoon, I was right there to show him the light. Where I'd normally be on the phone the second dinner ended, rounding up friends to go have a drink, he'd do the dishes and we'd watch a movie, maybe sit outside on the porch, weather permitting, to listen to coyotes howl, and contemplate life.

We lived life at entirely different paces. His day began before 5:00 A.M., and his work was backbreaking, sweaty, grueling. I worked so I'd have something to do during the daylight hours, so I'd have a place to wear my black pumps, and so I could fund a nightlife full of gourmet food and colorful drinks. For Marlboro Man, nightlife meant relaxation, an earned reward for a long day of labor. For me, nightlife meant an opportunity to wear something new and gloss my lips.

At times the differences concerned me. Could I ever be with a man who'd never, in his entire life, eaten sushi? Could I, a former vegetarian, conceivably spend the rest of my life with a man who ate red meat at every meal? I'd never thought about it before. And, most concerning, could I ever—in a million years—live so far out in the country that I'd have to traverse five miles of gravel road to reach my house?

The Magic 8-Ball in my head revealed its answer: OUTLOOK NOT SO GOOD.

And what was I doing even thinking about marriage, anyway? I knew good and well that with Marlboro Man, a rancher who lived on land that had been in his family for years, one thing was a certainty: *he was where he was,* and any future plans involving him would have to take place on his turf, not mine. It wasn't as if I could take off for Chicago armed with even the faintest hope that Marlboro Man might relocate there one day. Downtown Chicago isn't known for its abundant wheat-grazing pasture. His life was on the ranch, where he would likely remain forever. His dad was getting older, which meant Marlboro Man and his brother held the future of the ranch in their capable and calloused hands.

And so I found myself in the all-too-familiar position of deciding whether to frame my life around the circumstances of the man in my life.

I'd faced the same situation with J, when he'd wanted me to move to northern California with him. It had been difficult, but I'd held tightly to my
pride and chosen to leave California instead. It had been a personal accom-
plishment, extricating myself from the comfortable shackles of a four-year
relationship, and it had been the right decision. And so would my decision
to stick to my plans to move to Chicago now, as hard as it would be to put
the skids on my two-week love affair with Marlboro Man. I was a strong
woman. I'd done it before—refused to follow a man—and I could do it
again. It might sting for a short time, sure, but in the long run I'd feel good
about it.

My phone rang, startling me smooth out of my internal feminist dia-
tribe. It was late. Marlboro Man had dropped me off half an hour earlier; he
was probably halfway home. I loved his phone calls. His late-at-night, I'm-
just-thinking-about-you, I-just-wanted-to-say-good-night phone calls. I
picked up the phone.

"Hello?"

"Hey," he said.

"Hey," I replied. You sizzling specimen you.

"What're you doing?" he asked, casually.

I glanced down at the pile of tank tops I'd just neatly folded. "Oh, just
reading a book," I replied. Liar.

He continued, "Feel like talking?"

"Sure," I said. "I'm not doing anything." I crawled onto the comfortable chair in my room and nestled in.

"Well . . . come outside," he said. "I'm parked in your driveway."

My stomach lurched. He wasn't joking.

*Y*OU'RE . . . *you're what? Where?*" I stood up and glimpsed myself
in the mirror. I was a vision, having changed into satin pajama

pants, a torn USC sweatshirt, and polka-dotted toe socks, and to top it off, my hair was fastened in a haphazard knot on the top of my head with a no. 2 Ticonderoga pencil. Who wouldn't want me?

"I'm outside," he repeated, throwing in a trademark chuckle just to be extra mean. "Get out here."

"But . . . but . . . ," I stalled, hurriedly sliding the pencil out of my hair and running around the room, stripping off my pathetic house clothes and searching in vain for my favorite faded jeans. "But . . . but . . . I'm in my pajamas."

Another trademark chuckle. "So?" he asked. "You'd better get out here or I'm comin' in. . . ."

"Okay, okay . . . ," I replied. "I'll be right down." Panting, I settled for my second-favorite jeans and my favorite sweater of all time, a faded light blue turtleneck I'd worn so much, it was almost part of my anatomy. Brushing my teeth in ten seconds flat, I scurried down the stairs and out the front door.

Marlboro Man was standing outside his pickup, hands inside his pockets, his back resting against the driver-side door. He grinned, and as I walked toward him, he stood up and walked toward me, too. We met in the middle—in between his vehicle and the front door—and without a moment of hesitation, greeted each other with a long, emotional kiss. There was nothing funny or lighthearted about it. That kiss meant business.

Our lips separated for a short moment. "I like your sweater," he said, looking at the light blue cotton rib as if he'd seen it before. I'd hurriedly thrown it on the night we'd met a few months earlier.

"I think I wore this to the J-Bar that night . . . ," I said. "Do you remember?"

"Ummm, yeah," he said, pulling me even closer. "I remember." Maybe the sweater had magical powers. I'd have to be sure to hold on to it.

We kissed again, and I shivered in the cold night air. Wanting to get me out of the cold, he led me to his pickup and opened the door so we could both climb in. The pickup was still warm and toasty, like a campfire was burning in the backseat. I looked at him, giggled like a schoolgirl, and asked, "What have you been doing all this time?"

"Oh, I was headed home," he said, fiddling with my fingers. "But then I just turned around; I couldn't help it." His hand found my upper back and pulled me closer. The windows were getting foggy. I felt like I was seventeen.

"I've got this problem," he continued, in between kisses.

"Yeah?" I asked, playing dumb. My hand rested on his left bicep. My attraction soared to the heavens. He caressed the back of my head, messing up my hair . . . but I didn't care; I had other things on my mind.

"I'm crazy about you," he said.

By now I was on his lap, right in the front seat of his Diesel Ford F250, making out with him as if I'd just discovered the concept. I had no idea how I'd gotten there—the diesel pickup or his lap. But I was there. And, burying my face in his neck, I quietly repeated his sentiments. "I'm crazy about you, too."

I'd been afflicted with acute boy-craziness for over half my life. But what I was feeling for Marlboro Man was indescribably powerful. It was a primal attraction—the almost uncontrollable urge to wrap my arms and legs around him every time I looked into his eyes. The increased heart rate and respiration every time I heard his voice. The urge to have twelve thousand of his babies . . . and I wasn't even sure I wanted children.

"So anyway," he continued.

That's when we heard the loud knocking on the pickup window. I jumped through the roof—it was after 2:00 A.M. Who on earth could it be? The Son of Sam—it had to be! Marlboro Man rolled down the window, and a huge cloud of passion and steam escaped. It wasn't the Son of Sam. Worse—it was my mother. And she was wearing her heather gray cashmere robe.

"Reeee?" she sang. "Is that yooooou?" She leaned closer and peered through the window.

I slid off of Marlboro Man's lap and gave her a halfhearted wave. "Uh . . . hi, Mom. Yeah. It's just me."

She laughed. "Oh, okay . . . whew! I just didn't know who was out here. I didn't recognize the car!" She looked at Marlboro Man, whom she'd met only one time before, when he picked me up for a date.

"Well, hello again!" she exclaimed, extending her manicured hand.

He took her hand and shook it gently. "Hello, ma'am," he replied, his voice still thick with lust and emotion. I sank in my seat. I was an adult, and had just been caught parking at 2:00 A.M. in the driveway of my parents' house by my robe-wearing mother. She'd seen the foggy windows. She'd seen me sitting on his lap. I felt like I'd just gotten grounded.

"Well, okay, then," my mom said, turning around. "Good night, you two!" And with that, she flitted back into the house.

Marlboro Man and I looked at each other. I hid my face in my hands and shook my head. He chuckled, opened the door, and said, "C'mon . . . I'd better get you home before curfew." My sweaty hands still hid my face.

He walked me to the door, and we stood on the top step. Wrapping his arms around my waist, he kissed me on the nose and said, "I'm glad I came back." God, he was sweet.

"I'm glad you did, too," I replied. "But . . ." I paused for a moment, gathering courage. "Did you have something you wanted to say?"

It was forward, yes—gutsy. But I wasn't going to let this moment pass. I didn't have many more moments with him, after all; soon I'd be gone to Chicago. Sitting in coffee shops at eleven at night, if I wanted. Working. Eventually going back to school. I'd be danged if I was going to miss what he'd started to say a few minutes earlier, before my mom and her cashmere robe showed up and spoiled everything.

Marlboro Man looked up at me and smiled, apparently pleased that I'd shown such assertiveness. An outgoing middle child all my life, with him I'd become quiet, shy—an unrecognizable version of myself. He'd captured my heart so unexpectedly, so completely, I'd been rendered utterly incapable of speaking. He had this uncanny way of sucking the words right out of me and leaving nothing but pure, unadulterated passion in their place.

He grabbed me even more tightly. "Well, first of all," he began, "I really . . . I really like you." He looked into my eyes in a seeming effort to transmit the true meaning of each word straight into my psyche. All muscle tone disappeared from my body.

Marlboro Man was so willing to put himself out there, so unafraid to put forth his true feelings. I simply wasn't used to this. I was used to head games, tactics, apathy, aloofness. When it came to love and romance, I'd developed a rock-solid tolerance for mediocrity. And here, in two short weeks, Marlboro Man had blown it all to kingdom come.

There was nothing mediocre about Marlboro Man.

He had more to say; he didn't even pause to wait for a response. That, in his universe, was what a real man did.

"And . . ." He hesitated.

I listened. His voice was serious. Focused.

"And I just flat don't want you to leave," he declared, holding me close, resting his chin on my cheek, speaking directly into my ear.

I paused. Took a breath. "Well—" I began.

He interrupted. "I know we've just been doing this for two weeks, and I know you've already made your plans, and I know we don't know what the future holds, but. . . ." He looked at me and cupped my face in his hand, his other hand on my arm.

"I know," I agreed, trying to muster some trite response. "I—"

He broke in again. He had some things to say. "If I didn't have the ranch, it'd be one thing," he said. My pulse quickened. "But I . . . my life is here."

"I know," I said again. "I wouldn't. . . ."

He continued, "I don't want to get in the middle of your plans. I just . . ." He paused, then kissed me on the cheek. "I don't want you to go."

I was tongue-tied as usual. This was so strange for me, so foreign— that I could feel so strongly for someone I'd known for such a short time. To talk about our future would be premature; but to totally dismiss that we'd happened upon something special wouldn't be right, either. Something extraordinary had occurred between us—that fact was indisputable. It was the timing that left so much to be desired.

We were both bleary eyed, tired. Falling asleep standing up in each other's arms. Nothing more could be said that night; nothing could be resolved. He knew it, I knew it; so we settled on a long, lasting kiss and an all-encompassing hug before he turned around and walked away. Starting his diesel pickup. Driving down my parents' street. Driving back to his ranch.

I couldn't think; bed was all I could manage. I crawled under the covers with a faint lump in my throat. *What is that doing there? Go away, stop it. Leave me alone. I hate crying. It makes my head hurt. Makes my eyes puffy.* The lump was suddenly twice the size. I couldn't swallow. Then, against my wishes, the tears began to roll just before I fell into a deep, deep sleep.

Y PHONE rang at eight the next morning, startling me from my coma.

"Hello, Ree?" the pleasant female voice said. It wasn't Marlboro Man.

"Yes?" I responded. I smelled Marlboro Man's delicious scent. Even in his absence, he was all around me.

"This is Rhonda," the voice continued. "I'm just calling about your one-bedroom on Goethe?"

It was a great place, close to where my older brother lived. White paint, wood floors, good location. Nothing overly large or fancy, judging from the photos they'd sent, but so perfect for what I needed. I'd plunked down a healthy deposit on the place as soon as it became available the week before my brother's wedding, knowing I'd be up there within the month. Reasonably priced for what it was, the apartment would soon be my home, my haven, my New Jerusalem. Tiny as it was. There was plenty of room for all of my black pumps, plenty of room for a comfy bed. And no room whatsoever for a boy.

But my original move-in date had come and gone. I was stalling, delaying, putting off the inevitable. Swapping kisses with a cowboy. Dying daily in his arms.

"Are you still planning to move in this week?" Rhonda the Realtor continued. "Because we'll need to go ahead and get your first month's rent as soon as possible."

"Oh." I sat up. "I'm so sorry; I've been packing and getting ready to go, and it's gone a little more slowly than I thought."

"Oh, no problem," she said. "That's fine. We'll just need it by the end of this week, otherwise we'll have to let the place go, as a few other people are interested."

"Okay, thanks for calling," I replied. "See you soon."

I hung up the phone and fell backward, staring at the ceiling. I had things to do—I had to get busy. Stumbling to my bathroom, I fastened my hair in a knot and splashed icy cold water on my face. Brushing my teeth and looking at my reflection in the mirror, I knew what I had to do. *Okay,* I told myself, nodding. *Let's get this show on the road.*

Returning to my bedroom, I picked up the phone and clicked the caller ID button to reveal Rhonda the Realtor's phone number. Dialing the number, I took a deep, cleansing breath and exhaled.

"Hi, Rhonda—this is Ree again," I said when she picked up her phone. "Listen, I'm so sorry—but my plans have changed. I'm going to have to let the place go after all."

"Oh . . . Ree, are you sure?" Rhonda asked. "But you'll lose your deposit."

"Yeah, I'm sure," I said, feeling my heart thumping through my chest. "Go ahead and let it go."

I fell on my bed, my face tingling with unease, feeling not unlike a psychotic horse running wildly into a flaming barn. That's how sure I was of my decision.

Chapter Seven
CHICAGO, ADIÓS

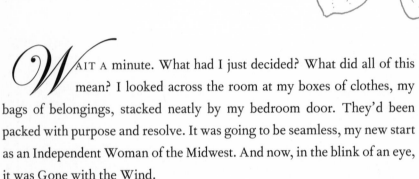

AIT A minute. What had I just decided? What did all of this mean? I looked across the room at my boxes of clothes, my bags of belongings, stacked neatly by my bedroom door. They'd been packed with purpose and resolve. It was going to be seamless, my new start as an Independent Woman of the Midwest. And now, in the blink of an eye, it was Gone with the Wind.

What had I done? I loved that apartment. I'd spent so much time picturing myself there—where I'd put my bed, where I'd hang my collection of black-and-white prints of Mikhail Baryshnikov. Months from now, when I'd eventually come to my senses and move to Chicago as originally planned, there's no way I'll find another apartment like this one.

In an internal panic, I picked up the phone and hurriedly pushed redial. I had to catch Rhonda the Realtor, had to tell her wait, hold off, don't let it go, I'm not sure, hang on, give me another day . . . or two . . . or three. But when the numbers finished dialing, I heard no ringing; instead, in a perfect moment of irony, coincidence, and serendipity, I heard Marlboro Man's voice on the other end.

"Hello?" he asked.

"Oh," I replied. "Hello?"

"Hey, you," he replied.

So much for calling Rhonda the Realtor. Three seconds into the phone call, Marlboro Man's voice had already taken hold. His voice. It weakened my knees, destroyed my focus, ruined my resolve. When I heard his voice, I could think of nothing but wanting to see him again, to be in his presence, to drink him in, to melt like butter in his impossibly strong arms. When I heard his voice, Chicago became nothing but a distant memory.

"What're you up to?" he continued. I could hear cattle in the background.

"Oh, just getting a few things done," I said. "Just tying up a few loose ends."

"You're not moving to Chicago today, are you?" he said with a chuckle. He was only halfway joking.

I laughed, rolling over in my bed and fiddling with the eyelet ruffle on my comforter. "Nope, not today," I answered. "What are you doing?"

"Coming to pick you up in a little bit," he said. I loved it when he took charge. It made my heart skip a beat, made me feel flushed and excited and thrilled. After four years with J, I was sick and tired of the surfer mentality. Laid-back, I'd discovered, was no longer something I wanted in a man. And when it came to his affection for me, Marlboro Man was anything but that. "I'll be there at five." Yes, sir. Anything you say, sir. I'll be ready. With bells on.

I started getting ready at three. I showered, shaved, powdered, perfumed, brushed, curled, and primped for two whole hours—throwing on a light pink shirt and my favorite jeans—all in an effort to appear as if I'd simply thrown myself together at the last minute.

It worked. "Man," Marlboro Man said when I opened the door. "You look great." I couldn't focus very long on his compliment, though—I was way too distracted by the way *he* looked. God, he was gorgeous. At a time of year when most people are still milky white, his long days of working cattle had afforded him a beautiful, golden, late-spring tan. And his typical denim button-down shirts had been replaced by a more fitted dark gray polo, the kind of shirt that perfectly emphasizes biceps born not from working out in a gym, but from tough, gritty, hands-on labor. And his prematurely gray hair, very short, was just the icing on the cake. I could eat this man with a spoon.

"You do, too," I replied, trying to will away my spiking hormones. He opened the door to his white diesel pickup, and I climbed right in. I didn't even ask him where we were going; I didn't even care. But when we turned west on the highway and headed out of town, I knew exactly where he was taking me: to his ranch . . . to his turf . . . to his home on the range. Though I didn't expect or require a ride from him, I secretly loved that he drove over an hour to fetch me. It was a throwback to a different time, a burst of chivalry and courtship in this very modern world. As we drove we talked and talked—about our friends, about our families, about movies and books and horses and cattle.

We talked about everything but Chicago.

I wanted so badly to tell him, but I couldn't. I wanted to tell him that I'd impulsively decided—within a period of five minutes earlier that morning—that I couldn't leave him. That I'd indefinitely put on hold—if not nixed altogether—my plans to move away. That I had a new plan now, and that was to be with him. But for some reason, the words just wouldn't come.

Instead of continuing on the highway to the gravel road that led to his house, Marlboro Man took an alternate route. "I've got to turn some cattle out of the horse trap," he said. I didn't even know what that meant, but I was game. He drove through a series of twisted, confusing roads—roads I could never imagine understanding or negotiating myself—and stopped at a pasture full of black cattle. Swinging open a couple of gates, he made a few gestures with his arms—and in no time at all, the cattle had gone where they were supposed to go. This man had a way of getting creatures of all kinds—whether it be bovine animals or redheaded women in their midtwenties—to bend to his influence.

We took the long way back toward his house and drove past the north-ernmost point of the ranch just as the sun was beginning to set. "That's so pretty," I exclaimed as I beheld the beauty of the sky.

Marlboro Man slowed to a stop and put his pickup in park. "It is, isn't it?" he replied, looking over the land on which he'd grown up. He'd lived there since he was four days old, had worked there as a child, had learned how to be a rancher from his dad and grandfather and great-grandfather. He'd learned how to build fences and handle animals and extinguish prai-rie fires and raise cattle of all colors, shapes, and sizes. He'd helped bury his older brother in the family cemetery near his house, and he'd learned to pick up and go on in the face of unspeakable tragedy and sadness. This ranch was a part of him. His love for it was tangible.

We got out of the pickup and sat on the back, holding hands and watch-ing every second of the magenta sunset as it slowly dissipated into the blackness underneath. The night was warm and perfectly still—so still we could hear each other breathing. And well after the sun finally dipped below the horizon and the sky grew dark, we stayed on the back of the pickup, hugging and kissing as if we hadn't seen each other in ages. The passion I felt was immeasurable.

"I have something to tell you," I said as the butterflies in my gut kicked into overdrive.

*M*ARLBORO MAN paused, his eyes piercing through to my mar-row. We'd started out watching the sunset over the ranch, sitting on the tailgate of his pickup, legs dangling playfully over the edge. By the time the sun had gone down, we were lying down, legs overlapping, as the sky turned blacker and blacker. And making out wildly. Making out, oh, so very wildly.

I didn't want to wait for him to bring it up again—the dreaded subject

of Chicago. I'd avoided it like the plague for the past several days, not wanting to face the reality of my impending move, of walking away from my new
love so soon after we'd found each other. But now the subject wasn't so scary;
it was safe. I'd made the decision, at least for now, to stay—I just had to tell
Marlboro Man. And finally, in between kisses, the words bubbled suddenly
and boldly to the surface; I could no longer contain them. But before I had
a chance to say them, Marlboro Man opened his mouth and began to speak.

"Oh no," he said, a pained expression on his face. "Don't tell me—
you're leaving tomorrow." He ran his fingers through my hair and touched
his forehead to mine.

I smiled, giggling inside at the secret I was seconds away from spilling.
A herd of cows mooed in the distance. Serenading us.

"Um . . . no," I said, finding it hard to believe what I was about to tell
him. "I'm not . . . I'm . . . I'm not going."

He paused, then pulled his face away from mine, allowing just enough
distance between us for him to pull focus. "What?" he asked, his strong
fingers still grasping my hair. A tentative smile appeared on his face.

I breathed in a deep dose of night air, trying to calm my schoolgirl
nervousness. "I, umm . . ." I began. "I decided to stick around here a little
while." There. I'd said it. This was all officially real.

Without a moment of hesitation, Marlboro Man wrapped his ample
arms around my waist. Then, in what seemed to be less than a second,
he hoisted me from my horizontal position on the bed of his pickup until
we were both standing in front of each other. Scooping me off my feet, he
raised me up to his height so his icy blue eyes were level with mine.

"Wait . . . are you serious?" he asked, taking my face in his hands.
Squaring it in front of his. Looking me in the eye. "You're not going?"

"Nope," I answered.

"Whoa," he said, smiling and moving in for a long, impassioned kiss
on the back of his Ford F250. "I can't believe it," he continued, squeezing
me tightly.

Our knees buckled under the heat, and before I knew it we were back where we'd been before, rolling around and kissing manically in the bed of his diesel pickup. Occasionally my arm would hit a crowbar and my head would slam against a spare tire or a cattle prod or a jack; I didn't care, of course. I'd said what I wanted to say that night. Everything else—even minor head injuries—was a piece of cake.

We stayed there a long, long time, the balmy night air giving us no good reason to leave. Under the innumerable stars, amidst all the embraces and kisses and sounds from the surrounding livestock, I suddenly felt more at peace in my decision than I had since my phone call with Rhonda the Realtor that morning. I felt at home, comfortable, nestled in, wonderful. My life had changed that day, changed in a way I never, ever, could have predicted. My big-city plans—plans many months in the making—had all at once been smashed to smithereens by a six-foot cowboy with manure on his boots. A cowboy I'd known, essentially, for less than three weeks. It was the craziest thing I'd ever done, deciding to take an impulsive walk down this new and unexpected path. And while I secretly wondered how long it would take for me to regret my decision, I rested easily, at least for that night, in the knowledge that I'd had the courage to step out on such an enormous limb.

It was late. Time to go. "Want me to drive you home now?" Marlboro Man asked, lacing our fingers together, kissing the back of my hand. "Or, do you. . . ." He paused, considering his words. "Do you want to come stay at my place?"

I DIDN'T ANSWER right away; I was too busy savoring the moment. The delicious night air, the music of mama cows in a distant pasture, the trillions of stars overhead, the feeling of his fingers entwined in mine. The night couldn't have gone any more perfectly. I'm not sure anything, even going home with him, could possibly make it any better.

I started to open my mouth, but Marlboro Man beat me to it. Standing up and lifting me off the tailgate of his pickup, he carried me, Rhett Butler–style, toward the passenger door. Setting me down and opening my door, he said, "On second thought . . . I think I'd better take you home." I smiled, convinced he must have read my mind.

Whether he had or not, the fact was that instantly and noticeably the whole vibe between us had changed. Before I'd dumped my Chicago apartment and told him my plans to stay, the passion between us had sometimes felt urgent, rushed, almost as if some imaginary force was compelling us to get it all out right here, right now, because before too long we wouldn't have the chance. There'd been a quiet desperation in our romance up until that point, feelings of excitement and lust mixed with an uncomfortable hint of doom and dread. But now that my move had all but been eliminated from the equation, the doom and dread had been replaced with a beautiful sense of comfort. In the blink of an eye, Marlboro Man and I, while madly and insanely in love, were no longer in any hurry.

"Yeah," I said, nodding my head. "I agree."

Man, did I ever have a way with words.

He drove me home, through all the windy roads of his ranch and down the two-lane highway that eventually led to my parents' house on the golf course. And when he walked me to the door, I marveled at how different it felt. Every time I'd stood with Marlboro Man on those same front porch steps, I'd felt the pull of my boxes beckoning me to come inside, to finish packing, to get ready to leave. Packing after our dates had become a regular activity, a ritual, an effort, on my part, to keep my plans moving along despite my ever-growing affection for this new and unexpected man in my life. And now, this night, standing here in his arms, the only thing left to do was unpack them. Or leave them there; I didn't care. I wasn't going anywhere. At least not for now.

"I didn't expect this," he said, his arms around my waist.

"I didn't expect it either," I said, laughing.

He moved in for one final kiss, the perfect ending for such a night. "You made my day," he whispered, before walking to his pickup and driving away.

As I turned to walk into the house and up the stairs to my bedroom, every nerve ending in my body tingled. If this wasn't love, I reflected, then love should just be discontinued entirely. As I walked into my room, I glanced at my boxes with a tickly mixture of melancholy and glee, then flopped onto my comfy bed, kicking off my shoes, and sighing dreamily.

The loud ring of my phone jarred me awake an hour later. Still exhausted from the night before, I'd fallen asleep in my clothes. "Hello?" I said, still almost entirely asleep. Disoriented, confused, drunk on lust and country air.

"Hey . . . it's me," the person on the line said. The voice was quiet. Grave. It was J.

I wasn't expecting this. "Hi," I said, forcing myself to a seated position on my bed, my comforter draped over my shoulders. "What are you doing?" *(Please say you're not at the airport.)*

"I just wanted to hear your voice," he said. He sounded depressed. "It's been a while."

It had been over a week, in fact—well over a week since he'd made his last-minute trip to my hometown. It had been a painful and difficult split, much more so for him, since he didn't have the cushion of a new, exciting romance to make everything seem okay. I hated how it had gone down. But J and I had to end sometime, and I suppose it was never going to be pleasant.

"How are you?" I asked, sounding sterile.

His voice was monotone. "I'm okay. You?"

"I'm okay," I said, deciding against expounding on how blissfully happy I was that night.

"So, when are you moving?" he asked. "I guess you're actually going, huh?"

Gulp. Now what?

"I'm not sure," I replied, stopping there. I didn't feel like being 100 percent honest.

"Well, like, next week? Next month? When?" J pushed.

Another gulp. "I really don't know," I said again, hesitating. "I've been rethinking my plans a little."

J paused. "What does that mean?"

"It means . . . that . . . ," I began. I had no idea what I was going to say.

"Last week all you could talk about was Chicago," J interrupted. "It's one of the reasons you said we couldn't be together anymore!"

"Well . . . ," I said, thinking. "Now it looks like I may not go for a while."

"What's going on?" J said.

I didn't respond.

"Wait, are you . . . are you going out with someone?" He asked pointedly. He was demanding, confrontational.

I was cornered; I had no choice but to spill it, though I wanted to hide under my bed instead. "Actually, J, yes . . . I am." Defiance oozed from my mouth. J brought out that side of me.

"I knew it," he said, as if he'd solved some mystery, cracked some ancient code. "I knew something like that must have been going on."

"You did, huh?" I asked, a smidgen of sarcasm in my weary voice.

"I just knew it," he continued. "You've been acting weird for the past three months."

He had it all wrong. "Hold on, J," I said, trying to find my calm. "I've only known him for three weeks."

Wrong thing to say. "You've only known him for *three weeks*, and suddenly you're not moving because of him?" J ranted. He was mad.

"Hey," I said, trying to bring the conversation back to neutral. "Let's not do this . . . okay?"

"Do what?" he continued, arguing. "Now I'm wondering what else you haven't told me!"

I was starting to get mad. J was clearly hurt; I understood that. He'd clearly felt blindsided by our split, even though it had been months and months in the making. But while I'd been busy not following him to San Francisco, not visiting him with any frequency, and involving him less and less in my life back home, J, by his account, had been happy as a clam with our relationship, taking for granted just about everything that mattered. *She'll be back*, he must have told himself. *She doesn't need me to call her. She knows I love her. She'll always be there.* Nothing egregious or unforgivable . . . but not near enough to cause me to want to stay with him for the rest of my life.

"So?" he said, his voice brimming with bitterness.

"What?" I asked defensively. I'd suddenly had enough.

"What else haven't you told me?"

I thought for a minute. "Actually, yes . . . there is," I replied, pausing to consider my words carefully, "I eat steak now."

I'd been a vegetarian for years, certainly the entire time I'd been with J, and had only recently crossed over to my new existence as a carnivore. I'd do anything for Marlboro Man, including forsake my longtime commitment to avoiding meat. This, I knew, would be the one way to get J's attention. This, I knew, would make everything crystal clear to him.

"My God," J said, his bitterness replaced with disgust. "What's happened to you?" He abruptly hung up the phone.

I guess it worked.

Now there was nothing left for him to do but face the reality that we were through. We'd simply run our course. There just wasn't enough left between us—enough respect, enough admiration, enough appreciation—to sustain us for the long haul.

*N*EXT, IT was time for me to tell my family, who'd started wondering what was going on. I started with my mom.

"I might go sometime later," I told her. "But I ain't going now."

"*Ain't* isn't a word, honey," my mom said, mildly concerned.

"I know, Mom," I replied. "It was for effect."

"Oh, good," she said, wiping the sweat from her freshly plucked brow. Then, smiling, she said, "I really do like his starched shirts . . . you know?"

"Oh, yes," I said, my eyes closing dreamily. "I know."

I told my dad next.

"Dad, I've decided not to go to Chicago right now," I said. "I'm sort of in love with that cowboy I told you about."

"Oh, yeah?" he asked.

"Yeah," I answered.

He paused for a minute, then asked, "Does J know?"

I spent the next fourteen hours filling him in.

I TOLD MY best friend in the world, my sister.

"Okay, so I'm not going now," I told Betsy over the phone. I'd awakened her from a deep collegiate sleep.

"Going where?" she asked groggily.

"Chicago," I continued.

"*What?*" she shrieked. That woke her up. That woke her up but good.

"I'm, like, totally in love," I said. "I'm totally in love with the Marlboro Man." I giggled wildly.

"Oh, God," she said. "Are you gonna get married to him and move out to the boonies and have his babies?"

"*No!*" I exclaimed. "I'm *not* moving to the boonies. But I might have his babies." I giggled wildly again.

"What about Chicago?" Betsy asked.

Well . . . but . . . ," I argued. "You have to see him in his Wranglers."

Betsy paused. "Well, so much for *this* conversation. I've gotta go back to sleep anyway—I've got class at noon and I'm exhausted. . . ."

"And you should see him in his cowboy boots," I continued.

"Alrighty, then . . ."

"Okay, well, don't worry about me," I continued. "I'll just be here, kissing the Marlboro Man twenty-four hours a day in case you need me."

"Whatever . . . ," Betsy said, trying hard not to laugh.

"Okay, well . . . study hard!" I told her.

"Yep," she replied.

"And don't sleep around," I admonished.

"Gotcha," Betsy replied. She was used to this.

"And don't smoke crack," I added.

"Righty-oh," she replied, yawning.

"Don't skip class, either," I warned.

"You mean, like you did?" Betsy retorted.

"Well, then, don't go all the way!" I repeated.

Click.

*N*EXT, IT was time to tell my brother Mike.

"Hey, Mike!" I announced. "Guess what?"

"Wh-wh-wh-what?" he asked.

"I'm staying here! I'm not moving away!" I said. "Aren't you excited?"

Mike thought for a minute, then asked, "C-c-c-can you drive me to duh fire station now?"

Finally I broke the news to my oldest brother. A resident of Chicago himself, he'd been looking forward to having a sister nearby.

"Have you lost your f*&%#ing *mind*?" he said. He'd never been one to mince words.

"Yes," I conceded, attempting to defuse him. "I do believe I have."

"What the hell are you going to do *back home*? You'll shrivel up and die there, it's so backward!" To my commodity-trading, world-traveling brother, any city with a population under three million was backward.

"What's the story with this guy, anyway?"

"Oh, you don't know him," I said. "We've only been going out about a month or so."

My brother's practical side came out swinging. "You've only known him for a *month*? What the hell does he do?"

"Well," I began, bracing myself. "He's . . . a cowboy."

"Oh, Christ." My brother exhaled loudly.

Chapter Eight

TROUBLE AT THE HITCHING POST

I'D FOUND love in the arms of a cowboy I called Marlboro Man. And what ample, amazing arms they were: bulging, with muscles wrought by a lifetime of intense physical labor; strong, in every literal sense of the word; but soft and protective, too, in all the right ways. I'd never been held by arms like these, never in my life. Arms that made me feel nine hundred different emotions at once—and all this time I'd thought there was only a handful of emotions to be felt. Happy. Sad. Angry. Glad. Excited. Bored.

Boy, had I been wrong. Just hearing his voice over the phone sent about two hundred different synapses firing in my central nervous system; an hour in his arms, and I'd pretty much felt them all, twice. Tingly elation, fizzy mania, utter contentment . . . and prickly fear at the thought of ever being without those arms in my life again.

Those arms. Beyond the obvious physical attractiveness, there was just something magical about them. They were filled with some kind of special chemical that seemed only to release itself when locked passionately around my waist. And the chemical was potent, intoxicating, like the second sip of red wine or the scent of burning patchouli. Times a million. Arms like that should be bronzed. Captured and preserved for all eternity.

We spent every possible moment together, driving around his ranch, cooking each other dinner, watching movies . . . trying our best to practice restraint on the comfortable couch in the living room of his isolated house on the ranch. And we largely remained alone on our dates, as nightclubs and parties weren't anywhere to be had. And we had no use for them anyway; socializing and meeting people weren't high on our agenda. We had way too much to learn about each other.

Soon, however, Marlboro Man decided it was time for me to meet his brother, Tim. The call came on my car phone as I drove to his ranch one evening, as I stared out of the windshield of my car and looked forward with eager anticipation to the glorious evening ahead of me. I'd have Marlboro Man all to myself. I'd get to crawl into those magical arms and forget the world around me. Though it had been less than twenty-four hours since I'd last seen him, I couldn't wait to get my fix.

"Hey," Marlboro Man said. "Where are you?"

Like I knew. I was somewhere between my house and his. "Oh . . . somewhere between my house and yours," I said, copping to my directional cluelessness.

He chuckled. "Okay, let me put it this way: are you more than halfway to my house? Or have you not gone that far?" He was already learning to speak my language.

"Umm . . . ," I said, looking around and trying to remember what time I'd left my house. "I would say . . . I would say . . . I'm exactly halfway there."

"Okay," he said, his smile evident through the phone. "When you get somewhere in the vicinity of the ranch, I want you to meet me at my brother's house."

Gulp. *Your brother's house? You mean, we actually have to introduce other people into our relationship? You mean, there are other people in the world besides us? I'm sorry. I forgot.*

"Oh, okay!" I said, enthusiastically, checking my makeup in the rearview mirror. "Um . . . how do I get there?" I felt butterflies in my gut.

"Okay, about a mile and a half before my turnoff, you'll see a white gate on the north side of the highway," he instructed. "You'll need to turn and head down that road a half a mile or so, and his house is right there."

"Okay . . . ," I said tentatively.

"Make sense?" he asked.

"Sure," I replied, pausing. "But . . . um . . . which way is north?"

I was only halfway kidding.

Miraculously, thirty minutes later I found Marlboro Man's brother's house. As I pulled up, I saw Marlboro Man's familiar white pickup parked next to a very large, imposing semi. He and his brother were sitting inside the cab.

Looking up and smiling, Marlboro Man motioned for me to join them. I waved, getting out of my car and obnoxiously taking my purse with me. To add insult to injury, I pressed the button on my keyless entry to lock my doors and turn on my car alarm, not realizing how out of place the dreadful *chirp!chirp!* must have sounded amidst all the bucolic silence. As I made my way toward the monster truck to meet my new love's only brother, I reflected that not only had I never in my life been inside the cab of a semi, but also I wasn't sure I'd ever been within a hundred feet of one. My armpits were suddenly clammy and moist, my body trembling nervously at the prospect of not only meeting Tim but also climbing into a vehicle nine times the size of my Toyota Camry, which, at the time, was the largest car I'd ever owned. I was nervous. What would I do in there?

Marlboro Man opened the passenger door, and I grabbed the large handlebar on the side of the cab, hoisting myself up onto the spiked metal steps of the semi. "Come on in," he said as he ushered me into the cab. Tim was in the driver's seat. "Ree, this is my brother, Tim."

Tim was handsome. Rugged. Slightly dusty, as if he'd just finished working. I could see a slight resemblance to Marlboro Man, a familiar twinkle in his eye. Tim extended his hand, leaving the other on the steering wheel of what I would learn was a brand-spanking-new cattle truck, just hours old. "So, how do you like this vehicle?" Tim asked, smiling widely. He looked like a kid in a candy shop.

"It's nice," I replied, looking around the cab. There were lots of gauges. Lots of controls. I wanted to crawl into the back and see what the sleeping quarters were like, and whether there was a TV. Or a Jacuzzi.

"Want to take it for a spin?" Tim asked.

I wanted to appear capable, strong, prepared for anything. "Sure!" I responded, shrugging my shoulders. I got ready to take the wheel.

Marlboro Man chuckled, and Tim remained in his seat, saying, "Oh, maybe you'd better not. You might break a fingernail." I looked down at my fresh manicure. It was nice of him to notice. "Plus," he continued, "I don't think you'd be able to shift gears." Was he making fun of me? My armpits were drenched. Thank God I'd worn black that night.

After ten more minutes of slightly uncomfortable small talk, Marlboro Man saved me by announcing, "Well, I think we'll head out, Slim."

"Okay, Slim," Tim replied. "Nice meeting you, Ree." He flashed his nice, familiar smile. He was definitely cute. He was definitely Marlboro Man's brother.

But he was nothing like the real thing.

Marlboro Man opened the passenger door of the semi and allowed me to climb out in front of him, while Tim exited the driver-side door to see us off. *That wasn't so bad*, I thought as I made my way down the steps. Aside from the manicure remark and my sweating problem, meeting Marlboro Man's brother had gone remarkably well. I looked okay that evening, had managed a couple of witty remarks, and had worn just the right clothing to conceal my nervousness. Life was good.

Then, because the Gods of Embarrassment seemed hell-bent on making me look bad, I lost my balance on the last step, hooking the heel of my stupid black boots on the grate of the step and awkwardly grabbing the handlebar to save myself from falling to my death onto the gravel driveway below. But though I stopped myself from wiping out, my purse flew off my arm and landed, facedown, on Tim's driveway, violently spilling its contents all over the gravel.

Only a woman can know the dreaded feeling of spilling her purse in the company of men. Suddenly my soul was everywhere, laid bare for Marlboro Man and his brother to see: year-old lip gloss, a leaky pen, wadded gum wrappers, and a hairbrush loaded up with hundreds, if not thousands, of my stringy auburn hairs. And men don't understand wads of long hair—for all they knew, I had some kind of follicular disorder and was going bald. There were no feminine products, but there was a package of dental floss, with a messy, eight-inch piece dangling from the opening and blowing in the wind.

And there were Tic Tacs. Lots and lots of Tic Tacs. Orange ones.

Then there was the money. Loose ones and fives and tens and twenties that had been neatly folded together and tucked into a pocket inside my purse were now blowing wildly around Tim's driveway, swept away by the strengthening wind from an approaching storm.

Nothing in my life could have prepared me for the horror of watching Marlboro Man, my new love, and his brother, Tim, whom I'd just met, chivalrously dart around Tim's driveway, trying valiantly to save my wayward dollars, all because I couldn't keep my balance on the steps of their shiny new semi.

I left my car at Tim's for the evening, and when we pulled away in Marlboro Man's pickup, I stared out the window, shaking my head and apologizing for being such a colossal dork. When we got to the highway, Marlboro Man glanced at me as he made a right-hand turn. "Yeah," he said, consoling me. "But you're my dork."

*S*OMETIMES MARLBORO Man and I would venture out into the world—go to the city, see a movie, eat a good meal, be among other humans. But what we did best was stay in together, cooking dinner and washing dishes and retiring to the chairs on his front porch or the couch in his living room, watching action movies and finding new and inventive ways to wrap ourselves in each other's arms so not a centimeter of space existed between us. It was our hobby. And we were good at it.

It was getting more serious. We were getting closer. Each passing day brought deeper feelings, more intense passion, love like I'd never known it before. To be with a man who, despite his obvious masculinity, wasn't at all afraid to reveal his soft, affectionate side, who had no fears or hang-ups about declaring his feelings plainly and often, who, it seemed, had never played a head game in his life . . . *this* was the romance I was meant to have.

Occasionally, though, after returning to my house at night, I'd lie awake in my own bed, wrestling with the turn my life had taken. Though my feelings for Marlboro Man were never in question, I sometimes wondered where "all this" would lead. We weren't engaged—it was way too soon for that—but how would that even work, anyway? It's not like I could ever live out here. I tried to squint and see through all the blinding passion I felt and envision what such a life would mean. Gravel? Manure? Overalls? Isolation?

Then, almost without fail, just about the time my mind reached full capacity and my what-ifs threatened to disrupt my sleep, my phone would ring again. And it would be Marlboro Man, whose mind was anything but scattered. Who had a thought and acted on it without wasting even a moment calculating the pros and cons and risks and rewards. Who'd whisper words that might as well never have existed before he spoke them: "I miss you already . . ." "I'm thinking about you . . ." "I love you. . . ." And then I'd smell his scent in the air and drift right off to Dreamland.

This was the pattern that defined my early days with Marlboro Man. I was so happy, so utterly content—as far as I was concerned, it could have gone on like that forever. But inevitably, the day would come when reality would appear and shake me violently by the shoulders.

And, as usual, I wasn't the least bit ready for it.

ARLBORO MAN lived twenty miles from the nearest town, a small town at that. There was no nightlife to speak of, save a local bar where retired oilfield workers and cowboys gossip and spin yarns over whiskey. His childhood friends were mostly gone, having moved on to larger lives in larger places. But after college he'd wound up back here, back in the same place he'd grown up. Back on the land that, apart from the telephone poles and oil wells, looked the same as it had a hundred years earlier, when his great-great-grandfather had first moved to America from Scotland. It was a quiet, isolated life. But it was where his heart was.

Strangely, I understood. There was something about the prairie. It was so drastically different from the crashing waves of the California coast, or from the rocky cliffs of Laguna, or from the palm trees and the mountains and the sunshine and the smog. It was wide open—not a freeway or high-rise in sight—and it whispered history and serenity. Apart from the horses and cattle, it was scarcely populated, with miles from one cowboy house to the next. Though I'd been away from L.A. for months, its pace and clutter were still so much a part of me, I could sometimes hear it ringing in my ears. I'd still get road rage pulling out of my parents' driveway. I'd still allow an hour for a ten-minute drive.

But five minutes on the prairie, and I'd forget about all of it. My soul would settle, relax, let go. The ranch was so removed from any semblance of society, it was easy to completely forget society even existed, let alone a society brimming with traffic, hustle and bustle, and stress. And stripped of all the noise and pounding distractions that had ruled my life for the previous seven years, I found it so easy to think clearly, to focus on my growing relationship with Marlboro Man, to take in and reflect on every delicious moment.

Absent all the friends, acquaintances, and party buddies with which I'd surrounded myself in L.A., I quickly grew accustomed to having Marlboro Man all to myself. And with the exception of a few brief meet-and-greet encounters with his brother and my mom, we'd spent hardly any time with other people. I'd loved it. But it wasn't reality.

And it couldn't last forever.

"Come over early tomorrow morning," Marlboro Man asked over the phone one night. "We're gathering cattle, and I want you to meet my mom and dad."

"Oh, okay," I agreed, wondering to myself why we couldn't just remain in our own isolated, romantic world. And the truth was, I wasn't ready to meet his parents yet. I still hadn't successfully divorced myself from California J's dear, dear folks. They'd been so wonderful to me during my years of dating their son and had become the California version of my parents, my home away from home. I hated that our relationship couldn't continue despite, oh, the minor detail of my breaking up with their son. And already? Another set of parents? I wasn't ready.

"What time do you want me there?" I asked. I'd do anything for Marlboro Man.

"Can you be here around five?" he asked.

"In the evening . . . right?" I responded, hopeful.

He chuckled. Oh, no. This was going to turn out badly for me. "Um . . . no," he said. "That would be five A.M."

I sighed. To arrive at his ranch at 5:00 A.M. would mean my rising by *4:00* A.M.—*before* 4:00 A.M. if I wanted to shower and make myself presentable. This meant it would still be dark outside, which was completely offensive and unacceptable. There's no way. I'd have to tell him no.

"Okay—no problem!" I responded. I clutched my stomach in pain.

Chuckling again, he teased, "I can come pick you up if you need me to. Then you can sleep all the way back to the ranch."

"Are you kidding?" I replied. "I'm usually up by four anyway. That's when I usually do my running, as you well know."

"Uh . . . huh," he said. "Gotcha." Another chuckle. Lifeblood to my soul.

I hung up the phone and darted to my closet. What does one wear to a ranch early in the morning? I wondered. I was stumped. I had enough good sense, thank God, to know my spiked black boots—the same boots I'd worn on basically every date with Marlboro Man thus far—were out of the question. I wouldn't want them to get dirty, and besides that, people might look at me funny. I had a good selection of jeans, yes, but would I go for the dark, straight-leg Anne Kleins? Or the faded, boot-cut Gaps with contrast stitching? And what on earth would I wear on top? This could get dicey. I had a couple of nice, wholesome sweater sets, but the weather was turning warmer and the style didn't exactly scream "ranch" to me. Then there was the long, flax-colored linen tunic from Banana Republic—one I loved to pair with a chunky turquoise necklace and sandals. But that was more Texas Evening Barbecue than Oklahoma Early-Morning Cattle Gathering. Then there were the myriad wild prints with sparkles and stones and other obnoxious adornments. But the last thing I wanted to do was spook the cattle and cause a stampede. I'd seen it happen in *City Slickers* when Billy Crystal fired up his cordless coffee grinder, and the results weren't the least bit pretty.

I considered canceling. I had absolutely nothing to wear. Every pair of shoes I owned was black, except for a bright yellow pair of pumps I'd bought on a whim in Westwood one California day. Those wouldn't exactly work, either. And I didn't own a single shirt that wouldn't loudly broadcast *CLUELESS CITY GIRL!* *CLUELESS CITY GIRL!* *CLUELESS CITY GIRL!* I wanted to crawl under my covers and hide.

I wandered into Betsy's room. Five years younger than me, she was away at college and deeply into grunge and hippie attire, but maybe I'd luck out and find a T-shirt she'd left behind that didn't have Kurt Cobain's or Bob Marley's face on it. Maybe. I opened her closet, looked inside, and magically, there it was, bathed in a glorious light: a faded denim button-down shirt—big enough for her, in all her scrawniness, to wear open and sloppy with her dirty Birkenstocks, but still small enough for me to tuck into my jeans and somewhat look the part. I tried it on and sang praises to the heavens. It was the perfect solution. This left only the shoes.

As fate would have it, I looked up and saw Betsy's brown Ralph Lauren waffle-soled hiking boots she'd gotten for Christmas three years earlier. She'd forsaken them for her too-cool-for-school hippie/grunge Birkenstocks, and they'd sat on the top shelf of her closet for ages. They laced up the front, were chunky, and were a size smaller than my feet; but considering my options—spiked black go-go boots or bright yellow pumps—these were the most appealing. I laid out my clothes, set my alarm for 3:40 A.M., and ran downstairs to place two spoons in the freezer. I was going to need them.

My parents were talking quietly in the den. They were always talking in the den, it seemed. "I'm getting up at four," I announced, waving. "Then I'm going out to the ranch to do something having to do with cattle. Wish me luck!"

My parents waved back, smiling. "Have fun," they said. Then I returned to my room and climbed under my covers, readying myself for the morning.

I darted out of bed to the sound of the screaming alarm. This had to be a joke. *It was nighttime.* Were these people crazy? I took a shower, my heart beating anxiously at the prospect of meeting Marlboro Man's parents on their turf. Wrapped in my towel, I slipped downstairs and retrieved my frozen spoons, which I carried upstairs and laid on both my eyes. I wanted none of that annoying puffiness. And within twenty-five minutes, I was thoroughly made up, blow-dried, curled, dressed, and out the door—dressed to the nines in my denim button-down shirt, Gap boot-cut jeans, and Betsy's brown lace-up Ralph Lauren waffle-soled hiking boots—

though something told me they weren't necessarily designed for outdoor durability. I hopped in the car and headed toward the ranch. I almost fell asleep at the wheel. Twice.

Marlboro Man met me at the road that led to his parents' house, and I followed him down five miles of graveled darkness. When we pulled into the paved drive, I saw the figure of his mother through the kitchen window. She was sipping coffee. My stomach gurgled. I should have eaten something. A croissant, back at my parents' house. A bowl of Grape-Nuts, maybe. Heck, a Twinkie at QuikTrip would have been nice. My stomach was in knots.

When I exited my car, Marlboro Man was there. Shielded by the dark of the morning, we were free to greet each other not only with a close, romantic hug but also a soft, sweet kiss. I was glad I'd remembered to brush my teeth.

"You made it," he said, smiling and rubbing my lower back.

"Yep," I replied, concealing a yawn. "And I got a five-mile run in before I came. I feel awesome."

"Uh-huh," he said, taking my hand and heading toward the house. "I sure wish I were a morning person like you."

When we walked into the house, his parents were standing in the foyer.

"Hey!" his dad said with a gravelly voice the likes of which I'd never heard before. Marlboro Man came by it honestly.

"Hello," his mom said warmly. They were there to welcome me. Their house smelled deliciously like leather.

"Hi," I said. "I'm Ree." I reached out and shook their hands.

"You sure look nice this morning," his mom remarked. She looked comfortable, as if she'd rolled out of bed and thrown on the first thing she'd found. She looked natural, like she hadn't set her alarm for 3:40 A.M. so she could be sure to get on all nine layers of mascara. She was wearing tennis shoes. She looked at ease. She looked beautiful. My palms felt clammy.

"She always looks nice," Marlboro Man said to his mom, touching my back lightly. I wished I hadn't curled my hair. That was a little over-the-top. That, and the charcoal eyeliner. And the raspberry shimmer lip gloss.

We needed to drive down the road a couple of miles to meet the rest of the cowboys and gather the cattle from there. "Mom, why don't you and Ree go ahead in her car and we'll be right behind you," Marlboro Man directed. His mother and I walked outside, climbed in the car, and headed down the road. We exchanged pleasant small talk. She was poised and genuine, and I chattered away, relieved that she was so approachable. Then, about a mile into our journey, she casually mentioned, "You might watch that turn up ahead; it's a little sharp."

"Oh, okay," I replied, not really listening. Clearly she didn't know I'd been an L.A. driver for years. Driving was not a problem for me.

Almost immediately, I saw a ninety-degree turn right in front of my face, pointing its finger at me and laughing—cackling—at my predicament. I whipped the steering wheel to the left as quickly as I could, skidding on the gravel and stirring up dust. But it was no use—the turn got the better of me, and my car came to rest awkwardly in the ditch, the passenger side a good four feet lower than mine.

Marlboro Man's mother was fine. Lucky for her, there's really nothing with which to collide on an isolated cattle ranch—no overpasses or concrete dividers or retaining walls or other vehicles. I was fine, too—physically, anyway. My hands were trembling violently. My armpits began to gush perspiration.

My car was stuck, the right two tires wedged inextricably in a deep crevice of earth on the side of the road. On the list of the Top Ten Things I'd Want Not to Happen on the First Meeting Between My Boyfriend's Mother and Me, this would rate about number four.

"Oh my word," I said. "I'm sorry about that."

"Oh, don't worry about it," she reassured, looking out the window. "I just hope your car's okay."

Marlboro Man and his dad pulled up beside us, and they both hopped out of the pickup. Opening my door, Marlboro Man said, "You guys okay?"

"We're fine," his mother said. "We just got a little busy talking." I was Lucille Ball. Lucille Ball on steroids and speed and vodka. I was a joke, a caricature, a freak. This couldn't possibly be happening to me. Not today. Not now.

"Okay, I'll just go home now," I said, covering my face with my hands. I wanted to be someone else. A normal person, maybe. A good driver, perhaps.

Marlboro Man examined my tires, which were completely torn up. "You're not goin' anywhere, actually. You guys hop in the pickup." My car was down for the count.

Despite the rocky start, I wound up enjoying a beautiful day on the ranch with Marlboro Man and his parents. I didn't ride a horse—my legs were still shaky from my near-murder of his mother earlier in the day—but I did get to watch Marlboro Man ride his loyal horse Blue as I rode alongside him in a feed truck with one of the cowboys, who gifted me right off the bat with an ice-cold Dr Pepper. I felt welcome on the ranch that day, felt at home, and before long the memory of my collision with a gravel ditch became but a faint memory—that is, when Marlboro Man wasn't romantically whispering sweet nothings like "Drive much?" softly into my ear. And when the day of work came to an end, I felt I knew Marlboro Man just a little better.

As the four of us rode away from the pens together, we passed the sad sight of my Toyota Camry resting crookedly in the ditch where it had met its fate. "I'll run you home, Ree," Marlboro Man said.

"No, no . . . just stop here," I insisted, trying my darnedest to appear strong and independent. "I'll bet I can get it going." Everyone in the pickup burst into hysterical laughter. I wouldn't be driving myself anywhere for a while.

On the ride back to my house, I asked Marlboro Man all about his parents. Where they'd met, how long they'd been married, what they were like together. He asked the same about mine. We held hands, reflecting on how remarkable it was that both his and my parents had been married in excess of thirty years. "That's pretty cool," he said. "It's unusual nowadays."

And it was. During my years in Los Angeles, I'd always taken comfort in the fact that my parents' marriage was happy and stable. I was among the few in my California circle of friends who'd come from an intact family, and I felt fortunate that I'd always been able to declare that my parents were still together. I was happy that Marlboro Man could say the same. It gave me some sense of security, an assurance that the man I was falling more in love with every day had parents who still loved each other. Marlboro Man kissed my hand, caressing my thumb with his. "It's a good sign," he said. The sun was beginning to set. We rode to my house in peaceful silence.

He walked me to the door, and we stopped at the porch step, my favorite porch step in the whole world. Some of the most magical moments had happened there, and that night was no different. "I'm so glad you came today," he said, wrapping his arms around me in an affectionate embrace. "I liked you being there."

"Thanks for having me," I said, gladly receiving his soft, sweet kiss on my cheek. "I'm sorry I wrecked with your mom in the car."

"That's okay," he replied. "I'm sorry about your car."

"It's no big deal," I said. "I'll be out there at five A.M. tomorrow with a crowbar and get to fixing those tires."

He laughed, then wrapped his arms tighter for a final, glorious hug. "Good night," he whispered. You beautiful man, you.

I floated into the house on clouds, despite the fact that I no longer had a car. I noticed my dad was in the kitchen. I flitted in to say hi.

"Hi, Dad!" I said, patting him on the shoulder. I grabbed a Diet Coke from the fridge.

"Hey," he replied, taking a seat on a barstool. "How was your day?"

"Oh my gosh, it was great—I loved it! We went. . . ." I looked at my dad. Something was wrong. His expression was grave. Troubled.

"What's *wrong*, Dad?" My face felt flushed.

He began to speak, then stopped.

"Dad . . . *what*?" I repeated. Something had happened.

"Your mother and I are having trouble," he said.

My knees immediately went weak. And my secure little world, as I'd always known it, changed in an instant.

I STOOD THERE frozen, unable to feel my feet beneath me. My cheeks turned hot and tingled, and the back of my neck tightened. My heart skipped a beat. I suddenly felt sick. All standard reactions to finding out that the longest, most stable personal relationship you'd ever witnessed wasn't so stable anymore.

In trouble? I couldn't believe what I was hearing. But they're just pulling into the home stretch. They'd raised four children, after all. They'd made it through the fight. Their youngest, my sister, was in college, for Pete's sake—the hard part was over and done with.

My dad gave me a brief rundown of the situation, then I walked slowly up the stairs, remnants of my soul dragging behind me. I felt gutted. My face still tingled as I entered my bedroom and pulled off my clothes—clothes dusty and grimy from my glorious day of working cattle with Marlboro Man and his parents. As I showered, I reflected on the turn my day had just taken: I'd felt so great that night when my love had brought me home—so elated, so in love, so full. Just an hour earlier, in Marlboro Man's pickup, I'd rattled on about how nice it was that both our parents' marriages were still intact. It was all nonsense now. I'd worn that label like a badge, that pride of being one of the minority of twenty-somethings whose parents' marriage was still going strong, whose family's foundation hadn't been shaken by divorce. And just now, in the blink of an eye, all my illusions of a stable, perfect home life had been shattered. And though I'd always been a life-long optimist, a glass-is-half-full type, a Suzy Sunshine Supreme, I also had enough weathered L.A. girl in me to know that my dad was deadly serious. And that this didn't look good at all.

I flopped onto my bed facedown, utterly deflated. Oh, what a beautiful day I'd had: meeting Marlboro Man's parents. Getting to know his mom. Nearly killing her on a ninety-degree turn in my Toyota Camry. Laughing with her. Seeing so much of Marlboro Man in her smile. Messing up my car. Leaving it all askew in the ditch on a rural county road. Embarrassing myself, but being okay with that. Talking with Marlboro Man as he chivalrously drove me all the way back to my house. Falling more in love with him with each mile we drove, with each sexy grin he flashed. But now—good God, what was the point? Love obviously didn't last forever—it couldn't possibly. Not when two people in their fifties, married thirty years, four children, two dogs, and a lifetime of memories, couldn't even keep it together. What was I doing? Why was I even bothering with this romance thing . . . this love thing? Where would it even lead? An uncharacteristic hopelessness suddenly flooded my insides, filling me with doom and dread. Reality, ugly and raw, grabbed me around the neck and began to squeeze.

As I lay in bed and looked at the innumerable stars outside my bedroom window, I tried to make sense of it all, even as my tired eyes bled painful, salty tears. Then, as had become customary, my phone began to ring. I knew who it was, of course. It was Marlboro Man, the source of so much joy that at times I could hardly handle it. He was calling to torture me with his strong, yet whispery, voice. He was calling to say good night. I'd come to expect his postdate phone calls; I drank them in like a potion, inhaled them like a powerful, mellowing drug. I'd become totally and completely addicted.

But that night, instead of jumping up and darting to the phone like a

lovesick schoolgirl, I rolled away and pulled the comforter farther over my head, trying my best to drown out the ringing. After four rings, the phone stopped, leaving me in the dark, depressing silence of my room—the same room in which I'd grown up. Tears of pain and confusion dampened my pillow as everything I'd ever understood about stability and commitment melted away. And for the first time in weeks—for the first time since Marlboro Man and I shared our first beautiful kiss—love was suddenly the last thing I wanted.

Chapter Nine
SWEET SURRENDER

EELING AWFUL, I dragged myself out of bed the next morning. My stomach felt hollow; I was a child lost in the woods. Overnight, I'd been excommunicated from my exalted position in the Church of the Stable Home, and I was ill-prepared to handle it.

I couldn't even bring myself to think about Marlboro Man, to find the emotional energy to escape to my normally vivid and delicious daydreams of him. I was weighted down, suddenly unsure of where I stood with anything. I'd never been one to look forward to marriage, to sharing my life with someone forever; I'd always lived way too much in the moment to think that far ahead, and besides, I just hadn't had the kind of relationships that had given me cause not to be cynical about love. But Marlboro Man had changed that. While we hadn't yet talked of marriage, he was the first man I'd ever been with who filled my thoughts twenty-four hours a day; who, four seconds after dropping me off at night, I longed to be with again; who I couldn't imagine ever being without.

But now, that morning, my cynicism had crept back in. I was back to feeling like it was all a foolish pipe dream, this idea of finding the one true love of one's life. Sure, I was in love with Marlboro Man *now*, but where might we be in five years? Fifteen years? Thirty? Right where my parents are, I supposed—struggling with dead love and apathy and ambivalence. After all, they'd been in love once, too.

"Mom, what's going on?" I asked after walking downstairs. She was scurrying around the kitchen, clearly on her way out the door.

"Oh, I'm going to go get ready for the soup kitchen," she said. "I've gotta run, sweetie. . . ."

"Mom," I said, more assertively. "What's going on with you and Dad?" My face tingled as I spoke. I still couldn't believe what I'd heard the night before.

"Sweetie," my mom repeated. "We can talk about it later. . . ."

"Well, I mean . . . ," I began. I couldn't figure out what to say. "What's the problem?"

"It's . . . it's too complicated to go into right now," she answered, acting busier as she went about her business in the kitchen. "We can talk about it some other time."

She clearly wasn't in the mood to share. Within minutes, she was pulling out of the driveway, leaving her older daughter behind to wallow around in her parents' empty house. I shivered; a cold air had moved into our once-warm home.

I made myself a scrambled egg and sat on the back porch in my pajamas, looking out at the seventh fairway. It was a beautiful summer morning—cool, quiet, serene. A stark contrast to the chaos erupting in my soul. I wouldn't be able to stay here—it was all different now. I was no longer the Prodigal Daughter lovingly welcomed home after a long stint of unrighteous living in Los Angeles. I was now the Intruder—barging in on my parents' lives at the most inopportune time. I'd have to get my own place somewhere to give my parents their space. But where? Not here, in my hometown; that would make no sense. I wished I was back in Los Angeles. Chicago. Somewhere anonymous. Anywhere but home.

I needed air. The golf course looked inviting. Throwing on my favorite black Gap leggings, a USC tank, and tennis shoes, I took off on a brisk walk, using the cart path as my guide. I loved walking on the golf course; it looked and smelled just as it did when I was a little girl. I began on the seventh fairway, the same fairway I'd always crossed to get to the club-house so I could order Shirley Temples to go, and before long I was near the eighth green, which was situated near a busy residential intersection. The horn of a passing black Cadillac sounded; a friend of my parents smiled and waved. I waved back, wondering if she knew of my parents' marital prob-lems, wondering if anyone did. My parents had always been "one of those couples"—not just to me but to an entire community. They were, simply, the Smiths, the king and queen of Suburban Stability, Success, and Bliss. If the worst happened, if they were unable to resolve their conflict and wound up divorcing, I wasn't sure the town would survive the shock.

I headed west and broke into a jog. I'd always hated jogging. Not that I could ever be confused with Dolly Parton, but running had always hurt my chest. It was jarring. Bouncy. Disruptive. Also, as a lifelong ballerina, running was something that always had to be done with turned-out feet, pointed toes, and long, lanky, outstretched arms resembling those of swans. I looked bad—really bad—whenever I tried to run like an athlete. I looked like a psychotic stork . . . but that morning, I didn't care. My jog turned into a run, and soon became a sprint, and before I knew it I was running like I'd never run before. I ran hard and fast, the pain of my panting lungs masking the sadness over my parents' marital woes. And when I finally arrived at the eighteenth hole, I stopped for a rest.

Glorious, cleansing sweat trickled down my back, and my face and torso burned like a furnace. I bent over, propping my hands on my knees, gasping for breath. I stood at the top of a huge hill—the hill on the eigh-teenth hole. It was an ideal hill for sledding in the wintertime, and on heavy snow days it was peppered with country club kids and their adventure-seeking parents, sliding down the hill at lightning speed and trudging back up to the top for another go. Standing there on that hot summer morning, I could almost see my dad pushing my brothers on the red plastic disc, the

one with thick rope handles, and could hear my mom giggling and screaming wildly as she gave my sister and me a healthy shove on our toboggan.
We were a happy family, weren't we? I hadn't imagined it, had I?

The run had helped. My body felt renewed, refreshed, even if my thinking was a little off balance. I walked slowly back home, breathing deeply
and taking in all the sights and sounds of a private country club golf course:
the beeping of a distant golf cart driving in reverse, the barking of the bird
dogs Dr. Burris took hunting with him every fall and winter, millions of
tiny birds in triumphant song. It was the closest thing to the country that
I'd known until now.

And my thoughts turned to Marlboro Man.

I was thinking of him when I walked back into the house, imagining his
gorgeous voice in my ear when I heard the phone ringing in my room. I ran up
the stairs, skipping three steps at a time, and answered the phone, breathless.

"Hello?" I gasped.

"Hey there," Marlboro Man said. "What are you doing?"

"Oh, I just went for a run on the golf course," I answered. As if I did it
every day.

"Well, I just want you to know I'm coming to get you at five," he said.
"I'm having Ree withdrawals."

"You mean since *midnight,* when we last saw each other?" I joked.
Actually, I knew exactly what he meant.

"Yeah," he said. "That's way, way too long, and I'm not gonna put up
with it anymore." I loved it when he took charge.

"Okay, then—fine," I said, surrendering. "I don't want to argue. I'll
see you at five."

$\mathcal{M}$ARLBORO MAN showed up five minutes early, before my second coat of mascara had a chance to dry. He looked gorgeous

standing at the front door, his strong, tan arms looking like sculpted mas-
terpieces in his charcoal gray polo shirt. He moved in for a hug, holding me
close for a minute and rubbing his hand on my back.

Climbing into his pickup, we headed toward the ranch for the evening,
talking as the road before us grew more rural by the mile. I didn't mention my parents and did a pretty good job of keeping it shoved into a quiet
corner in my mind. But the sting of it lingered, and a tiny cloud of gloom
followed us on our trip. Though I knew with every ounce of my being that
I was sitting next to the love of my life, I had no idea what the future held
for us. I wasn't even sure what "future" meant at that point. My mind trailed
off, and I looked out the window at the approaching prairie.

"You're awfully quiet," Marlboro Man said, his hand resting on the
back of my head.

"Am I?" I asked, playing dumb. "I don't mean to be."

"You're not your usual self," he responded, his hand finding the back of
my neck. A million tingles traveled down my spine.

"Oh, I'm fine," I said, trying to appear strong and together. "I think
that twenty-mile run got the best of me today."

Marlboro Man chuckled. I'd hoped that would happen. "Twenty miles?
That's a mighty big golf course," he remarked. We both laughed, well aware
that I was way too much of a pansy-ass to run such a distance.

But there was no way I was bringing up what was really troubling
me that night. I wasn't ready to admit it yet, to acknowledge that things
in my family weren't as peachy as I'd always thought. I certainly wasn't
ready to risk that dreaded quivering bottom lip that was always a distinct
possibility lately whenever I vocalized something upsetting. I still hadn't
forgiven myself for breaking down in Marlboro Man's kitchen after running over Puggy Sue. There was no telling what deluge might come if the
subject matter turned to my mom and dad. I didn't think I could handle the
humiliation.

When we pulled up to Marlboro Man's house, I saw my Camry sitting in his driveway. I didn't expect it to be there; I figured it was still on Marlboro Man's parents' road, sitting all crooked in the ditch where I'd left it the night before. Marlboro Man had already fixed it, fishing it out of the ditch and repairing the mangled tires and probably, knowing him, filling the tank with gas.

"Oh, thank you so much," I said as we walked toward the front door. "I thought maybe I'd killed it."

"Aw, it's fine," he replied. "But you might want to learn to drive before you get in it again." He flashed his mischievous grin.

I slugged him in the arm as he laughed. Then he lunged at me, grabbing my arms and using his leg to sweep my supporting leg right out from under me. Within an instant, he had me on the ground, right on the soft, green grass of his front yard. I shrieked and screamed, trying in vain to wrestle my way out of his playful grasp, but my wimpy upper body was no match for his impossible strength. He tickled me, and being the most ticklish human in the Northern Hemisphere, I screamed bloody murder. Afraid I'd wet my pants (it was a valid concern), I fought back the only way I knew how—by grabbing and untucking his shirt from his Wranglers . . . and running my hand up his back, poking at his rib cage.

The tickling suddenly stopped. Marlboro Man propped himself on his elbows, holding my face in his hands. He kissed me passionately and seriously, and what started as a playful wrestling match became an impromptu make-out session in his front yard. It was an unlikely place for such an event, and considering it was at the very beginning of our night together, an unlikely time. But it was also strangely perfect. Because sometime during all the laughing and tickling and wrestling and rolling around in the grass, my worry and concern over my parents' troubles had magically melted away.

Only when the chiggers began biting did Marlboro Man suggest an alternate plan. "Let's go inside," he said. "I'm cooking dinner." *Yummy,* I thought. *That means steak.* And as we walked into the house, I smiled contentedly, realizing that the stress of the previous twenty-four hours had all but disappeared from view. And I knew it, even then: Marlboro Man, not only that night but in the months to come, would prove to be my savior, my distraction, my escape in the midst of troubles, my strength in the face of upheaval, my beauty in times of terrible, heartbreaking ugliness. He held my heart entirely in his hands, this cowboy, and for the first time in my life, despite everything I'd ever believed about independence and feminism and emotional autonomy, I knew I'd be utterly incomplete without him.

Talk about a terrifying moment.

Part Two

Chapter Ten

THE GOOD, THE BAD, AND THE SWEATY

THE SUMMER months rolled by, marked by hot, humid days and beautiful, romantic evenings. During the day, I'd help my dad convert his antiquated medical bookkeeping system to modernized computers. In the evenings I'd rest in Marlboro Man's ample arms, grasping them affectionately as we watched old westerns together on his worn leather sofa. We were inseparable, conjoined, together every possible moment . . . and the passion between us showed no signs of cooling.

My life had taken such a turn; this was most clear to me as I relaxed in this cowboy's house on an isolated ranch and watched John Wayne's swagger on the television screen before me. Just months earlier, living in L.A., I'd found it difficult not to live by plans. I had schedules and meetings and dinner dates with friends . . . and the colorful cocktails flowed forth as abundantly as the L.A. colloquialisms that poured from my glossy red lips. Some days, I was stoked. Other days I was full-on pumped. I lived in a rad apartment in Marina del Rey, and generally speaking, life was totally awesome. Like, totally.

I was a ninny of the highest order.

Somewhere along the way, though, the sushi, the high heels, the 110 and the 405 and the 10 had become nooses around my neck. Daily, the air was being choked from my lungs; I'd begun noticing a brutally slow death of the person inside me. And I might have stayed forever, might have carried on and continued my ambitious quest of sampling every restaurant in Greater Los Angeles and married J, my electrical engineer. I might have settled into an enviable existence as an Orange County housewife with 1.698 kids, a flat stomach, and a three-car garage. Oh, was I well on my way.

But before my eyes, in a matter of a few short months, sushi had metamorphosed into steak, and nightclubs had changed into the front porch of Marlboro Man's quiet house in the country. I hadn't felt the reverb of a thumping club beat in months and months. My nervous system had never known such calm.

That is, until Marlboro Man called one morning that August with his simple request: "My cousin Kim is getting married next weekend," he said. "Can you come?"

An uncomfortable wave washed over my body.

"You there?" he asked. I'd paused longer than I'd intended.

"Yeah . . . I'm here," I replied. "But, um . . . will I . . . will I have to meet anyone?"

Marlboro Man laughed. The answer, obviously, was yes. Yes, I'd have to meet "anyone." In fact, I'd have to meet *everyone:* everyone in his extended family of cousins, aunts, uncles, grandparents, and friends; and his family, by all accounts, was large. We'd talked about our families before, and he knew good and well that I had all of three cousins. *Three.* He, on the other hand, had fifty. He knew how intimidating a family wedding would be to an outsider, especially when the family is as large as his. He knew this would be way out of my comfort zone. And he was right.

I turned my focus to clothes, immediately endeavoring to find just the right dress for the occasion. This was huge—my debut as the girlfriend of Marlboro Man—and I shopped with that in mind. Should I go for a sleek, sexy suit? That might seem too confident and brazen. A floral silk skirt? Too obvious for a wedding. A little black dress? Too conservative and safe. The options pummeled my brain as I browsed the choices on the racks.

I tried on dress after dress, suit after suit, outfit after outfit, my frustration growing more acute with each zip of the zipper. I wanted to be a man. Men don't agonize over what to wear to a wedding. They don't spend seven hours trying on clothes. They don't think of wardrobe choices as life-or-death decisions.

That's when I found it: a drop-dead gorgeous fitted suit the exact color of a stick of butter. It was snug, with just a slight hint of sexy, but the lovely, pure color made up for it. The fabric was a lightweight wool, but since the wedding would be at night, I knew it would be just fine. I loved the suit—not only would I feel pretty for Marlboro Man, but I'd also appear moderately, but not overly, confident to all his cousins, and appropriate and proper to his elderly grandmothers.

When we arrived at the wedding at Marlboro Man's grandparents' house, I gasped. People were absolutely everywhere: scurrying and mingling and sipping champagne and laughing on the lawn. Marlboro Man's mother was the first person I saw. She was an elegant, statuesque vision in her brown linen dress, and she immediately greeted and welcomed me. "What a pretty suit," she said as she gave me a warm hug. *Score. Success.* I felt better about life. After the ceremony, I'd meet Cousin T., Cousin H., Cousin K., Cousin D., and more aunts, uncles, and acquaintances than I ever could have counted. Each family member was more gracious and welcoming than the one before, and it didn't take long before I felt right at home. This was going well. This was going really, really well.

It was hot, though, and humid, and suddenly my lightweight wool suit didn't feel so lightweight anymore. I was deep in conversation with a group of ladies—smiling and laughing and making small talk—when a trickle of perspiration made its way slowly down my back. I tried to ignore it, tried to will the tiny stream of perspiration away, but one trickle soon turned into two, and two turned into four. Concerned, I casually excused myself from the conversation and disappeared into the air-conditioned house. I needed to cool off.

I found an upstairs bathroom away from the party, and under normal circumstances I would have taken time to admire its charming vintage pedestal sinks and pink hexagonal tile. But the sweat profusely dripping from all pores of my body was too distracting. Soon, I feared, my jacket would be drenched. Seeing no other option, I unbuttoned my jacket and removed it, hanging it on the hook on the back of the bathroom door as I frantically looked around the bathroom for an absorbent towel. None existed. I found the air vent on the ceiling, and stood on the toilet to allow the air-conditioning to blast cool air on my face.

Come on, Ree, get a grip, I told myself. Something was going on . . . this was more than simply a reaction to the August humidity. I was having some kind of nervous psycho sweat attack—think Albert Brooks in *Broadcast News*—and I was being held captive by my perspiration in the upstairs bathroom of Marlboro Man's grandmother's house in the middle of his cousin's wedding reception. I felt the waistband of my skirt stick to my skin. Oh, God . . . I was in trouble. Desperate, I stripped off my skirt and the stifling control-top panty hose I'd made the mistake of wearing; they peeled off my legs like a soggy banana skin. And there I stood, naked and clammy, my auburn bangs becoming more waterlogged by the minute. *So this is it,* I thought. *This is hell.* I was in the throes of a case of diaphoresis the likes of which I'd never known. And it had to be on the night of my grand entrance into Marlboro Man's family. Of course, it just had to be. I looked in the mirror, shaking my head as anxiety continued to seep from my pores, taking my makeup and perfumed body cream along with it.

Suddenly, I heard the knock at the bathroom door.

"Yes? Just a minute . . . yes?" I scrambled and grabbed my wet control tops.

"Hey, you . . . are you all right in there?"

God help me. It was Marlboro Man.

ACK IN L.A., I'd remained friends with my freshman-year boyfriend, Collin, and we'd become even closer after he confided in me one dark and emotional night that he'd finally come to terms with his homosexuality. Around that time, his mother was visiting from Dallas, and Collin invited me to meet them at Hotel Bel Air for brunch. I wore the quintessential early-1990s brunch outfit: a copper-brown silk tank with white, dime-size polka dots and a below-the-knee, swinging skirt to match. A flawless *Pretty Woman*–Julia Roberts polo match replica. I loved that outfit.

It was silk, though, and clingy, and the second I sat down at the table I knew I was in trouble. My armpits began to feel cool and wet, and slowly I noticed the fabric around my arms getting damper and damper. By the time our mimosas arrived, the ring of sweat had spread to the level of my third rib; by mealtime, it had reached the waistline of my skirt, and the more I tried to will it away, the worse it got. I wound up eating my Eggs Florentine with my elbows stuck to my hip bones so Collin and his mother wouldn't see. But copper-brown silk, when wet, is the most unforgiving fabric on the planet. Collin had recently come out to his parents, so I'd later determined I'd experienced some kind of sympathetic nervousness on Collin's behalf. I never wore that outfit again. Never got the stains out.

Nor would I ever wear this suit again.

"Hey . . . you okay?" Marlboro Man repeated.

My heart fluttered in horror. I wanted to jump out of the bathroom window, scale down the trellis, and hightail it out of there, forgetting I'd ever met any of these people. Only there wasn't a trellis. And outside the window, down below, were 150 wedding guests. And I was sweating enough for all of them combined.

I was naked and alone, enduring the flop sweat attack of my life. It figured. It was usually the times I felt and looked my absolute best when I wound up being humbled in some colossally bizarre way. There was the time I traveled to my godmother's son's senior prom in a distant city and partied for an hour before realizing the back of my dress was stuck inside my panty hose. And the time I entered the after-party for my final *Nutcracker* performance and tripped on a rug, falling on one of the guest performers and knocking an older lady's wineglass out of her frail arms. You'd think I would have come to expect this kind of humiliation on occasions when it seemed like everything should be going my way.

"You need anything?" Marlboro Man continued. A drop of sweat trickled down my upper lip.

"Oh, no . . . I'm fine!" I answered. "I'll be right out! You go on back to the party!" *Go on, now. Run along. Please. I beg you.*

"I'll be out here," he replied. Dammit. I heard his boots travel a few steps down the hall and stop. I had to get dressed; this was getting ridiculous. Then, as I stuck my big toe into the drenched leg of my panty hose, I heard what I recognized as Marlboro Man's brother Tim's voice.

"What's she *doing* in there?" Tim whispered loudly, placing particularly uncomfortable emphasis on "doing." I closed my eyes and prayed fervently. *Lord, please take me now. I no longer want to be here. I want to be in Heaven with you, where there's zero humidity and people aren't punished for their poor fabric choices.*

"I'm not sure," Marlboro Man answered. The geyser began spraying again.

I had no choice but to surge on, to get dressed, to face the music in all my drippy, salty glory. It was better than staying in the upstairs bathroom of his grandmother's house all night. God forbid Marlboro Man or Tim start to think I had some kind of feminine problem, or even worse, *constipation* or *diarrhea*! I'd sooner move to another country and never return than to have them think such thoughts about me.

Working quickly, I pulled on my panty hose and stepped into the skirt of my godforsaken butter yellow lightweight wool suit. Then, with a wad of toilet paper, I dabbed the sweat from my chin, the back of my neck, my armpits, and my lower back. I caught a glimpse of myself in the mirror and mouthed *loser* to the sweaty freak looking back at me. I slipped on my jacket, buttoned it up, and opened my purse, working quickly to salvage what little makeup remained on my face. I didn't look pretty. I didn't look pretty at all. The outer corners of my eyes were caked with melted mascara, and the taupe shimmer eye shadow I'd painstakingly applied to my lids was now adorning both my cheeks. It wasn't a good look.

But it didn't matter anymore. I was doing much more damage holing up in the bathroom by myself than this new streaky, splotchy complexion ever could. So I combed my damp, sticky bangs, slung my handbag over my shoulder, and walked out of the bathroom to face the sharks.

Marlboro Man and Tim were standing in the hall, not seven steps from the bathroom door. "*There* she is," Tim remarked as I walked up to them and stood. I smiled nervously.

Marlboro Man put his hand on my lower back, caressing it gently with his thumb. "You all right?" he asked. A valid question, considering I'd been in the bathroom for over twenty minutes.

"Oh yeah . . . I'm fine," I answered, looking away. I wanted Tim to disappear.

Instead, the three of us made small talk before Marlboro Man asked, "Do you want something to drink?" He started toward the stairs.

Gatorade. I wanted Gatorade. Ice-cold, electrolyte-replacing Gatorade. That, and vodka. "I'll go with you," I said.

Marlboro Man and I grabbed ourselves a drink and wound up in the backyard, sitting on an ornate concrete bench by ourselves. Miraculously, my nervous system had suddenly grown tired of sending signals to my sweat glands, and the dreadful perspiration spell seemed to have reached its end. And the sun had set outside, which helped my appearance a little. I felt like a circus act.

I finished my screwdriver in four seconds, and both the vitamin C and the vodka went to work almost instantly. Normally, I'd know better than to replace bodily fluids with alcohol, but this was a special case. At that point, I needed nothing more than to self-medicate.

"So, did you get sick or something?" Marlboro Man asked. "You okay?" He touched his hand to my knee.

"No," I answered. "I got . . . I got hot."

He looked at me. "Hot?"

"Yeah. Hot." I had zero pride left.

"So . . . what were you doing in the bathroom?" he asked.

"I had to take off all my clothes and fan myself," I answered honestly. The vitamin C and vodka had become a truth serum. "Oh, and wipe the sweat off my neck and back." This was sure to reel him in for life.

Marlboro Man looked at me to make sure I wasn't kidding, then burst into laughter, covering his mouth to keep from spitting out his Scotch. Then, unexpectedly, he leaned over and planted a sweet, reassuring kiss on my cheek. "You're funny," he said, as he rubbed his hand on my tragically damp back.

And just like that, all the horrors of the evening disappeared entirely from my mind. It didn't matter how stupid I was—how dumb, or awkward, or sweaty. It became clearer to me than ever, sitting on that ornate concrete bench, that Marlboro Man loved me. Really, really loved me. He loved me with a kind of love different from any I'd felt before, a kind of love I never knew existed. Other boys—at least, the boys I'd always bothered with— would have been embarrassed that I'd disappeared into the bathroom for half the night. Others would have been grossed out by my tale of sweaty woe or made jokes at my expense. Others might have looked at me blankly, unsure of what to say. But not Marlboro Man; none of it fazed him one bit. He simply laughed, kissed me, and went on. And my heart welled up in my soul as I realized that without question, I'd found the one perfect person for me.

Because more often than not, I was a mess. Embarrassing, clumsy things happened to me with some degree of regularity; this hadn't been the first time and it sure wouldn't be the last. The truth was, despite my best efforts to appear normal and put together on the outside, I'd always felt more like one of the weird kids.

But at last, miraculously, I'd found the one man on earth who would actually love that about me. I'd found the one man on earth who would appreciate my spots of imperfection . . . and who wouldn't try to polish them all away.

Chapter Eleven
ALONG THE DUSTY ROAD

I'D NEVER been with anyone like Marlboro Man. He was attentive—the polar opposite of aloof—and after my eighteen-month-long college relationship with my freshman love Collin, whose interest in me had been hampered by his then-unacknowledged sexual orientation, and my four-year run with less-than-affectionate J, attentive was just the drug I needed. Not a day passed that Marlboro Man—my new cowboy love—didn't call to say he was thinking of me, or he missed me already, or he couldn't wait to see me again. Oh, the beautiful, unbridled honesty.

We loved taking drives together. He knew every inch of the countryside: every fork in the road, every cattle guard, every fence, every acre. Ranchers know the country around them. They know who owns this pasture, who leases that one, whose land this county road passes through, whose cattle are on the road by the lake. It all looked the same to me, but I didn't care. I'd never been more content to ride in the passenger seat of a crew-cab pickup in all my life. I'd never *ridden* in a crew-cab pickup in all my life. Never once. In fact, I'd never personally known anyone who'd driven a pickup; the boys from my high school who drove pickups weren't part of my scene, most likely because their families had a farm or ranching operation, and in their spare time they were needed at home to contribute to the family business. Either that, or they were cowboy wannabes—the kind that only wore cowboy hats to bars—and that wasn't really my type either. For whatever reason, pickup trucks and I had never once crossed paths. And now, with all the time I was spending with Marlboro Man, I practically lived in one.

The only thing I knew about pickups was this: growing up, I always inwardly mocked the couples I saw who drove around in them. The girl would be sitting in the middle seat right next to the boy, and the boy's right arm would be around her shoulders, and his left arm would be on the wheel. I'm not sure why, but there was something about my golf course upbringing that had always caused me to recoil at this sight. *Why is she sitting in the middle seat?* I'd wonder. *Why is it important that they press against each other as they drive down the road? Can't they wait until they get home?* I looked at it as a sign of weakness—something pitiable. *They need to get a life* may have even crossed my mind once or twice, as if their specific brand of public affection was somehow directly harming me. But that's what happens to people who, by virtue of the geography of their childhood, are deprived of the opportunity to ride in pickup trucks. They become really, really judgmental about otherwise benign things.

Still, every now and then, as Marlboro Man showed me the beauty of the country in his white Ford F250, I couldn't help but wonder . . . had he been one of those boys in high school? I knew he'd had a serious girlfriend back in his teenage years. Julie. A beautiful girl and the love of his adolescent life, in the same way Kev had been mine. And I wondered: had Julie scooched over to the middle seat when Marlboro Man picked her up every Friday night? Had he hooked his right arm around her neck, and had she then reached her left hand up and clasped his right hand with hers? Had they then dragged Main in this position? Our hometowns had been only forty miles apart; maybe he'd brought her to my city to see a movie. Was it remotely possible I'd actually seen Marlboro Man and Julie riding around in his pickup, sitting side by side? Was it possible this man, this beautiful, miraculous, perfect man who'd dropped so magically into my life, had actually been one of the innocent recipients of my intolerant, shallow pickup-related condemnation?

And if he had done it, was it something he'd merely grown out of? How come *I* wasn't riding around in his middle seat? Was I supposed to initiate this? Was this expected of me? Because I probably should know early on. But wouldn't he have gestured in that direction if he'd wanted me to move over and sit next to him? Maybe, just maybe, he'd liked those girls better than he liked me. Maybe they'd had a closeness that warranted their riding side by side in a pickup, a closeness that he and I just don't share? *Please don't let that be the reason. I don't like that reason.* I had to ask him. I had to know.

"Can I ask you something?" I said as we drove down the road separating a neighboring ranch from his.

"Sure," Marlboro Man answered. He reached over and touched my knee.

"Did you ever used to drive around in your pickup with a girl sitting in the middle seat right next to you?" I tried not to sound accusatory.

A grin formed in the corner of Marlboro Man's mouth. "Sure I did," he said. His hand was still on my knee. "Why?"

"Oh, no reason. I was just curious," I said. I wanted to leave it at that.

"What made you think of that?" he said.

"Oh, I was really just curious," I repeated. "Growing up, I'd sometimes see boys and girls riding right next to each other in pickups, and I just wondered if you ever did. That's all." I stopped short of telling him I never understood the whole thing or asking him why he loved Julie more than me.

"Yep. I did," he said.

I looked out the window and thought for a minute. *What am I? Chopped liver? Is there some specific reason he never pulls me over close to him as we drive around the countryside? Why doesn't he hook his right arm affectionately around my neck and claim me as the woman of his pickup?* I never knew I had such a yearning to ride right next to a man in a pickup, but apparently it had been a suppressed lifelong dream I knew nothing about. Suddenly, sitting in that pickup with Marlboro Man, I'd apparently never wanted anything so badly in my life.

I couldn't keep quiet about it any longer. "So . . . ," I began. *Was it just a high school thing? Or worse,* I imagined, *is it just that I'm not and never will be a country girl? Is it that country girls have some wild sense of abandon that I wasn't born with? A reckless side, a fun, adventurous side that makes them worthy of riding next to boys in pickups? Am I untouchable? Am I too prim? Too proper? I'm not! I'm really not! I'm fun and adventurous. Reckless, too! I have a pair of jeans: Anne Kleins! And I want to be Middle Seat Worthy. Please, Marlboro Man . . . please. I've never wanted anything this much.* "So, um . . . why don't you do it anymore?" I asked.

"Bucket seats," Marlboro Man answered, his hand still resting on my leg.

Made sense. I settled in and relaxed a bit.

But I had another question I'd been mulling over.

"Mind if I ask you another question?" I said.

"Go ahead," he replied.

I cleared my throat and sat up straight in my seat. "How come . . . how come it took you so long to call me?" I couldn't help but grin. It was one of the most direct questions I'd ever asked him.

He looked in my direction, then back toward the road.

"You don't have to tell me," I said. And he didn't. But I'd wondered more than a handful of times, and as long as he was coming clean about bucket seats and other important matters, I thought it would be a good time to ask him why four months had passed between the first night we'd met in the smoky bar and the night he'd finally called to invite me to dinner. I remembered being knocked over by his magnetism that night during Christmas vacation. What had he thought of me? Had he forgotten me instantly, then remembered me in a flash that April night after my brother's wedding? Or had he intentionally waited four months to call? Was it some kind of country boy protocol I didn't know about?

I was a girl. I simply had to know.

"I was . . . ," he began. "Well, I was dating someone else."

I'll kill her with my bare hands. "Oh," I said in return. It was all I could muster.

"Plus, I was running a herd of cows in Nebraska and having to drive up there every week," he continued. "I just wasn't here enough to break things off with her in the right way . . . and I didn't want to call you and ask you out until that was all resolved."

I repeated myself. "Oh." *What was her name? She's dead to me.*

"I liked you, though," he said, flashing me a smile. "I thought about you."

I couldn't help but smile back. "You did?" I asked quietly, still wondering what the girl's name was. I wouldn't rest till I knew.

"I did," he said sweetly, stroking my leg with his hand. "You were different."

I stopped short of interrogating him further, of asking him to specify what he meant by "different." And it didn't take much imagination to figure it out. As he drove me around his familiar homeland, it was obvious what he would have considered "different" about me.

I didn't know anything about the country.

I LOVED DRIVING with Marlboro Man. I saw things I'd never seen before, things I'd never even considered in my two and a half decades of city life. For the first time ever, I began to grasp the concept of north, south, east, and west, though I imagine it would take another twenty-five years before I got them straight. I saw fence lines and gates made of welded iron pipe, and miles upon miles of barbed wire. I saw creeks—rocky, woodsy creeks that made the silly water hazard in my back-yard seem like a little mud puddle. And I saw wide open land as far as the eye could see. I'd never known such beauty.

Marlboro Man loved showing me everything, pointing at pastures and signs and draws and lakes and giving me the story behind everything we saw. The land, both on his family's ranch and on the ranches surrounding it, made sense to him: he saw it not as one wide open, never-ending space, but as neatly organized parcels, each with its own purpose and history. "Betty Smith used to own this part of our ranch with her husband," he'd say. "They never had kids and were best friends with my grandparents." Then he'd tell some legend of Betty Smith's husband's grandfather, remembering such vivid details, you'd think he'd been there himself. I absorbed it all, every word of it. The land around him pulsated with the heartbeats of all who'd lived there before . . . and as if it were his duty to pay honor to each and every one of them, he told me their names, their stories, their relationship, their histories.

I loved that he knew all those things.

One late afternoon, we crossed a creek and came upon a thicket of trees in the middle of a pasture quite a ways from Marlboro Man's homestead. As I looked more closely, I saw that the trees were shrouding a small white house. A white picket fence surrounded the lot, and as we drove closer to the property, I noticed movement in the yard. It was a large, middle-aged woman, with long, gray hair cascading down her shoulders. She was push-ing a lawn mower around her yard, and two wagtail dogs yipped and fol-lowed her every step. Most notably, she was wearing only underwear and what appeared to be a late model Playtex bra. And as we passed by her house, she glanced up at us for a moment . . . then kept on mowing.

Trying to appear nonchalant, I asked Marlboro Man, "So . . . who was that?" Maybe this could be the start of another story.

He looked at me and replied, "I have absolutely no idea."

We never spoke of her again.

Chapter Twelve

GUNFIGHT AT THE O.K. CORRAL

AFTER OUR drives, we made dinner together in his kitchen. I cooked my pasta primavera, which burst with the bright colors of zucchini, carrots, and peas. Marlboro Man grilled medium-rare rib eye steaks that sizzled in melted butter and garlic. I prepared my favorite Spago-inspired pizza: a thin, chewy crust topped with tomatoes, basil, and fresh mozzarella, which I had to order by mail from a mom-and-pop outfit in Dallas, since no Oklahoma shops carried it. He showed me the art of making white gravy in an iron skillet, how important it was to brown the roux to a deep golden brown before pouring in the milk. We discovered each other's histories while cooking in his kitchen in the country, me whipping out my arsenal of L.A. vegetarian delights with the same pride and enthusiasm that Marlboro Man shared his carnivorous ones. Our two worlds collided in rich, calorie-laden dinners. I began doing step aerobics at my hometown YMCA every morning to keep from growing out of my Anne Kleins. Now was the time for love, not jiggle.

Meanwhile, back in my hometown, my parents' marriage was crumbling before my eyes. I loved my parents, loved them dearly. But as an adult, watching the thirty-year marriage of your mother and father implode and disintegrate is like watching a train wreck happen in slow motion. And your parents are the conductors, and the passengers on the train are family, and many lifelong friends, and all the future grandchildren, and a community, and memories and hopes and dreams. And they're all about to die in a fiery, deadly accident. Oh, and you're on the train, too. But you're also watching from outside the tracks. You want to scream, to try to warn the operators of the train of the devastation that's about to come. But it's a nightmare, and your voice is squeezed and squelched and nothing comes out. And you're powerless to stop it.

I wanted to leave; I wanted out of there so badly. It's not as if my parents' difficulties manifested themselves in dish throwing or screaming or slamming doors or loud, unpleasant histrionics. No, instead it was hushed conversations, tense expressions, ashen faces, and, occasionally, tired, puffy eyes. The screaming might actually have been better; this slow, excruciating death was agonizing to watch. Every time I passed through the house and felt the stifling tension in the air, all I wanted was to be somewhere else. I wanted to pack my bags, withdraw all my cash from the bank, and bolt.

But I was stuck—stuck in a delicious, glorious, beautiful, inescapable La Brea tar pit of romance with a rough, rugged, impossibly tender cowboy. As soon as I'd have any thoughts of escaping to Chicago to avoid my parents' problems, within seconds I'd shoot myself down. Something major would have to happen to pry me out of his arms.

Marlboro Man filled my daydreams, filled my thoughts, my time, my heart, my mind. When I was with him, I was able to forget about my parents' marital problems. On our drives together, preparing our dinners, watching our VHS action movies, all of those unhappy things disappeared from view. This became a crutch for me, an addictive drug of escape. Ten seconds in Marlboro Man's pickup, and I saw only goodness and light. And the occasional bra-and-panty-wearing grandma mowing her yard.

Further complicating matters was the passion and lust I felt for Marlboro Man; it was stronger than anything I'd felt in my life. And sometimes I worried about it, in the same way a heavy drinker might occasionally

MECHANICS' INSTITUTE LIBRARY
57 Post Street
San Francisco, CA 94104
(415) 393-0101

question his second, third, or fourth pour of whiskey. This couldn't be good
for me, could it?

But deep, deep down, I didn't care. And even if I did care, there wasn't
a thing on earth I could do about it. If Marlboro Man were moonshine during Prohibition, I'd smuggle crates of it across state lines and guzzle it on
the journey; if he were a street drug, I'd sell my hair to score a fix; if he were
standing below a cliff, I'd jump off to be with him.

If Marlboro Man was wrong, I didn't want to be right.

Where would all of this lead? At times I asked myself and wondered.
Despite having put my plans for Chicago on hold, despite my knowledge
that trying to go one day without seeing Marlboro Man was futile, despite
how desperately in love I knew I was, I still at times thought this might all
just be a temporary glitch in my plans, a wild hair I needed to work out of
my system before getting on with the rest of my life. Like I was at Romance
Camp for a long, hot summer, playing the part of the cowgirl.

The time was drawing near, however, when Marlboro Man would take
the bull by the horns and answer that question for me, once and for all.

O NE DAY Marlboro Man invited my sister, Betsy, and me to the
ranch to work cattle. She was home from college and bored, and
Marlboro Man wanted Tim to meet another member of my family.

"Working cattle" is the term used to describe the process of pushing
cattle, one by one, through a working chute, during which time they are
branded, dehorned, ear tagged, and "doctored" (temperature taken, injec-
tions given). The idea is to get all the trauma and mess over with in one fell
swoop so the animals can spend their days grazing peacefully in the pasture.

When Betsy and I pulled up and parked, Tim greeted us at the chute and
immediately assigned us our duties. He handed my sister a hot shot, which
is used to gently zap the animal's behind to get it to move through the chute.

It's considered the easy job.

"You'll be pushing 'em through," Tim told Betsy. She dutifully took the hot shot, studying the oddly shaped object in her hands.

Next, Tim handed me an eight-inch-long, thick-gauge probe with some kind of electronic device attached. "You'll be taking their temperature," Tim informed me.

Easy enough, I thought. *But how does this thing fit into its ear? Or does it slide under its arm somehow? Perhaps I insert it under the tongue? Will the cows be okay with this?*

Tim showed me to my location—at the hind end of the chute. "You just wait till the steer gets locked in the chute," Tim directed. "Then you push the stick all the way in and wait till I tell you to take it out."

Come again? The bottom fell out of my stomach as my sister shot me a worried look, and I suddenly wished I'd eaten something before we came. I felt weak. I didn't dare question the brother of the man who made my heart go pitter-pat, but . . . *in the bottom? Up the bottom? Seriously?*

Before I knew it, the first animal had entered the chute. Various cowboys were at different positions around the animal and began carrying out their respective duties. Tim looked at me and yelled, "Stick it in!" With utter trepidation, I slid the wand deep into the steer's rectum. This wasn't natural. This wasn't normal. At least it wasn't for me. This was definitely against God's plan.

I was supposed to check the monitor and announce if the temperature was above ninety-nine degrees. The first one was fine. But before I had a chance to remove the probe, Tim set the hot branding iron against the steer's left hip. The animal let out a guttural *Moooooooooooooo!*, and as he did, the contents of its large intestine emptied all over my hand and forearm.

Tim said, "Okay, Ree, you can take it out now." I did. I didn't know what to do. My arm was covered in runny, stinky cow crap. Was this supposed to happen? Should I say anything? I glanced at my sister, who was looking at me, completely horrified.

The second animal entered the chute. The routine began again. I stuck it in. Tim branded. The steer bellowed. The crap squirted out. I was amazed at how consistent and predictable the whole nasty process was, and how nonchalant everyone—excluding my sister—was acting. But then slowly . . . surely . . . I began to notice something.

On about the twentieth animal, I began inserting the thermometer. Tim removed his branding iron from the fire and brought it toward the steer's hip. At the last second, however, I fumbled with my device and had to stop for a moment. Out of the corner of my eye, I noticed that when I paused, Tim did, too. It appeared he was actually waiting until I had the thermometer fully inserted before he branded the animal, ensuring that I'd be right in the line of fire when everything came pouring out. He had planned this all along, the dirty dog.

Seventy-eight steers later, we were finished. I was a sight. Layer upon layer of manure covered my arm. I'm sure I was pale and in shock. The cowboys grinned politely. Tim directed me to an outdoor faucet where I could clean my arm. Marlboro Man watched as he gathered up the tools and the gear . . . and he chuckled.

*A*S MY sister and I pulled away in the car later that day, she could only say, "Oh. My. God." She made me promise never to return to that awful place.

I didn't know it at the time, but I'd found out later that this, from Tim's perspective, was my initiation. It was his sick, twisted way of measuring my worth.

Chapter Thirteen

HIGH NOON

*I*N THE first week of my relationship with Marlboro Man, I'd spent more time alone with him, it seemed, than I'd ever spent with J in the four years we were together. And now, so many months later, I realized how important it really is for a couple in love to sit in silence every once in a while. To be still. To trace your thumbs along each other's hand and let the sounds of the atmosphere be your music for a while. J and I had never had that. There were always too many people around.

I'd been reflecting on this—the drastic turn my life and my outlook on love had taken—more and more on the evenings Marlboro Man and I spent together, the nights we sat on his quiet porch, with no visible city lights or traffic sounds anywhere. Usually we'd have shared a dinner, done the dishes, watched a movie. But we'd almost always wind up on his porch, sitting or standing, overlooking nothing but dark, open countryside illuminated by the clear, unpolluted moonlight. If we weren't wrapped in each other's arms, I imagined, the quiet, rural darkness might be a terribly lonely place. But Marlboro Man never gave me a chance to find out.

It was on this very porch that Marlboro Man had first told me he loved me, not two weeks after our first date. It had been a half-whisper, a mere thought that had left his mouth in a primal, noncalculated release. And it had both surprised and melted me all at once; the honesty of it, the spontaneity, the unbridled emotion. But though everything in my gut told me I was feeling exactly the same way, in all the time since I still hadn't found the courage to repeat those words to him. I was guarded, despite the affection Marlboro Man heaped upon me. I was jaded; my old relationship had done that to me, and watching the crumbling of my parents' thirty-year marriage hadn't exactly helped. There was just something about saying the words "I love you" that was difficult for me, even though I knew, without a doubt, that I did love him. Oh, I did. But I was hanging on to them for dear life—afraid of what my saying them would mean, afraid of what might come of it. I'd already eaten beef—something I never could have predicted I'd do when I was living the vegetarian lifestyle. I'd gotten up before 4:00 A.M. to work cattle. And I'd put my Chicago plans on hold. At least, that's what I'd told myself all that time. I put my plans *on hold*.

That was enough, wasn't it? Putting my life's plans on hold for him? Marlboro Man had to know I loved him, didn't he? He was so confident when we were together, so open, so honest, so transparent and sure. There was no such thing as "give-and-take" with him. He gave freely, poured out his heart willingly, and either he didn't particularly care what my true feelings were for him, or, more likely, he already knew. Despite my silence, despite my fear of totally losing my grip on my former self, on the independent girl that I'd wanted to believe I was for so long . . . he knew. And he had all the patience he needed to wait for me to say it.

*I*T WAS a Tuesday when I finally threw caution to the wind, when I decided, finally, to articulate the words I knew I so desperately felt but that, for whatever reason, I'd always been too scared to say. It was impromptu, unexpected. But there was something about the night.

He'd greeted me at the car. "Hey, you," he said as I closed the door behind me and, still out of habit, armed the theft alarm of my car. "Do you think you might ever get to a point where you'll actually leave your car unlocked out here?" he asked with a chuckle.

I hadn't even noticed. "Oh," I said, laughing. "I don't know why I even do that!" My face turned red. Freakazoid.

Marlboro Man smiled, wrapped his arms around my waist, and lifted me off the ground—my favorite move of his. "Hi," he said, the right side of his mouth turned upward in a grin.

"Hi," I replied, smiling back. He looked so beautiful in his worn-out, comfortable jeans and his starched charcoal button-down shirt. God, did he look good in charcoal.

Charcoal, the color, was created with Marlboro Man in mind.

And then came the kiss—the kind usually reserved for couples who spend weeks and weeks apart and store up all their passions for the moment when they say hello again. For us, it had been less than twenty-four hours. At that moment, there was no one in the world but the two of us, and as closely as we were pressed together in our embrace, there weren't really two of us at all anymore.

My whole body tingled as we walked into the house. I was feeling the love that night.

Marlboro Man cooked a tenderloin on the grill. The most unimaginably scrumptious cut of beef there is, tenderloin, when prepared properly, can be easily cut with a fork. Marlboro Man had made it for me a couple of times during the previous few months, and there were moments, usually after the first bite or two, when I would nearly shed a tear over its beauty. To cook the tenderloin, Marlboro Man would nestle it on a sturdy ship of heavy foil, then sprinkle it generously with salt and coarsely ground pepper. To finish it off, he'd pour a saucepanful of butter over the top, set the whole thing on a hot grill, and cook it for twenty to thirty minutes until it was a perfect, warm medium-rare inside. I was sure that a more beautiful piece of animal flesh had never existed.

We ate dinner and talked, and I sipped chilled wine slowly, savoring every single swallow, even as I savored every single moment with the man sitting next to me. I loved looking at him when he talked, loved the movement of his mouth. *He has the best mouth,* I'd think to myself. His mouth drove me absolutely wild.

We wound up on his couch, watching a submarine movie and making out, with the chorus of "The Navy Hymn" in the background. And just like that, it happened: the executive officer had just relieved the captain of command of the ship. It was a tense, exciting moment in the movie, and I was suddenly so overcome with emotion, I couldn't control myself. My head rested on his shoulder, my heart rested entirely in his hands. And in a whisper, my words escaped: "I love you." He probably hadn't heard them. He was too focused on the movie.

But he had heard me; I could tell. His arms enveloped me even further; his embrace tightened. He breathed in and sighed, and his hand played with my hair. "Good," he said softly, and his gentle lips found mine.

DRIVING HOME that night, I felt so much better. I was no longer a freak of nature—the kind of freak that spends every waking hour with a man for months on end but has some sort of bizarre mental defect that prevents her from articulating her feelings for him—the kind of freak that allows the man to express his love time after time but gives nothing in return. I felt good about it, too, that I'd had the uncharacteristic boldness to tell him I loved him before he'd had a chance to say it to me first that night. I wanted to say *I love you,* not *I love you, too.* I knew there was a reason I liked submarine movies.

I had no idea where our relationship was headed. But I did know that I meant what I'd said.

I slept like a baby that night.

MARLBORO MAN'S call woke me up the next morning. It was almost eleven.

"Hey," he said. "What's up?"

I hopped out of bed, blinking and stumbling around my room. "Who me? Oh, nothing." I felt like I'd been drugged.

"Were you *asleep?*" he said.

"Who, me?" I said again, trying to snap out of my stupor. I was stalling, trying my darnedest to get my bearings.

"Yes. You," he said, chuckling. "I can't believe you were asleep!"

"I wasn't asleep! I was . . . I just . . . " I was a loser. A pathetic, late-sleeping loser.

"You're a real go-getter in the mornings, aren't you?" I loved it when he played along with me.

I rubbed my eyes and pinched my own cheek, trying to wake up. "Yep. Kinda," I answered. Then, changing the subject: "So . . . what are you up to today?"

"Oh, I had to run to the city early this morning," he said.

"Really?" I interrupted. The city was over two hours from his house. "You got an early start!" I would never understand these early mornings. When does anyone ever sleep out there?

Marlboro Man continued, undaunted. "Oh, and by the way . . . I'm pulling into your driveway right now."

Huh?

I ran to my bathroom mirror and looked at myself. I shuddered at the sight: puffy eyes, matted hair, pillow mark on my left cheek. Loose, faded pajamas. Bag lady material. Sleeping till eleven had not been good for my appearance. "No. No you're not," I begged.

"Yep. I am," he answered.

"No you're not," I repeated.

"Yes. I am," he said.

I slammed my bathroom door and hit the lock. *Please, Lord, please,* I prayed, grabbing my toothbrush. *Please let him be joking.*

I brushed my teeth like a crazed lunatic as I examined myself in the mirror. Why couldn't I look like the women in commercials who wake up in a bed with ironed sheets and a dewy complexion with their hair perfectly tousled? I wasn't fit for human eyes, let alone the piercing eyes of the sexy, magnetic Marlboro Man, who by now was walking up the stairs to my bedroom. I could hear the clomping of his boots.

The boots were in my bedroom by now, and so was the gravelly voice attached to them. "Hey," I heard him say. I patted an ice-cold washcloth on my face and said ten Hail Marys, incredulous that I would yet again find myself trapped in the prison of a bathroom with Marlboro Man, my cowboy love, on the other side of the door. What in the world was he doing there? Didn't he have some cows to wrangle? Some fence to fix? It was broad daylight; didn't he have a ranch to run? I needed to speak to him about his work ethic.

"Oh, hello," I responded through the door, ransacking the hamper in my bathroom for something, anything better than the sacrilege that adorned my body. Didn't I have any respect for myself?

I heard Marlboro Man laugh quietly. "What're you doing in there?" I found my favorite pair of faded, soft jeans.

"Hiding," I replied, stepping into them and buttoning the waist.

"Well, c'mere," he said softly.

My jeans were damp from sitting in the hamper next to a wet washcloth for two days, and the best top I could find was a cardinal and gold FIGHT ON!

T-shirt from my 'SC days. It wasn't dingy, and it didn't smell. That was the best I could do at the time. Oh, how far I'd fallen from the black heels and glitz of Los Angeles. Accepting defeat, I shrugged and swung open the door.

He was standing there, smiling. His impish grin jumped out and grabbed me, as it always did.

"Well, good morning!" he said, wrapping his arms around my waist. His lips settled on my neck. I was glad I'd spritzed myself with Giorgio.

"Good morning," I whispered back, a slight edge to my voice. Equal parts embarrassed at my puffy eyes and at the fact that I'd slept so late that day, I kept hugging him tightly, hoping against hope he'd never let go and never back up enough to get a good, long look at me. Maybe if we just stood there for fifty years or so, wrinkles would eventually shield my puffiness.

"So," Marlboro Man said. "What have you been doing all day?"

I hesitated for a moment, then launched into a full-scale monologue. "Well, of course I had my usual twenty-mile run, then I went on a hike and then I read *The Iliad*. Twice. You don't even want to know the rest. It'll make you tired just hearing about it."

"Uh-huh," he said, his blue-green eyes fixed on mine. I melted in his arms once again. It happened any time, every time, he held me.

He kissed me, despite my gold FIGHT ON! T-shirt. My eyes were closed, and I was in a black hole, a vortex of romance, existing in something other than a human body. I floated on vapors.

Marlboro Man whispered in my ear, "So . . . ," and his grip around my waist tightened.

And then, in an instant, I plunged back to earth, back to my bedroom, and landed with a loud thud on the floor.

"R-R-R-R-Ree?" A thundering voice entered the room. It was my brother Mike. And he was barreling toward Marlboro Man and me, his arms outstretched.

"*Hey!*" Mike yelled. "W-w-w-what are you guys doin'?"And before either of us knew it, Mike's arms were around us both, holding us in a great big bear hug.

"Well, hi, Mike," Marlboro Man said, clearly trying to reconcile the fact that my adult brother had his arms around him.

It wasn't awkward for me; it was just annoying. Mike had interrupted our moment. He was always doing that. "Yo, Mike," I said. "Where the heck did you come from?"

"Carl just brought me home from the ambulance," he said. The ambulance was one of Mike's favorite haunts, second only to Fire Station no. 3.

I wriggled loose of his and Marlboro Man's grip. "So, Mike," I said. "What can I do for you this fine morning?" (Translation: *What do you want?*)

"W-w-w-well . . . I am fixin' to meet Dan at the mall for lunch because he said he has not had a vacation in a l-l-l-long time and his wife has been really stressed-out so he is gettin' ready to go on vacation with his wife and he said he wants to spend some time with me before he leaves." Mike always liked to provide plenty of detail.

"Okay, cool," I said. (Translation: *Bye, Mike. Scram.*)

"And I need a ride to the mall." There it was. I knew he wanted something.

"Well, Mike," I said. "I'm kinda busy right now. I've got company, as you can see."

"B-b-b-but I am gonna be late and Dan will think somethin' is wrong!" Oh, no. He was getting amped up.

"Well, how come you didn't just have Carl drop you off there?" I asked. Mike didn't always take the most reasonable course.

"Because I t-t-t-told him my sister would be glad to take me!" Mike replied. Mike liked to sign me up for things without my consent.

I wasn't budging, though; I wasn't going to let Mike bully me. "Well, Mike," I said, "I'll take you to the mall in a little bit, but I've got

to finish getting dressed. So just chill out, dude!" I loved telling Mike to chill out.

Marlboro Man had been watching the whole exchange, clearly amused by the Ping-Pong match between Mike and me. He'd met Mike several times before; he "got" what Mike was about. And though he hadn't quite figured out all the ins and outs of negotiating him, he seemed to enjoy his company.

Suddenly, Mike turned to Marlboro Man and put his hand on his shoulder. "C-c-c-can you please take me to the mall?"

Still grinning, Marlboro Man looked at me and nodded. "Sure, I'll take you, Mike."

Mike was apoplectic. *"Oh my gosh!"* he said. *"You will? R-r-r-really?"* And with that he grabbed Marlboro Man in another warm embrace.

"Okeydoke, Mike," Marlboro Man said, breaking loose of Mike's arms and shaking his hand instead. "One hug a day is enough for guys."

"Oh, okay," Mike said, shaking Marlboro Man's hand, apparently appreciating the tip. "I get it now."

"No, no, no! You don't need to take him," I intervened. "Mike, just hold your horses—I'll be ready in a little bit!"

But Marlboro Man continued. "I've gotta get back to the ranch anyway," he said. "I don't mind dropping him off."

"Yeah, *Ree*!" Mike said belligerently. He stood beside Marlboro Man in solidarity, as if he'd won some great battle. "M-m-m-mind your own beeswax!"

I gave Mike the evil eye as the three of us walked downstairs to the front door. *"Are we gonna take your white pickup?"* Mike asked. He was about to burst with excitement.

"Yep, Mike," Marlboro Man answered. "Wanna go start it?" He dangled the keys in front of Mike's face.

"What?" Mike said, not even giving Marlboro Man a chance to answer. He snatched the keys from his hand and ran to the pickup, leaving Marlboro Man and me alone on our old familiar front step.

"Well, uh," I said playfully. "Thanks for taking my brother to the mall." Mike fired up the diesel engine.

"No problem," Marlboro Man said, leaning in for a kiss. "I'll see you tonight." We had a standing date.

"See you then." Mike laid on the horn.

Marlboro Man headed toward his pickup, then stopped midway and turned toward me once again. "Oh, hey—by the way," he said, walking back toward the front step. "You wanna get married?" His hand reached into the pocket of his Wranglers.

My heart skipped a beat.

*H*E REMOVED his hand from his worn, pleasantly snug jeans . . . and it held something small. *Holy Lord*, I said to myself. *What in the name of kingdom come is going on here?* His face wore a sweet, sweet smile.

I stood there completely frozen. "Um . . . what?" I asked. I could formulate no words but these.

He didn't respond immediately. Instead he took my left hand in his, opened up my fingers, and placed a diamond ring onto my palm, which was, by now, beginning to sweat.

"I said," he closed my hand tightly around the ring. "I want you to marry me." He paused for a moment. "If you need time to think about it, I'll understand." His hands were still wrapped around my knuckles. He touched his forehead to mine, and the ligaments of my knees turned to spaghetti.

Marry you? My mind raced a mile a minute. Ten miles a second. I had three million thoughts all at once, and my heart thumped wildly in my chest.

Marry you? But then I'd have to cut my hair short. Married women have short hair, and they get it fixed at the beauty shop.

Marry you? But then I'd have to make casseroles.

Marry you? But then I'd have to wear yellow rubber gloves to do the dishes.

Marry you? As in, move out to the country and actually live with you? In your house? In the country? But I . . . I . . . I don't live in the country. I don't know how. I can't ride a horse. I'm scared of spiders.

I forced myself to speak again. "Um . . . what?" I repeated, a touch of frantic urgency to my voice.

"You heard me," Marlboro Man said, still smiling. He knew this would catch me by surprise.

Just then my brother Mike laid on the horn again. He leaned out of the window and yelled at the top of his lungs, *"C'mon! I am gonna b-b-be late for lunch!"* Mike didn't like being late.

Marlboro Man laughed. "Be right there, Mike!" I would have laughed, too, at the hilarious scene playing out before my eyes. A ring. A proposal. My developmentally disabled and highly impatient brother Mike, waiting for Marlboro Man to drive him to the mall. The horn of the diesel pickup. Normally, I would have laughed. But this time I was way, way too stunned.

"I'd better go," Marlboro Man said, leaning forward and kissing my cheek. I still grasped the diamond ring in my warm, sweaty hand. "I don't want Mike to burst a blood vessel." He laughed out loud, clearly enjoying it all.

I tried to speak but couldn't. I'd been rendered totally mute. Nothing could have prepared me for those ten minutes of my life. The last thing I remember, I'd awakened at eleven. Moments later, I was hiding in my bathroom, trying, in all my early-morning ugliness, to avoid being seen by Marlboro Man, who'd dropped by unexpectedly. Now I was standing on the front porch, a diamond ring in my hand. It was all completely surreal.

Marlboro Man turned to leave. "You can give me your answer later," he said, grinning, his Wranglers waving good-bye to me in the bright noon-day sun.

But then it all came flashing across my line of sight. The boots in the bar, the icy blue-green eyes, the starched shirt, the Wranglers . . . the first date, the long talks, my breakdown in his kitchen, the movies, the nights on his porch, the kisses, the long drives, the hugs . . . the all-encompassing, mind-numbing passion I felt. It played frame by frame in my mind in a steady stream.

"Hey," I said, walking toward him and effortlessly sliding the ring on my finger. I wrapped my arms around his neck as his arms, instinctively, wrapped around my waist and raised me off the ground in our all-too-familiar pose. "Yep," I said effortlessly. He smiled and hugged me tightly. Mike, once again, laid on the horn, oblivious to what had just happened. Marlboro Man said nothing more. He simply kissed me, smiled, then drove my brother to the mall.

As for me, I went inside, walked up to my bedroom, and fell on the floor. *What . . . just happened?* Staring at the ceiling, I tried to take it all in. My mind began to race, trying to figure out what it all meant. *Do I need to learn how to whittle? Cook fried chicken? Ride a horse? Use a scythe?* My face began to feel flushed. *And children? Oh, Lord. That means we might have children! What will we name them? Travis and Dolly? Oh my gosh. I have children in my future.* I could see it plainly in front of me. *They'll be little redheaded children with green eyes just like mine, and they'll have lots of freckles, too. I'll have ten of them, maybe eleven. I'll have to squat in the garden and give birth while picking my okra.* Every stereotype of domestic country life came rushing to the surface. A lot of them involved bearing children.

Then my whole body relaxed in a mushy, contented heap as I remembered all the times I'd walked back into that very room after being with Marlboro Man, my cowboy, my savior. I remembered all the times I'd fallen onto my bed in a fizzy state of euphoria, sighing and smelling my shirt to try to get one last whiff. All the times I'd picked up the phone early in the morning and heard his sexy voice on the other end. All the times I'd longed to see him again, two minutes after he'd dropped me off. This was right, this was oh, so right. If I couldn't go a day without seeing him, I certainly couldn't go a lifetime. . . .

Just then my phone rang, startling me. It was Betsy, my younger sister.

"Yo, what up?" she asked. She was driving home from college for a visit.

I twirled my hair on my finger, not the least bit prepared to answer frankly.

"Oh, nothin'," I answered as my thumb played with the new engagement ring around my finger.

We spent the next five minutes in sisterly small talk, and we hung up without my sharing the news. I wanted to wait awhile before telling anyone. I still needed to grasp it myself. Still lying on the floor of my bedroom, I took a deep breath and looked at my hand. I felt strange and tingly, almost separated from my body. I wasn't really here, I told myself. I was in Chicago, and I was watching all of this happen to someone else. It was a movie, maybe on the big screen, maybe cable. But it couldn't be my life . . . could it?

My phone rang again. It was Marlboro Man.

"Hey," he said. I heard the diesel engine rattling in the background. "I just dropped Mike at the mall."

"Hi," I said, smiling. "Thanks for doing that."

"I just wanted to tell you that . . . I'm happy," he said. My heart leapt out of my chest and shot through the roof.

"I am, too," I said. "Surprised . . . and happy."

"Oh," he continued. "I told Mike the news. But he promised he wouldn't tell anybody."

Oh, Lord, I thought. *Marlboro Man obviously has no idea who he's dealing with.*

Chapter Fourteen

SHE ALMOST DIED WITH HER BOOTS ON

I WAS CERTAIN that by now Mike had told half the shopping mall in my hometown that "M-m-m-my sister is gonna get m-m-m-*married*!" This would mean that within an hour or two, the entire state would probably know. It would all be very real in no time. The guy behind the Subway counter would hear the news first, followed by the sweet high school girl at Candy Craze, who probably knew my sister from high school, so she'd call her mom, who'd probably been a patient of my dad's at some point, and who likely knew my mom. And the gal at the cosmetics counter in Dillards, who sold my grandmother Estée Lauder foundation once a month—she'd soon know, too. And so would all the security guards and janitors on-site—they would all hear the news within the hour, though very few of them would likely care. But everyone would know: this was a fact. To Mike, news—any news at all—was meant to be shared. And if he could be the first person to spread the word, the happier he'd be. Thank God he didn't have a cell phone, or he would have already called the local radio station and asked that they announce it during the rush hour drive.

That was one of Mike's tactics. He loved being the bearer of any kind of news.

But I couldn't allow myself to worry about that. Still lying on the ground, half tingly, half stunned, I held my left hand in front of my face and lightly spread my fingers, examining what Marlboro Man had given me that morning. I couldn't have chosen a more beautiful ring, or a ring that was a more fitting symbol of my relationship with Marlboro Man. It was unadorned, uncontrived, consisting only of a delicate gold band and a lovely diamond that stood up high—almost proudly—on its supportive prongs. It was a ring chosen by a man who, from day one, had always let me know exactly how he felt. The ring was a perfect extension of that: strong, straightforward, solid, direct. I liked seeing it on my finger. I felt good knowing it was there.

My stomach, though, was in knots. I was engaged. *Engaged.* I was ill-prepared for how weird it felt. Why hadn't I ever heard of this strange sensation before? Why hadn't anyone told me? I felt simultaneously grown up, excited, shocked, scared, matronly, weird, and happy—a strange combination for a weekday morning. I was engaged—holy moly. My other hand picked up the receiver of the phone, and without thinking, I dialed my little sister.

"Hi," I said when Betsy picked up the phone. It hadn't been ten minutes since we'd hung up from our last conversation.

"Hey," she replied.

"Uh, I just wanted to tell you"—my heart began to race—"that I'm, like . . . engaged."

What seemed like hours of silence passed.

"Bullcrap," Betsy finally exclaimed. Then she repeated: "Bull*crap.*"

"Not bullcrap," I answered. "He just asked me to marry him. I'm *engaged,* Bets!"

"*What?*" Betsy shrieked. "Oh my God . . ." Her voice began to crack. Seconds later, she was crying.

A lump formed in my throat, too. I immediately understood where her tears were coming from. I felt it all, too. It was bittersweet. Things would change. Tears welled up in my eyes. My nose began to sting.

"Don't cry, you butthead." I laughed through my tears.

She laughed it off, too, sobbing harder, totally unable to suppress the tears. "Can I be your maid of honor?"

This was too much for me. "I can't talk anymore," I managed to squeak through my lips. I hung up on Betsy and lay there, blubbering on my floor.

The phone rang again almost immediately. It was Mike, calling from a pay phone in the mall. *Oh Lord*, I thought. *He probably has a whole roll of quarters.*

"Hey!" Mike shouted. I heard shoppers in the background.

"Hey, Mike," I answered, wiping tears from my face.

His voice was playful. "I heard s-s-s-somethin' about s-s-s-someone today. . . ." He burst out in mischievous laughter.

I played along. "Oh yeah, Mike? What's that?"

"I heard . . . that . . . s-s-s-someone I know is gettin' m-m-m-m-*married*!" He shrieked and cackled as only Mike can.

"Now, Mike," I began. "You haven't *told* anyone . . . have you?"

He didn't respond.

"Mike?" I pressed.

Finally, he replied, "I . . . don't . . . think so."

"*Mike* . . . ," I teased. "Remember, you promised you wouldn't tell anyone!"

"I h-h-h-have to go," Mike said. And with that, he hung up and went about his business.

Yep, it was sure to be in that evening's paper . . . figuratively speaking.

I spent the next couple of hours preemptively informing the rest of my immediate family that I, their daughter/sister/granddaughter, would be marrying a cowboy from the next county. I was met with very little resistance—other than a couple of *"Oh, Jesus"* remarks from my oldest brother, who, as I once had, believed that life outside a big city wasn't worth living. By and large, my family approved. They obviously knew how crazy I was about Marlboro Man; they'd hardly seen me since we'd gotten together. The glaring precariousness of my own parents' marriage loomed large.

It was a nasty, dark thundercloud, threatening to move in on my perfect spring day. But I tried to ignore it, at least for now, and enjoy this moment.

This beautiful, extraordinary moment.

ARLY THE next morning, I was driving westward toward the ranch. Marlboro Man had called the night before—a rare evening we'd spent apart—and had asked me to come out early.

I'd just turned onto the highway that led out of my hometown when my car phone rang. It was dewy outside, foggy. "Hurry up," Marlboro Man's voice playfully commanded. "I want to see my future wife." My stomach lurched. Wife. It would take me a while to get used to that word.

"I'm coming," I announced. "Hold your horses!" We hung up, and I giggled. Hold your horses. Heh-heh. I had a lifetime of these jokes ahead. This was going to be loads of fun.

He met me at my car, wearing jeans, boots, and a soft, worn denim shirt. I climbed out of the car and stepped right into his arms. It was just after 8:00 A.M., and within seconds we were leaning against my car, sharing a passionate, steamy kiss. Leave it to Marlboro Man to make 8:00 A.M. an acceptable time to make out. I never would have known this if I hadn't met him.

"So . . . what are we gonna do today?" I asked, trying to remember what day it was.

"Oh, I thought we'd drive around for a while . . . ," he said, his arms still grasping my waist, "and talk about where we might want to live." I'd heard him mention before, in passing, that someday he wanted to move to a different spot on the ranch, but I'd never paid much attention to it. I'd never really cared much where he lived, just as long as he took his Wranglers with me. "I want it to be your decision, too."

We spent the morning driving, my Marlboro Man and me. We drove around the hidden places and the far reaches of his family's ranch: through rippling creeks, across innumerable cattle guards, over this hill, past that thicket of trees—all of this in search of the ideal spot for us to start our life together. Marlboro Man liked the house in which he'd been living, but it was far removed from the heart of the ranch, and he'd always planned to set up a more permanent spot somewhere. That we were now engaged to be married made it the perfect time to make the transition.

I'd always liked his house; it was rustic and unadorned, yet beautiful in its simplicity. I could live there. Or I could live in another house. Or I could live in his pickup, or in his barn, or in a teepee in a pasture . . . as long as he was there. But he wanted to drive and look together, so we drove. And we looked. And we held hands. And we talked. And somewhere along the way, in the bright morning sunshine, Marlboro Man stopped his pickup under the shade of a tree, crossed the great divide between our leather bucket seats, and grabbed me in a sexy, warm embrace. And we sat there and kissed, like two teenagers parked at a drive-in. A 1958 drive-in, though. Before the sexual revolution. Before Cinemax, though my mind remained very much in the 1990s. It was hard to practice restraint in the pickup that morning. There was nobody around to see us.

We did practice restraint, though, ending our make-out fest within minutes instead of hours, which would have been my choice. But we had a lifetime ahead. Things to do. Cattle guards to cross. So we continued our drive, checking out some of the more obvious locations we might one day call our home. We started at the Home Place—the quaint, modest homestead where his grandfather used to live back when he was a newly married rancher just beginning to raise a family. The well-maintained road on which we drove wasn't always there, Marlboro Man told me, and when any amount of rain would fall, his grandmother would find herself trapped at the Home Place for days because of the roaring, impassable creek. His grandmother had been a town girl much like me, Marlboro Man said, and had resisted living on the ranch at the beginning. But because she wanted to marry his grandfather, she'd bitten the bullet and made the move.

"How sweet," I remarked. "Did she eventually wind up liking it?"

"Well, she tried to," he said. "But the first time she got on a horse my grandpa made the mistake of laughing at her," Marlboro Man explained. "She got off and said that was the last time she was ever riding a horse." Marlboro Man chuckled his signature chuckle.

"Oh," I said, smiling nervously. "Well, how long did it take her to get used to it?"

"Well, she never really did," Marlboro Man said. "They eventually bought a house and moved to town." He chuckled again.

I looked out the window, twirling my hair. Something about the Home Place didn't seem like the best fit.

We continued our drive, not making any permanent decisions that day about where we'd live. We'd been engaged less than twenty-four hours, after all; there was no huge rush. When we finally returned to his house, we curled up on his couch and watched a movie. *Gone With the Wind,* of all things. He was a fan. And as I lay there that afternoon and watched the South crumble around Scarlett O'Hara's knees for what had to have been the 304th time in my life, I touched the arms that held me so sweetly and securely . . . and I sighed contentedly, wondering how on earth I'd ever found this person.

When he walked me to my car late that afternoon, minutes after Scarlett had declared that tomorrow is another day, Marlboro Man rested his hands lightly on my waist. He caressed my rib cage up and down, touching his forehead to mine and closing his eyes—as if he were recording the moment in his memory. And it tickled like crazy, his fingertips on my ribs, but I didn't care; I was engaged to this man, I told myself, and there'll likely be much rib caressing in the future. I needed to toughen up, to be able to with-stand such displays of romance without my knees buckling beneath me and without my forgetting my mother's maiden name and who my first grade teacher had been. Otherwise I had lots of years of trouble—and decreased productivity—ahead. So I stood there and took it, closing my eyes as well and trying with all my might to will away the ticklish sensations. They had no place here. Begone, Satan! Ree, hold strong.

My mind won, and we stood there and continued to thumb our nose at the reality that we were two separate bodies . . . and the western sun behind us changed from yellow to orange to pink to a brilliant, impossible red—the same color as the ever-burning fire between us.

On the drive home, my whole torso felt warm. Like when you've awakened from the most glorious dream you've ever had, and you're still half-in, half-out, and you still feel the dream and it's still real. I forced myself to think, to look around me, to take it all in. One day, I told myself as I drove down that rural county road, I'm going to be driving down a road like this to run to the grocery store in town . . . or pick up the mail on the highway . . . or take my kids to cello lessons.

Cello lessons? That would be possible, right? Or ballet? Surely there was an academy nearby.

We'd casually thrown some wedding dates around: August? September? October? After next summer, when the weather was cool again. When shipping season was over. When we could relax and celebrate and enjoy a nice, long honeymoon without the pressures of cattle work. Our wedding would likely be months and months away, which was fine with me. It would take me that long to address enough invitations for his side of the family, what with the cousins and uncles and aunts and extended relatives, who all seemed to live within a fifty-mile radius, who all would want to celebrate the first wedding in Marlboro Man's immediate family—a family that had been rocked by the tragic death of the oldest son some ten years before. And it would take me that long to break away from my old life, to cut the cord between my former and future selves.

Meanwhile, word of our engagement had begun to spread through my hometown of 35,000, thanks in no small part to my brother Mike and his patented Bullhorn Policy of announcing our engagement at the mall—or over the telephone lines—the day before. My return to my hometown after

living in Los Angeles had been somewhat noteworthy, since I'd always given off the air—sometimes obnoxiously so—of someone who thought she belonged in a larger, more cosmopolitan locale. The fact that I would now be hanging up my L.A.-acquired black pumps to move to an isolated ranch in the middle of nowhere was enough to raise a few eyebrows. I could almost hear the whispers through the grapevine.

"Ree? Is getting married?"

"Seriously? Ree's marrying . . . a rancher?"

"She's going to live in the *country*?"

"I can't picture Ree . . . riding a horse."

"She's the last person I would ever imagine in the country."

"Whatever happened to her boyfriend in California?"

Halfway through my trip, my car phone rang. It was my sister, Betsy, who'd been home visiting for the past twenty-four hours.

"Mom just saw Carolyn at the gift shop." Betsy laughed. "She said she'd just heard about you getting engaged and she could not *believe* you were actually going to be living in the country. . . ." We both laughed, knowing this was going to become a regular thing.

I couldn't blame people for their doubts. The truth was, I still didn't even know how I'd manage it. Country life? As much time as I'd spent at Marlboro Man's house, the reality of a day-to-day rural existence was still a big unknown to me. I closed my eyes and tried to reconcile my future— a future in an as-yet-unidentified house, likely at the end of an as-yet-unidentified dusty gravel road far away from restaurants and shops and makeup counters—with my citified, pampered, self-absorbed existence. What would I do every day? What time would I have to get out of bed? Would there be hens involved? Though I'd dated Marlboro Man for some time, I'd never really spent the night with him . . . I'd never woken up to his schedule and watched how it all played out once his feet hit the floor. I couldn't imagine what I'd do with him in the morning. Would I eat Grape-Nuts in front of him, or wait till he left for the office? Wait—there was no office. Would I go to work with him, or would I have to spend the day scrubbing clothes on the washboard . . . and hanging them on a clothesline? Where would Bounce come into play? If I sat still, my mind wandered. All the stereotypes I'd ever heard about country life swam around in my mind like a school of tiny fish. I was completely powerless to shake them.

I finally arrived back home and entered my house. Betsy had gone out with friends from high school, and when I walked into the kitchen I saw it—the elephant in the room: the door leading to the family room was closed; my parents were on the other side. The air was thick and suffocating. I could actually see, floating around my childhood home, what is normally invisible: tension, strife, conflict, pain. I realized I was a person split in two—giddy and fizzy and ecstatic about my future with Marlboro Man . . . and, simultaneously, devastated and filled with doom and dread over the knowledge my stable, normal, happy family life was coming apart before my eyes. How could this perfect, shiny house have spiraled downward into such a den of sadness? That it happened to coincide with my finding the greatest love of my life had to be a joke.

Dragging myself up to my bedroom, I kicked off my shoes and curled up on the soft chair next to my bed. I so wanted to leave, to avoid the whole godforsaken mess altogether. It was my parents' problem, after all—not mine. I certainly had no power to reunite them. But instead of being liberated and resigned to that reality, all I could think about was how on earth I'd be able to negotiate the next several months of my engagement. I could see it all in front of me—a never-ending, schizophrenic cycle of euphoric highs from being with my beloved . . . and abysmal lows the second I walked back into my parents' house. I wasn't sure I had the intestinal fortitude to withstand the roller coaster.

That's when my savior called. He called as he always did after we'd spent a day or evening together. He called to say good night . . . I had a good time today . . . what are you doing tomorrow . . . I love you. His calls

were a panacea; they instantly lifted me, reassured me, healed me, made everything whole again. This call was no different.

"Hey, you," he said, his voice reaching new heights of sexiness.

"Hey," I said, quietly sighing.

"What are you doing?" he asked.

"Sitting here," I answered, hearing the muffled voices of my parents through my upstairs bedroom floor. "And thinking . . ."

"What about?" he said.

"Oh, I was thinking . . . ," I began, hesitating for a moment. "That I think I want to elope."

Marlboro Man laughed at first. But when he realized I wasn't laughing, too, he stopped, and we both sat in silence.

*Y*OU DO?" Marlboro Man responded. "You want to elope?"

"Well yeah . . . kinda," I responded. "What do you think?"

"Well," he began. "What brought this on?" He didn't say it, but I knew he didn't want to elope. He wanted to have a wedding. He wanted to celebrate.

"Oh, I don't know." I hesitated, not really knowing how I felt or what to say. "I was just thinking about it when you called."

He paused for a moment. "You okay?" he asked. He'd detected the change in my voice, that a dark cloud had descended.

"Oh, I'm fine!" I reassured him. "I'm totally fine. I just . . . oh, I just thought it might be fun to run off together."

But that wasn't at all what I meant.

What I meant was that I didn't want to have anything whatsoever to do with family celebrations, tensions, stress, or marital problems. I didn't want to have to worry from one day to the next whether my folks were going to hold it together through the next several months of wedding preparations. I just didn't want to deal with it anymore. I wanted to bail. I wanted it to go away.

But I didn't say that; it was too much for that late-night phone call, too much for me to explain.

"Well, I'm open," Marlboro Man responded, yawning through his words. "We can just figure it out tomorrow."

"Yeah," I said, yawning in return. "Good night . . ."

I fell asleep on my comfortable chair, hugging Fox Johnson, a worn-out Steiff animal my parents had given me back when we were a happy, perfect family.

"COME OUT today," he said the next morning. "You can come help me finish burnin'."

I smiled, knowing he didn't need my help at all. But I loved it when he phrased it that way.

"Oh, okay!" I said, rubbing my eyes. "What should I wear?"

Marlboro Man laughed, probably wondering how many years would pass before I'd quit asking that question.

Controlled burning, or, simply, burnin', as landowners usually call it, is usually done in the spring just as new grass growth would begin. Burning gets rid of the old, dead grass from the winter months and makes room for fresh, green grass to push through the ground more robustly. It also kills new weeds that have already popped up, since many weeds sprout first in early spring. Normally, burning is carried out from a Jeep or other open vehicle, the driver holding a torch out of the side, lighting grass as he goes. I'd seen Marlboro Man do it from afar but had never been up close and personal with the flames. *Maybe he needs me to drive the Jeep!* I thought. *Or, better yet, man the torch!* This could be really fun.

He asked me to meet him at the barn near his house, where his Jeep was parked. Just as I pulled up, I saw Marlboro Man exiting the barn . . .

with two horses in hand. My stomach felt funny as I scrunched up my nose and mouthed the word *crap*. I wasn't comfortable riding a horse, and like my parents' marital problems, I'd been secretly hoping this whole "horse thing" would just up and magically disappear.

When it came to horses, the problem wasn't that I was afraid—not at all. I thought horses were beautiful, and I'd never been nervous around animals. The problem wasn't my ability to get on or off the horse—this was one of the few things on the ranch in which a background in ballet was an asset. Neither did the smell bother me—I actually kind of liked it. My problem with horses had to do with the fact that any time the horse broke into a trot, my bottom wouldn't stay in the saddle. No matter what level of instruction Marlboro Man gave me, no matter how many pointers, a horse trot for me meant a repeated and violent *Slap! Slap! Slap!* on the seat of my saddle. My feet were fine—they'd stay securely in the stirrups. But I just couldn't figure out how to use the muscles in my legs correctly, and I hadn't yet learned how to post. It was so unpleasant, the whole riding-a-horse business: my bottom would slap, my torso would stiffen, and I'd be sore for days—not to mention that I looked like a complete freak while riding—kind of like a tree trunk with red, stringy hair. Short of taking the rectal temperatures of cows, I'd never felt more out of place doing anything in my life.

All of this rushed to the surface when I saw Marlboro Man walking toward me with two of his horses, one of which was clearly meant for me. *Where's my Jeep?* I thought. *Where's my torch? I don't want a horse. My bottom can't take it. Where's my Jeep?* I'd never wanted to drive a Jeep so much.

"Hey," I said, walking toward him and smiling, trying to appear not only calm but also totally unconcerned about the reality that faced me. "Uh . . . I thought we were going burning."

I clearly sounded out the *g*. It was a loud, clanging cymbal.

"Oh, we are," he said, smiling. "But we've got to get to some areas the Jeep can't reach."

My stomach lurched. For more than a couple of seconds, I actually considered feigning illness so I wouldn't have to go. What can I say? I wondered. That I feel like I'm going to throw up? Or should I just clutch my stomach, groan, then run behind the barn and make dramatic retching sounds? That could be highly effective. Marlboro Man will feel sorry for me and say, "It's okay . . . you just go on up to my house and rest. I'll be back later." But I don't think I can go through with it; vomiting is so embarrassing! And besides, if Marlboro Man thinks I vomited, I might not get a kiss today. . . .

"Oh, okay," I said, smiling again and trying to prevent my face from betraying the utter dread that plagued me. I hadn't noticed, through all my inner torture and turmoil, that Marlboro Man and the horses had been walking closer to me. Before I knew it, Marlboro Man's right arm was wrapped around my waist while his other hand held the reins of the two horses. In another instant, he pulled me toward him in a tight grip and leaned in for a sweet, tender kiss—a kiss he seemed to savor even after our lips parted.

"Good morning," he said sweetly, grinning that magical grin.

My knees went weak. I wasn't sure if it was the kiss itself . . . or the dread of riding.

We mounted our horses and began walking slowly up the hillside. When we reached the top, Marlboro Man pointed across a vast prairie. "See that thicket of trees over there?" he said. "That's where we're headed." Almost immediately, he gave his horse a kick and began to trot across the flat plain. With no prompting from me at all, my horse followed suit. I braced myself, becoming stiff and rigid and resigning myself to looking like a freak in front of my love and also to at least a week of being too sore to move. I held on to the saddle, the reins, and my life as my horse took off in the same direction as Marlboro Man's.

Not two minutes into our ride, my horse slightly faltered after stepping in a shallow hole. Having no experience with this kind of thing, I reacted,

shrieking loudly and pulling wildly on my reins, simultaneously stiffen-
ing my body further. The combination didn't suit my horse, who decided,
understandably, that he pretty much didn't want me on his back anymore.
He began to buck, and my life flashed before my eyes—for the first time,
I was deathly afraid of horses. I held on for dear life as the huge creature
underneath me bounced and reared, but my body caught air, and I knew it
was only a matter of time before I'd go flying.

In the distance, I heard Marlboro Man's voice. "Pull up on the reins!
Pull up! Pull up!" My body acted immediately—it was used to responding instantly to that voice, after all—and I pulled up tightly on the horse's
reins. This forced its head to an upright position, which made bucking vir-
tually impossible for the horse. Problem was, I pulled up too tightly and
quickly, and the horse reared up. I leaned forward and hugged the saddle,
praying I wouldn't fall off backward and sustain a massive head injury. I
liked my head. I wasn't ready to say good-bye to it.

By the time the horse's front legs hit the ground, my left leg was
dangling out of its stirrup, even as all my dignity was dangling by a
thread. Using my balletic agility, I quickly hopped off the horse, trip-
ping and stumbling away the second my feet hit the ground. Instinctively, I began hurriedly walking away—from the horse, from the
ranch, from the burning. I didn't know where I was going—back to
L.A., I figured, or maybe I'd go through with Chicago after all. I didn't
care; I just knew I had to keep walking. In the meantime, Marlboro Man
had arrived at the scene and quickly calmed my horse, who by now was
eating a leisurely morning snack of dead winter grass that had yet to be
burned. The nag.

"You okay?" Marlboro Man called out. I didn't answer. I just kept on
walking, determined to get the hell out of Dodge.

It took him about five seconds to catch up with me; I wasn't a very fast
walker. "Hey," he said, grabbing me around the waist and whipping me
around so I was facing him. "Aww, it's okay. It happens."

I didn't want to talk about it. I didn't want to hear it. I wanted him to let go of me and I wanted to keep on walking. I wanted to walk back down the hillside, start my car, and get out of there. I didn't know where I'd go, I just knew I wanted to go. I wanted away from all of it—riding horses, saddles, reins, bridles—I didn't want it anymore. I hated everything on that ranch. It was all stupid, dumb . . . and stupid.

Wriggling loose of his consoling embrace, I squealed, "I seriously can't *do this*!" My hands trembled wildly and my voice quivered. The tip of my nose began to sting, and tears welled up in my eyes. It wasn't like me to display such hysteria in the presence of a man. But being driven to the brink of death had brought me to this place. I felt like a wild animal. I was powerless to restrain myself. "I don't want to do this for the rest of my life!" I cried.

I turned to leave again but decided instead to give up, choosing to sit down on the ground and slump over in defeat. It was all so humiliating—not just my rigid, freakish riding style or my near collision with the ground, but also my crazy, emotional reaction after the fact. This wasn't me. I was a strong, confident woman, for Lord's sake; I don't slump on the ground in the middle of a pasture and cry. What was I doing in a pasture, anyway? Knowing my luck, I was probably sitting on a pile of manure. But I couldn't even walk anymore; my knees were even trembling by now, and I'd lost all feeling in my fingertips. My heart pounded in my cheeks.

If Marlboro Man had any sense, he would have taken the horses and gotten the hell out of there, leaving me, the hysterical female, sobbing on the ground by myself. *She's obviously in the throes of some hormonal fit*, he probably thought. *There's nothing you can say to her when she gets like this. I don't have time for this crap. She's just gonna have to learn to deal with it if she's going to marry me.*

But he didn't get the hell out of there. He didn't leave me sobbing on the ground by myself. Instead he joined me on the grass, sitting beside me and putting his hand on my leg, reassuring me that this kind of thing happens, and there wasn't anything I did wrong, even though he was probably lying.

"Now, did you really mean that about not wanting to do this the rest of your life?" he asked. That familiar, playful grin appeared in the corner of his mouth.

I blinked a couple of times and took a deep breath, smiling back at him and reassuring him with my eyes that no, I hadn't meant it, but I did hate his horse. Then I took a deep breath, stood up, and dusted off my Anne Klein straight-leg jeans.

"Hey, we don't have to do this now," Marlboro Man said, standing back up. "I'll just do it later."

"No, I'm fine," I answered, walking back toward my horse with newfound resolve.

I took another deep breath and climbed back on the horse. As Marlboro Man and I rode back toward the thicket of trees, I suddenly understood: if I was going to marry this man, if I was going to live on this isolated ranch, if I was going to survive without cappuccino and takeout food . . . I sure wasn't going to let this horse beat me. I'd have to toughen up and face things.

As we rode, it became even more clear. I'd have to apply this same courage to *all* areas of my life—not just the practical, day-in and day-out activities of ranch life, but also the reality of my parents' marital collapse and any other problems that would arise in the coming years. Suddenly, running off and getting married no longer seemed like the romantic adventure I was trying to convince myself it would be. Suddenly I realized that if I did that, if I ran away and said *"I do"* in some dark, hidden corner of the world, I'd never be able to handle the rigors and stresses of country life. And that wouldn't be fair to Marlboro Man . . . or myself.

As we started moving, I noticed that Marlboro Man was riding at my pace. "The horses need to be shod," he said, grinning. "They didn't need to trot today anyway."

I glanced in his direction.

"So we'll just go slow and easy," he continued.

I looked toward the thicket of trees and took a deep, calming breath, grabbing on to the saddle horn so firmly my knuckles turned pasty white.

Chapter Fifteen
TALL IN THE SADDLE

So," MARLBORO Man began over dinner one night. "How many kids do you want to have?" I almost choked on my medium-rare T-bone, the one he'd grilled for me so expertly with his own two hands.

"Oh my word," I replied, swallowing hard. I didn't feel so hungry anymore. "I don't know . . . how many kids do *you* want to have?"

"Oh, I don't know," he said with a mischievous grin. "Six or so. Maybe seven."

I felt downright nauseated. Maybe it was a defense mechanism, my body preparing me for the dreaded morning sickness that, I didn't know at the time, awaited me. Six or seven kids? Righty-oh, Marlboro Man.

Righty . . . no.

"Ha-ha ha-ha ha. Ha." I laughed, tossing my long hair over my shoulder and acting like he'd made a big joke. "Yeah, right! Ha-ha. Six kids . . . can you imagine? Ha-ha. Ha. Ha." The laughter was part humor, part nervousness, part terror. We'd never had a serious discussion about children before.

"Why?" He looked a little more serious this time. "How many kids do you think we should have?"

I smeared my mashed potatoes around on my plate and felt my ovaries leap inside my body. This was not a positive development. *Stop that!* I ordered, silently. *Settle down! Go back to sleep!*

I blinked and took a swig of the wine Marlboro Man had bought me earlier in the day. "Let's see . . . ," I answered, drumming my fingernails on the table. "How 'bout one? Or maybe . . . one and a half?" I sucked in my stomach—another defensive move in an attempt to deny what I didn't realize at the time was an inevitable, and jiggly, future.

"One?" he replied. "Aw, that's not nearly enough of a work crew for me. I'll need a lot more help than that!" Then he chuckled, standing up to clear our plates as I sat there in a daze, having no idea whether or not he was kidding.

It was the strangest conversation I'd ever had. I felt like the roller coaster had just pulled away from the gate, and the entire amusement park was pitch-black. I had no idea what was in front of me; I was entering a foreign land. My ovaries, on the other hand, were doing backflips, as if they'd been wandering, parched, in a barren wasteland and finally, miraculously, happened upon a roaring waterfall. And that waterfall was about six feet tall, with gray hair and bulging biceps. They never knew they could experience such hope.

After dinner, as we had so many times during our months and months together, Marlboro Man and I adjourned to his porch. It was dark—we'd eaten late—and despite my silent five-minute battle with the reality of my reproductive system, there was definitely something special about the night. I stood at the railing, breathing in the dewy night air and taking in all the sounds of the countryside that would one day be my home. The pumping of a distant oil well, the symphony of crickets, the occasional moo of a mama cow, the manic yipping of coyotes . . . the din of country life was as present and reassuring as the cacophony of car horns, traffic sounds, and sirens had been in L.A. I loved everything about it.

He appeared behind me; his strong arms wrapped around my waist. Oh, it was real, all right—he was real. As I touched his forearms and ran the palms of my hands from his elbows down to his wrists, I'd never been more sure of how very real he was. Here, grasping me in his arms,

was the Adonis of all the romance-novel fantasies I clearly never realized I'd been having; they'd been playing themselves out in steamy detail under the surface of my consciousness, and I never even knew I'd been missing it. I closed my eyes and rested my head back on his chest, just as his impossibly soft lips and subtle whiskers rested on my neck. Romancewise, it was perfection—the night air was still—almost imperceptible. Physically, viscerally, it was almost more than I could stand. Six babies? Sure. How 'bout seven? Is that enough? Standing there that night, I would have said eight, nine, ten. And I could have gotten started right away.

But getting started would have to wait. There'd be plenty of time for that. For that night, that dark, perfect night, we simply stayed on the porch and locked ourselves in kiss after beautiful, steamy kiss. And before too long, it was impossible to tell where his arms ended and where my body began.

*S*OON WE found the place where we would one day live, the perfect spot on earth to start our lives together. It was an old yellow brick "Indian Home," as everyone called it, on a separate, newer area of the family ranch. It had been built in the 1920s by a Native American who'd reaped the windfall of a recent oil boom, and after changing hands a few times through the years, the inside of the house was a mess of seven-foot ceilings, avocado appliances, and shag carpeting that had long since been inhabited by every kind of creature on earth. Smaller remodeling projects throughout the house had never been finished, and the stench of mouse urine was strong.

"I love it," I exclaimed as Marlboro Man showed me around, raising up boards so I could walk down hallways and holding my hand so I wouldn't hurt myself. And I really did—I loved it. The house was old, very old. It told many, many stories.

"You do?" he asked, smiling. "You like it?"

"Oh, yeah," I repeated, looking around. "It's really something!"

"Well, we obviously couldn't live here till we fixed a few things," he said. "But I've always loved this old house." He looked around with an obvious regard for the place in which we stood.

Remnants of the most recent owner—an aged area rancher who'd owned the land before selling it to Marlboro Man and his brother in recent years—peppered the dusty areas of the house. An ancient, polished urn-shaped trophy sat toppled over in a corner. I picked it up, wiping away the grime. *Upperclassman of the Year, 1936.* The rancher's name was etched below. A box of unused ranch letterhead sat beside it—old, yellowed letter-head with a watercolor image of the old man, not so old at the time, stand-ing next to a herd of Hereford cattle, wearing horn-rimmed glasses. Khaki trousers were tucked into his big, brown boots. The stationery was from the 1950s, I estimated. I held it in my hands and smelled the paper.

There was dust and grime, cobwebs, and memories . . . on the floor, on the ceiling, and floating in the air. It was strange, almost haunting, that amidst the avocado appliances and layers of dirt, I felt so instantly con-nected to this old yellow brick house. Maybe it was because I sensed imme-diately that Marlboro Man loved it; maybe it was the uniqueness of the old house itself; maybe it was the fact that I knew it would be ours, the first thing of ours, together; or maybe it was just a sense of knowing that I was standing exactly where I belonged.

"Watch that step." Marlboro Man pointed as we walked up the rick-ety staircase to look around. A spacious landing awaited us, a white iron-framed mirror still hanging on the wall. Marlboro Man led me down a short passageway to the master bedroom, which was brilliantly lit by wall-to-wall windows around the room. Through them I could see at least a mile or two to the east, over a woodsy creek that wound its way through the property. Through the bathroom door I noticed old hexagonal tile, dingy and dirty; and a hole in the floor where a toilet once had been. And in the

closet across the room, I spied a rickety, faded yellow dresser—the same golden shade of the bricks outside. Why has it been left here? I wondered. What's inside the drawers?

"Well . . . what do you think?" Marlboro Man asked, looking around.

"Oh my gosh . . . I love it," I said, hugging him tightly around the neck. The fact was, I had no idea how we'd ever make this house habitable again, or how long it would even take. It might be a several-year process; it might suck us into an evil, hairy money pit of doom. I'd seen *The Money Pit;* I knew how quickly things could spiral downhill. But for some reason, I wasn't worried; it just felt so right, standing in the bedroom of the house where Marlboro Man and I would start our life together. Where we'd wake up together in the morning; or where, if it was before 8:00 A.M., I'd pull the covers over my head and stay in bed while Marlboro Man woke up and went to work. It was where we'd eventually put a bed, and a nightstand, and a lamp or two . . . and probably, knowing us, a TV so we could watch submarine movies and Schwarzenegger flicks and *Gone With the Wind* without ever leaving the sanctity of our sheets.

As I pictured it all, Marlboro Man led me back down the hallway, past the landing again, and toward the other bedrooms in the house.

"There are two other bedrooms," Marlboro Man said, stepping over a pile of debris. "They're in pretty good shape, too."

I couldn't help but grin. As I walked into one of the two bedrooms and looked around, I snickered and teased, "So much for that whole 'seven kids' thing, huh?" I giggled smugly and kept looking around at the empty spaces of the room.

Undeterred, Marlboro Man looked at me slyly. "Ever heard of bunk beds?"

I gulped and braced myself, even as my ovaries cheered triumphantly.

EFORE I knew it, demolition work had begun on the interior of our yellow brick home even as plans for a six-hundred-guest wedding moved ahead at full steam. It happens, even if you've never in your life thought about your ideal wedding day, even if, not long before, you were ready to elope. When faced with hundreds of choices and hundreds of thousands of permutations and combinations relating to everything from the wedding date to invitations to food choices to flowers, you convince yourself that if all these choices even exist, they must be really important. And you set about the business of making sure all your choices are the only right choices on earth.

For me, though, becoming obsessed with planning my wedding to Marlboro Man served a much higher purpose. Aside from ensuring that the wedding machine would keep moving forward and that our eventual celebration would accommodate our ever-growing list of guests—a large chunk of which was Marlboro Man's extended family—drowning myself in wedding plans became the Great Distraction for me, the perfect escape from the black, nasty cloud that loomed over my formerly happy, normal family. The problems in my parents' marriage hadn't been helped by the prospect of a happy family celebration; in fact, they'd gotten worse. After making the decision not to run away and elope, I'd tried to think positively. *Maybe by the time the wedding date rolls around, they'll be back on track*, I told myself.

I didn't realize at the time that my mom already had one foot out the door. And not just out the door—running down the driveway, sprinting down the street. And her other foot wasn't far behind. That I didn't see it clearly at the time is a testament to the power of wishful thinking. Wishful thinking wrapped in a cloak of denial.

"We're thinking September," I told my mom when she pressed me for the wedding date.

"Oh . . . ," she replied, hesitating. "Really? September?" She seemed surprised; it was many months away. "Wouldn't you rather do . . . May or

June?" I could sense where she was headed with this. But that only made me dig in my heels further.

"Well, summer's busy on the ranch," I said. "And we want to be able to go on a honeymoon. And besides, it'll be much cooler by then."

"Okay . . ." Her voice trailed off. I knew what she wanted to say. She didn't want to hold it together that long. She didn't want my wedding to prolong the inevitable. I wouldn't fully know this until much later, but I wouldn't have had the guts to do anything about it even if I had known. The wedding plans were in full swing, and rather than digging deeper to find out the gravity of what was happening, I simply batted the fly away and began registering for china. With all the patterns and details and flowers and butterflies and blue transferware, it kept my brain wonderfully busy.

Of course, no china—however intricate and inviting—was as seductive as my fiancé, my future husband, who continued to eat me alive with one glance from his icy-blue eyes. Who greeted me not at the door of his house when I arrived almost every night of the week, but at my car. Who welcomed me not with a pat on the arm or even a hug but with an all-enveloping, all-encompassing embrace. Whose good-night kisses began the moment I arrived, not hours later when it was time to go home.

We were already playing house, what with my almost daily trips to the ranch and our five o'clock suppers and our lazy movie nights on his thirty-year-old leather couch, the same one his parents had bought when they were a newly married couple. We'd already watched enough movies together to last a lifetime. *Giant* with James Dean, *The Good, the Bad, and the Ugly*, *Reservoir Dogs*, *Guess Who's Coming to Dinner*, *The Graduate*, *All Quiet on the Western Front*, and, more than a handful of times, *Gone With the Wind*. I was continually surprised by the assortment of movies Marlboro Man loved to watch—his taste was surprisingly eclectic—and I loved discovering more and more about him through the VHS collection in his living room. He actually owned *The Philadelphia Story*. With Marlboro Man, surprises lurked around every corner.

We were already a married couple—well, except for the whole "sleepover thing" and the fact that we hadn't actually gotten hitched yet. We stayed in, like any married couple over the age of sixty, and continued to get to know everything about each other completely outside the realm of parties, dates, and gatherings. All of that was way too far away, anyway—a minimum hour-and-a-half drive to the nearest big city—and besides that, Marlboro Man was a fish out of water in a busy, crowded bar. As for me, I'd been there, done that—a thousand and one times. Going out and painting the town red was unnecessary and completely out of context for the kind of life we'd be building together.

This was what we brought each other, I realized. He showed me a slower pace, and permission to be comfortable in the absence of exciting plans on the horizon. I gave him, I realized, something different. Different from the girls he'd dated before—girls who actually knew a thing or two about country life. Different from his mom, who'd also grown up on a ranch. Different from all of his female cousins, who knew how to saddle and ride and who were born with their boots on. As the youngest son in a family of three boys, maybe he looked forward to experiencing life with someone who'd see the country with fresh eyes. Someone who'd appreciate how miraculously countercultural, how strange and set apart it all really is. Someone who couldn't ride to save her life. Who didn't know north from south, or east from west.

If that defined his criteria for a life partner, I was definitely the woman for the job.

Chapter Sixteen
FIRE IN THE WESTERN SKY

*I*T WAS time for me to go that Thursday night. We'd just watched *Citizen Kane*—a throwback to my Cinema 190 class at USC—and it was late. And though a soft, cozy bed in one of the guest rooms sounded much more appealing than driving all the way home, I'd never really wanted to get into the habit of sleeping over at Marlboro Man's house. It was the Pretend-I'm-a-Proper-Country-Club-Girl in me, mixed with a healthy dose of fear that Marlboro Man's mother or grandmother would drop by early in the morning to bring Marlboro Man some warm muffins or some such thing and see my car parked in the driveway. Or even worse, come inside the house, and then I'd have to wrestle with whether or not to volunteer that *"I slept in a guest room! I slept in a guest room!"*, which only would have made me look more guilty. *Who needs that?* I'd told myself, and vowed never to put myself in that predicament.

With Marlboro Man's strong hands massaging my tired shoulders, I walked in front of him down the narrow porch toward the driveway, where my dusty car awaited me. But before I could take the step down he stopped me, grabbing a belt loop on the back of my Anne Kleins, and pulling me back toward him with rapid—almost shocking—force.

"Woooo!" I exclaimed, startled at the jolt. My cry was so shrill, the coyotes answered back. I felt awkward. Marlboro Man moved in for the

kill, pulling my back tightly against his chest and wrapping his arms slowly around my waist. As I rested my arms on top of his hands and leaned my head back toward his shoulder, he buried his face in my neck. Suddenly, September seemed entirely too far away. I had to have this man to myself 24/7, as soon as humanly possible.

"I can't wait to marry you," he whispered, each word sending a thousand shivers to my toes. I knew exactly what he meant. He wasn't talking about the wedding cake.

I was speechless, as usual. He had that effect on me. Because whatever he said, when it came to his feelings about me or his reflections on our relationship, made whatever I'd respond with sound ridiculous . . . lame . . . bumbling . . . awkward. If ever I said anything to him in return, it was something along the lines of "Yeah . . . me, too" or "I feel the same way" or the equally dumb "Aww, that's nice." So I'd learned to just soak up the moment and not try to match him . . . but to show him I felt the same way. This time was no different; I reached my arm backward, caressing the nape of his neck as he nuzzled his face into mine, then turned around suddenly and threw my arms around him with every ounce of passion in my body.

Minutes later, we were back at the sliding glass door that led inside the house—me, leaning against the glass, Marlboro Man anchoring me there with his strong, convincing lips. I was a goner. My right leg hooked slowly around his calf.

And then, the sound—the loud ringing of the rotary phone inside. Marlboro Man ignored it through three rings, but it was late, and curiosity took over. "I'd better get that," he said, each word dripping with heat. He ran inside to answer the phone, leaving me alone in a sultry, smoky cloud. *Saved by the bell*, I thought. Damn. I was dizzy, unable to steady myself. Was it the wine? Wait . . . I hadn't had any wine that night. I was drunk on his muscles. Wasted on his masculinity.

Within seconds, Marlboro Man was running back out the door.

"There's a fire," he said hurriedly. "A big one—I've got to go." Without pausing, he ran toward the pickup.

I stood there, still dazed and fizzy, still unable to feel my knees. And then, just as I was beginning to reflect on the utter irony that a prairie fire may have just saved my eternal soul from burning in hell for carnal sin, Marlboro Man's pickup flew into reverse and screeched abruptly to a halt at the edge of The Porch—our porch. Rolling down his window, he leaned out and yelled, "You comin'?"

"Oh . . . um . . . sure!" I replied, running toward the pickup and hopping inside.

A prairie fire. A real, live prairie fire, I thought as Marlboro Man's diesel pickup peeled out of his gravel driveway. *Cool! This'll be so neat!* Moments later, as the pickup reached the top of the hill by his house, I could see an ominous orange glow in the distance.

I shuddered as I felt a chill go through me.

MARLBORO MAN'S whole demeanor changed; a seriousness descended. Looking straight ahead, Marlboro Man drove with a clear purpose: to get to the scene of the fire as soon as humanly possible. I shivered with anticipation—I'd never seen a prairie fire before, let alone a prairie fire in the dead of night. I felt adventurous and excited, feeling twinges of the thrill I used to feel when my friends and I would explore the seedier parts of Los Angeles. There was always a rush, a jolt of energy I'd feel driving into the more dangerous areas of the city. It had been so far away from the idyllic seventh fairway on which I'd grown up.

So was the tallgrass of Marlboro Man's ranch. It was so natural, so wild, and it waved beautifully in the late-night breeze—the same breeze that was rapidly fueling the fire on the horizon. It was nothing like the grass on the golf course, which was always a precise, prescribed height—

usually measured in centimeters or inches—and was never unruly or out of control. Looking out in front of Marlboro Man's pickup at the impossibly tall bluestem, which was eerily lit by the headlights, I began to comprehend why prairie fires were such a serious business. And then, when his pickup reached the top of his hill and I could see the ranch in its entirety, I didn't have a hint of a doubt.

"Oh my . . . ," I gasped as I beheld the scope of the fire that engulfed the countryside.

"That's huge," Marlboro Man said, accelerating.

The sense of thrill I'd felt moments earlier was replaced by impending doom as the inferno ahead of us grew more and more enormous. When we arrived at the scene, other pickups—many with large machines in the back—were just pulling up. Area cowboys and ranchers—mere silhouettes against the huge wall of fire—scrambled around, hopped onto spray trucks, and began fighting the fire.

When Marlboro Man and I got out of his pickup, we could feel the heat immediately. *What am I doing here?* I asked myself, looking down at my shoes. Joan & David flats, adorned with bronze and silver jewels. Absolutely perfect for the occasion.

"C'mon!" Marlboro Man shouted, jumping onto the back of a nearby spray truck driven by an elderly man. "Hop in there with Charlie!" He pointed toward the door of the old, royal blue vehicle. Not having many other appealing options, I ran to the truck and hopped inside. "Well . . . hi, darlin'!" the old man said, putting his truck into gear. "You ready?"

"Um, sure," I replied. Who was Charlie? Had we met before? Why was I in his spray truck, and where was he taking me?

I would have asked Marlboro Man these questions, but he'd jumped onto the back of the truck too quickly. As far as I could tell, I was riding in the pickup with an elderly gentleman who was about to drive the both of us straight into hell. I guess I'd have to ask all my questions later . . . when they wouldn't be so relevant anymore. The fire seemed twice as large as it had when we'd arrived moments earlier. I wished I was somewhere else. A seedy area of L.A. would be great.

Charlie stopped just short of the flames, whose heat I could feel through the windshield, then turned to the right and began driving parallel to the blaze. I saw Marlboro Man hop off the back of the pickup and direct the hose toward the fire, occasionally shielding his face with his other arm. I could hardly see a thing. Just fire, silhouettes, and my own life passing before my eyes.

*W*HEN THERE'S a fire in the country, everyone shows up. It's an unwritten rule, a universal rural truth. Helping neighbors fight fire on their land is the ultimate show of support and goodwill, not to mention a clear acknowledgment that prairie fires are no respecters of persons or fence lines and can quickly jump from ranch to ranch, taking nutritive grass, animals, and structures along with it. Plus, while it's probably only a small part, it's an excuse for a bunch of men to get together and, well, fight fire . . . to gather around a huge inferno and start up the sprayers . . . to drive around and extinguish flames . . . to light backfires and try to anticipate changes in the direction of the wind. Men, whether they admit it or not, thrive on that kind of thing.

Women, on the other hand, are not like that in the least, and minutes after Charlie had driven us within three feet of the fire, the novelty had worn off and melted into a pool of irritability and fear caused by a combination of the lateness of the hour, fear for my personal safety, and, most of all, anxiety over having to watch the father of my ninety-four future children standing in the face of what seemed like an entire planet of violent, whipping flames. The childhood I'd spent looking at X-rays in my dad's office, seeing my surgeon father calculate the risks of everything from skiing to go-carts and skateboards, seeing medical tragedies and challenges firsthand . . . it all came rushing to the surface. It couldn't have helped that in high school, my best friend's sister had been critically burned in an explosion . . . and I'd seen firsthand how devastating burn injuries can be.

These were the thoughts that flooded my mind as I rode helplessly in the royal blue spray truck of some unknown man named Charlie, who was following closely behind Marlboro Man, who was, by now, following the fire down a steep, rocky slope. The vehicle rose and fell and bounced as its driver navigated the large stones, and Charlie occasionally had to accelerate to get over the larger humps . . . then slam on his brakes to keep from hitting Marlboro Man. My imagination went crazy—I could just see it: within minutes, Charlie would get the timing wrong and run over Marlboro Man. And then he'd be injured . . . and trapped . . . and burned. This was risky—ridiculously risky—behavior! It flew in the face of everything I understood about sensibly avoiding medical tragedies. Why did Marlboro Man have to bring me along, anyway? Why didn't he just let me go home earlier? I'd be close to home by now, home in my safe, smoke-free bed on the golf course. Away from burning bluestem. Away from the heat and the throbbing fear of something terrible happening and instantly changing my life. My life had already changed so drastically in the past year; I wasn't prepared for it to change again.

But what could I do? Roll down my window and tell Marlboro Man to stop that firefighting nonsense? Throw down his hose and drive me back to the house? Go back to his house with me? And stay there? We could watch a good action flick—that's so easy and so very danger free. *Yes*, I told myself. *That sounds like the perfect plan.*

Then I heard it—the voice over the CB radio. *"You're on fire! You're on fire!"* The voice repeated, this time with more urgency, *"Charlie! Get out! You're on fire!"*

I sat there, frozen, unable to process the reality of what I'd just heard "*Oh, shit!*" sweet little Charlie yelled, grabbing his door handle. "We've got to get *out, darlin'—get outta here!*" He opened his door, swung his feeble knees around, and let gravity pull him out of the pickup; I, in turn, did the same. Covering my head instinctively as I ditched, I darted away from the vehicle, running smack-dab into Marlboro Man's brother, Tim, in the process. He was spraying the side of Charlie's pickup, which, by now, was engulfed in flames. I kept running until I was sure I was out of the path of danger.

"Ree! Where'd *you* come from?!?" Tim yelled, barely taking his eyes off the fire on the truck, which, by then, was almost extinguished. Tim hadn't known I was on the scene. *"You okay?"* he yelled, glancing over to make sure I wasn't on fire, too. A cowboy rushed to Charlie's aid on the other side of the truck. He was fine, too, bless his heart.

By now Marlboro Man had become aware of the commotion, not because he'd seen it happen through the smoke, but because his hose had reached the end of its slack and Charlie's truck was no longer following behind. Another spray truck had already rushed over to Marlboro Man's spot and resumed chasing the fire—the same fire that might have gobbled up a rickety, old spray truck, an equally rickety man named Charlie, and me. Luckily Tim had been nearby when a wind gust blew the flames over Charlie's truck, and had acted quickly.

The fire on the truck was out by now, and Marlboro Man rushed over, grabbed my shoulders, and looked me over—trying, in all the confusion, to make sure I was in one piece. And I was. Physically, I was perfectly fine. My nervous system, on the other hand, was a shambles. *"You okay?"* he shouted over the crackling sounds of the fire. All I could do was nod and bite my lip to keep from losing it. *Can I go home now?* was the only thing going through my mind. That, and *I want my mommy.* The fire was farther away by now, but it seemed to be growing in intensity. Even I could tell the wind had picked up.

Marlboro Man and Tim looked at each other . . . and burst out in nervous laughter—the kind of laugh you laugh when you almost fall but don't; when your car almost goes off a cliff but comes to a stop right at the edge; when your winning team almost misses the winning pass but doesn't; or when your fiancée and a local cowboy are almost burned alive . . . but aren't. I might have laughed, too, if I could muster any breath. But my lungs were deflated; I couldn't get them to take in air. I wanted to believe it was the smoke; but I knew it was nothing but sheer panic.

Tim and Marlboro Man looked toward the fire. "C'mon, Charlie," Tim said. "Why don't you drive us around to the north side and we'll take to it that way." Charlie, who'd likely been through dozens of fires in his lifetime, jumped in Tim's driver's seat, undeterred. Did he realize how close he'd just come to being terribly injured? But Charlie, a tough, leathery cowboy, was completely unfazed.

I, on the other hand, was fazed. I was extremely fazed. Adrenaline poured from my eyeballs.

"C'mon," Marlboro Man said, grabbing my hand. But my feet were firmly planted. I wasn't moving another inch toward that fire. "Go ahead," I said, shaking my head. "I'll just go wait in your pickup."

"Okay," he said, giving me a quick glance. "You'll be fine." Then he broke into a run and jumped onto the back of the truck with Tim . . . and I watched as the three brave, psychotic men drove straight back into Hades.

I turned on my heels and walked briskly toward Marlboro Man's pickup, which glowed light orange from the fire behind me. After crawling into the backseat, I watched as the fire—and all the firefighters—traveled farther and farther away. The night air took over, and I rested my head against the door—eventually slumping over into a deep coma of a sleep. I dreamed that Marlboro Man and I were playing golf, and that he was wearing a kelly green Izod. He had a caddy named Teddy. Then, just as we started playing the back nine, I heard the door of the pickup open.

"Hey," he said, his hand gently rubbing my back. I heard the diesel rattle of vehicles driving away from the scene.

"Hey," I replied, sitting up and looking at my watch. It was 5:00 A.M. "Are you okay?"

"Yep," he said. "We finally got it out." Marlboro Man's clothes were black. Heavy soot covered his drawn, exhausted face.

"Can I go home now?" I said. I was only halfway kidding. And actually, I wasn't kidding at all.

"Sorry about that," Marlboro Man said, still rubbing my back. "That was crazy." He gave a half-chuckle and kissed my forehead. I didn't know what to say.

Driving back to his house, the pickup was quiet. My mind began to race, which is never good at five in the morning. And then, inexplicably, just as we reached the road to his house, I lost it.

"So, why did you even take me there, anyway?" I said. "I mean, if I'm just going to ride in someone's pickup, why even bring me along? It's not like I was any help to anyone. . . ."

Marlboro Man glanced over at me. His eyes were tired. "So . . . did you want to operate one of the sprayers?" he asked, an unfamiliar edge to his voice.

"No, I just . . . I mean. . . ." I searched for the words. "I mean, that was just ridiculous! That was *dangerous*!"

"Well, prairie fires are dangerous," Marlboro Man answered. "But that's life. Stuff like this happens."

I was cranky. The nap had done little to calm me down. "*What* happens? You just drive right into fires and throw caution to the wind? I mean, people could die out there. I could have died. *You* could have died! I mean, do you realize how crazy that was?"

Marlboro Man looked straight ahead, rubbing his left eye and blinking. He looked exhausted. He looked spent.

We arrived in his driveway just in time to see the eastern sun peeking over the horse barn. Marlboro Man stopped his pickup, put it into park, and said, still looking straight ahead, "I took you with me . . . because I thought you'd like to see a fire." He turned off the pickup and opened his door. "And because I didn't want to leave you here by yourself."

I didn't say anything. We both exited the pickup, and Marlboro Man began walking toward his house. And then, still walking, he said it—words that chilled me to the bone.

"I'll see you later." He didn't even turn around.

I stood there, not knowing what to say, though deep down I knew I wouldn't have to. I knew that just as he'd always done anytime I'd ever been rendered speechless in his presence, he'd speak up, turn around, come to my rescue, hold me in his arms . . . and infuse love into my soul, as only he could do. He always swooped in to save me, and this time would be no different.

But he didn't turn around. He didn't speak up. He simply walked toward the house, toward the door on his back porch—the same porch door where, hours earlier, he and I had stood in a complete fit of romance and lust, where the heat between us was but a foreshadowing of the fire waiting for us in that distant prairie. Where I was safe and cozy and secure, and had Marlboro Man just the way I wanted him: with no accompanying danger, no risk, no interruption from the outside world, no scariness. Where I'd had Marlboro Man on my terms. And now a dumb, out-of-control prairie fire had come along and ruined it.

He didn't run over, swoop me up in his arms, or whisper love into my ear. I just stood there, alone, in Marlboro Man's driveway, suddenly painfully aware of the glaring ugliness of my outburst. And the only sound in my ear that morning would be the quiet click of his back door closing behind him.

Chapter Seventeen

TORMENT TRAIL

I STOOD THERE in his driveway, not knowing whether to run after him or leave; the latter was certainly the easier of the two options. I'd never felt so exhausted; I felt needles in my eyes when I blinked. Never mind how Marlboro Man's eyes must have felt after staring into a blazing prairie fire for over four hours. I heard a mama cow moo in the distance. What was she telling me? *You were stooooooopid. Go in after him.* I wasn't sure what the right move was; he'd never put me in this position before. He always made the moves; he always flew in and saved the moment.

The romantic thing, the right thing, the brave thing would have been for me to follow him into his house. To grab him, to hug him, to embrace him . . . to say *I'm sorry*, whether I felt that way or not. Acknowledge that it had been a rough night for both of us. Admit that I'd overreacted. Show him that I'm here for him, no matter what life brings, and that I love him more than anything. That's what my heart commanded me to do.

But my head took over and reminded my heart, which by now was thumping inside me, of the tone of Marlboro Man's voice moments earlier—the cold, distant, detached "see you later" that plunged a thousand icicles into my chest. And within moments, I was quietly pulling out of Marlboro Man's gravel driveway, trying to convince myself that the past several hours had been a bad dream . . . that I'd soon wake up to the familiar sound of Marlboro

Man saying "Hey, you . . ." over the phone. It had to have been a bad dream. But all the way home, my car phone remained deafeningly silent.

An hour later, I was pulling into my parents' driveway, the site of so many long, impassioned embraces between Marlboro Man and me. I'd lived in this house since third grade—had walked up to this same porch in everything from Sperry Top-Siders to Reebok high-tops to Birkenstocks. I'd stood on that porch, saying good night to prom dates and boyfriends and band geeks and tennis pros. But the ghosts of those dates were long gone; this porch had been forever etched with the soles of Marlboro Man's boots. He'd taken over everything—every speck of my focus and attention since I'd laid eyes on him in that bar in my hometown. It had been a whirlwind, a tsunami—a natural disaster of my judgment and resolve and self. One week with a Wrangler-wearing cowboy, and the entire course of my life had changed.

As I walked up the same driveway where it had all begun with a kiss between us, I knew without a doubt that it was the only thing I'd ever really wanted. I fell onto my bed and buried my head in my pillow, wanting desperately to fall fast asleep. But sleep wouldn't come, no matter how much I wanted it to rescue me from the horrible feeling in my stomach. I didn't want to feel what I was feeling—that a bubble had burst, that I'd gotten so angry and lost it the way I had. Unable to sleep, I got up and took a long, refreshing shower and went for a walk on the golf course.

I walked counter to the direction of the golf course: first down the seventh fairway to the seventh tee, and on to the sixth hole. Seeing early golfers in the distance—retirees with socks stretching halfway up their calves—I cut across the sixth fairway to continue my walk in the rough, a perfect reflection of the state of things that day.

A bird dog, cooped up in a wire dog run, barked at me as I walked past. "Shut up," I snapped back, as if the dog even heard me, or cared. I was cranky; it had definitely set in. I looked around for any bird or squirrel who might want to cross me; I'd take them out with one cold stare. I'd been

awake for twenty-four hours, save for the deep, face-pressed-against-the-
pickup nap in Marlboro Man's pickup while he fought the blazing fire early
that morning. And we'd had our first fight since our delicious love affair
began. It hadn't been a knock-down, drag-out fight, though; in a way, I
wished it had been. Then I'd be able to put my finger on it, identify it, wrap
my brain around what had happened.

Instead I was left with the cold shiver of the sound of Marlboro Man's
voice—Marlboro Man, my beautiful love, saying "I'll see you later" as
he walked away. I didn't even remember what had happened before that
moment; I didn't even care. I just knew I felt tired and broken and wrong.

And the only person I had to talk to was a nameless bird dog on a golf
course.

By now I was walking near the third green, near the home of a retired
doctor. He was sitting on a wooden bench in his beautifully manicured
backyard, his arm around a very attractive older woman—a woman who
wasn't his wife of fifty years, who had died suddenly and unexpectedly two
years earlier. This woman's husband, who'd also been a physician in town,
had died of a heart attack just a short while before that. In their grief and
loneliness, they'd found a common bond and had married each other a few
months earlier.

"Good morning," I said, waving as I walked by, managing a weak
smile.

The couple waved and smiled, then resumed their original position: his
arm around her shoulder, her hand resting on the inside of his leg. I loved
the sight of two older adults showing each other physical attention sugges-
tive of a more intimate relationship. As a woman madly in love, it only made
me ache for Marlboro Man.

I wasn't the type to call. To pursue. To beg forgiveness. There was way
too much of my mother in me: too much *I'm fine . . . I'm strong . . . I don't
need you* to lay myself on the line with a phone call of contrition. But that
morning, inexplicably, I made a circle around an enormous elm tree and

took off in a sprint back toward my parents' house. I had to talk to Marlboro Man—I couldn't take this stand-my-ground approach anymore.

As I ran that humid morning, I thought about the old doctor and his new wife sitting on that wooden bench. They had joy on their faces. Contentment, despite the life-altering grief of losing their respective spouses, was all around them. Together they'd picked up the pieces and found happiness. Not through golf or bridge or shopping or friends, but each other.

That was the happiness I'd found with Marlboro Man. And I wasn't about to let my pride screw it up. I picked up the pace, finally reaching my parents' backyard.

I walked into a quiet house. My parents were away on a weekend getaway, one of what would be a handful of last-ditch efforts to save their troubled marriage. My eyes were puffy and tired, but my walk had gotten my heart pumping. And though I knew Marlboro Man was likely sleeping off the exhaustion of the night before, I just knew I had to call. Whether he was dreaming or awake, I didn't want another moment to pass without reaching out to him. I wanted him to know that it had been the same exhaustion that had driven me to my early-morning outburst—exhaustion mixed with the adrenaline that comes from a near-death experience, but that was another topic for another time. I wanted him to know that I wasn't actually a reactive, histrionic brat. That I'd been overwhelmed by the fire.

And that I wanted to sit on a wooden bench in our backyard when we were eighty, with his arm around my shoulder and my hand on the inside of his leg.

I was so busy going through it all in my mind, I didn't realize I'd already dialed Marlboro Man's house, and that it had rung over a dozen times. I caught myself and immediately hung up. Only psychos let the phone ring over a dozen times. *It's just as well*, I thought. He needs to sleep. Then, slowly, the building exhaustion took over . . . and I crawled onto my parents' bed—one that, once upon a time, had been a joyful, safe place in our house—and drifted off into a deep, deep sleep.

I woke up in a dimly lit room. Was it dawn? Had I slept all night? I looked at my dad's circa 1984 electronic alarm clock. It was 7:23. My body felt heavy and weak, as if I'd just resurfaced from a season-long hibernation. When I put my feet on my parents' carpet and tried to stand, my knees nearly buckled. I looked into the backyard, rubbing both eyes with my knuckles. It was evening—I could tell. I'd slept for over nine hours. I inhaled deeply, then dragged myself up to the shower. The nap had been so heavy, I had to wash it off.

After my shower, I felt reborn. I was sure Marlboro Man would be rested by then—he'd likely been asleep earlier when I'd called—so I put on my favorite jeans and my equally favorite pink tank top and poured myself a glass of my mom's Far Niente chardonnay. Snuggling into a comfy chair in the living room, I reached for the phone and dialed Marlboro Man's house. I couldn't wait to hear his voice. To know that everything was fine.

Instead I heard the sultry whisper of a quiet female voice.

"Hello?" the woman said softly, as if she was trying to keep from being heard.

Startled, I hung up the phone. *Wrong number,* I told myself, then I carefully redialed Marlboro Man.

The same voice answered: "Hello?" The woman was young, breathless, busy.

I froze in my seat, then hurriedly hung up the phone again.

What the . . .

What in the world is going on?

I SAT THERE utterly unable to move—the young woman's breathy voice still resonating in my ears. My cheeks tingled; my entire body seized up. In a million years, I never would have expected this. My thumbnail was between my front teeth, getting ripped to shreds.

What just happened? Who WAS that? I was at a total loss for words, even as countless horrific thoughts swam furiously around my brain. It certainly hadn't been his mother, whose low, sophisticated voice was way too distinctive to miss. Marlboro Man's brother, Tim, wasn't dating anyone—that wasn't a possibility, either. Marlboro Man didn't have a housekeeper, a personal chef, an acupuncturist, or even a sister . . . and he lived too far off the beaten path to have any drop-by visitors. No scenario—absolutely no scenario on earth—made sense.

But even if there had been a legitimate reason for the presence of another woman in his house, I couldn't get past the sexy, hushed, secretive tone to the voice. It was no voice any mother or aunt would use to answer someone else's phone. The woman sounded young. Intimate. Lusty.

The woman sounded naked. Naked and tan and extremely petite and busty. I could almost see her face—the violet-blue eyes and the full, bee-stung lips. I wanted to turn off my mind so she'd go away and fade back into The Land of People Who Don't Exist, where she'd lived before this phone call.

But she wouldn't go back to her homeland. I'd seen enough movies to know exactly what that woman's hushed voice had meant. Without even being there, I knew. She was there with Marlboro Man. She was as in love with him as I was. She'd been waiting on the sidelines ever since he and I had gotten together. And in his frustration with our argument early that morning, he'd reached out and sought comfort in this girl . . . this woman . . . this dripping-with-lust voice on the other end of the phone. They'd spent the whole day together—he, resting and reveling in her company . . . she, doctoring his wounds and pouring loving salve on his soul. He'd told her about the fire he'd fought, and she'd felt sorry for him and rubbed his shoulders . . . then his back. Then she'd kissed every inch of his body to make him feel better.

AAAAAAAAAAAAAAAAAAAAAAAAAAAAAGHHH! My hands clamped over my face, powerless to stop my imagination.

Marlboro Man has just jumped into the shower, closing the bathroom door behind him. The phone rings. The sex kitten jumps up wrapped in a crisp bed-sheet—the tightly woven white twill setting off her glistening bronze skin—and runs down the hallway to answer it. She has no freckles. Her sexy, tousled hair falls forward and tickles her cheeks as she picks up the phone. She suspects it's me—he'd warned her I might call—so she answers quietly, knowing Marlboro Man wouldn't want her to. But she had to answer—she wanted to mark her territory, to tell me "it's on" in her own way. She was there. And I was here. And Marlboro Man was in the shower. Naked. And she was ready to rub his back all night long.

AAAAAAAAAAAAAAAAAAAAAAAAAAAAAAGHGGH. I drew my legs up and curled up in a tight ball on the comfy chair on which I sat and cursed every movie I'd ever seen that involved a busty, petite, or bronze female character.

I took a deep breath, trying to suppress my building agitation. I felt sick. This wasn't an emotion I'd been remotely prepared to face—not that night, not in the past, not in the future. We'd just spent the past several months spending every evening together—how could this ever have happened? When? Of all the things I ever would have suspected, Marlboro Man seeking comfort in the arms of another woman was so far down the list, it had never even crossed my mind. It flew in the face of everything I'd come to know about him. He was way too transparent, I thought, to sneak around on the sidelines with another woman, no matter how petite and bronze she was. He couldn't possibly have been duplicitous all this time . . . could he?

Then again, it happens all the time. Maybe I'm one of those girls who doesn't have a clue until it blows up in a nuclear explosion of betrayal and pain. But . . . there's no way! Is there? My thumbnail was totally gone by now. My pupils were fixed and dilated. My pink tank top fluttered from the racing of my heart.

That's when the front door opened.

"He-he-he-hello?" the thundering voice announced. Great. It was Mike.

I took a deep breath. "Hi, Mike," I managed, my head resting on my hand. My mind was going a million miles a minute.

"Hey." Mike started in. I braced myself. I wasn't in the mood for Mike. I wasn't in the mood for anyone or anything. I just wanted to sit there and obsess. It had only been seven minutes since the sex kitten had entered my world, and I needed to figure it all out.

"*Yes*, Mike?" I answered, irritated.

Mike paused. "W-w-w-w-what's *your* problem?" Mike could always tell when I was in a bad mood.

"Nothing, Mike!" I snapped. Then I paused. Softened my voice a little. "I just . . . I just don't feel like talking right now. I'm thinking about some stuff."

"Well, c-c-c-c-can you take me to the mall?" Mike asked.

"Mike, who just dropped you off?" I asked.

"Karole C-C-C-Cozby," Mike replied.

"Well, why didn't you just have Karole take you to the *mall*?" I pleaded. This is exactly why I'd braced myself moments earlier. Nothing's ever easy when Mike's around.

"B-b-b-b-be*cause*!" Mike snapped. "I gots to . . . to change my *shirt* and I didn't want to make her wait for me, turkey damn butt!" And with that, he stomped upstairs to his room. Mike had a colorful arsenal of expletives.

I would have kept arguing with him, but I didn't have it in me. All I could do was go back and forth in my mind about how there had to be some explanation for the woman who'd answered Marlboro Man's phone moments earlier, but there was none. But there *had* to be an explanation. But there was none. If I sat there all night, I could never figure out the answer.

I stood up and walked over to the stairs. "I'll take you to the mall later, Mike," I hollered up to him. "But you're gonna have to wait awhile, okay?"

Mike didn't answer.

I turned to walk toward my parents' room, where I planned to crawl back under the covers and forget the world and, hopefully, go back to sleep in an effort to avoid the reality of the night, though after the nine-hour nap I'd just had, sleep was highly unlikely. I felt strange, out of my head, in a daze. And just as I passed by the front door, I was startled by a light knock. *Maybe it's one of Mike's cronies,* I thought. *Good!* Then I won't have to drive him anywhere.

When I swung open the door, there he was: Marlboro Man, wearing Wranglers and a crisp white shirt and boots. And a sweet, heart-melting smile.

What are you doing here? I thought. *You're supposed to be in the shower. You're supposed to be with the sex kitten.*

"Hey," he said, wasting no time in stepping through the door and winding his arms around my waist. My arms couldn't help but drape over his strong shoulders; my lips couldn't help but find his. He felt soft, warm, safe . . . and our first kiss turned into a third, and a sixth, and a seventh. It was the same kiss as the night before, when the phone call alerting him to the fire had come. My eyes remained tightly closed as I savored every second, trying to reconcile the present with the horror movie I'd imagined just moments earlier. I had no idea what was going on. At that point, I didn't even care.

"Ummmmm!!! I'm t-t-t-ttellin'!" Mike teased from the top of the stairs, just before running down and embracing Marlboro Man in a bear hug.

"Hi, Mike," Marlboro Man said, politely patting him on the back.

"Mike?" I said, smiling and blinking my eyes. "Will you excuse us for a couple of minutes?"

Mike obliged, giggling and *ooooh*-ing as he walked toward the kitchen.

Marlboro Man picked me up and brought my eyes to the level of his. Smiling, he said, "I've been trying to call you this afternoon."

"You have?" I said. I hadn't even heard the phone ring. "I, um . . . I sort of took a nine-hour nap."

Marlboro Man chuckled. Oh, that chuckle. I needed it badly that night.

He set my feet back down on the floor. "So . . . ," he teased. "You still cranky?"

"Nope," I finally answered, smiling. *So, who is that woman in your house? So . . . what did you do all day?* "Did you ever get any sleep?" *So, who is that woman in your house?*

"Well," he began. "I had to help Tim with something this morning, then I crashed on the couch for a few hours . . . it felt pretty good."

Who was the woman? What's her name? What's her cup size?

He continued. "I would've slept all day, but Katie and her family showed up in the middle of my nap," he said. "I forgot they were staying at my house tonight."

Katie. His cousin Katie. The one with the two young kids, who had probably just gone to bed when I'd called earlier.

"Oh . . . really?" I said, my chest relaxing with a long, quiet exhale.

"Yeah . . . but it's a little crowded over there," he said. "I thought I'd come over here and take you to a movie."

I smiled, stroking his back with my hand. "A movie sounds perfect." The busty, bronze mystery girl slowly faded into oblivion.

Mike came barreling out of the kitchen, where he'd been listening to every word.

"*Hey*—if you guys are goin' to the movie, c-c-c-can you drive me to the mall?" he yelled.

"Sure, Mike," Marlboro Man said. "We'll drive you to the mall. It'll cost you ten bucks, though."

And as the three of us made our way outside to Marlboro Man's diesel pickup, I had to bite my lip to keep myself from articulating the only seven words in the English language that were in my vocabulary at that moment:

God help me—I love that man.

Chapter Eighteen

SO LONG TO PARADISE

EDDING PLANS moved along, and the date was fast approaching. My dress was ordered—the last size six I would ever wear—and all the details of a beautiful Episcopal wedding were falling neatly into place, despite the turmoil brewing at my formerly happy, peaceful childhood home. My parents' marriage was hanging by a rapidly unraveling thread; every day I hoped beyond hope they'd hold it together until the wedding day. Sometimes I wished they'd hurry up and divorce so we could all get on with our lives. Then I'd see signs that things would improve . . . only to be disappointed by another argument or crisis or drama. At least once a week, I wished I'd followed my original instinct and just eloped.

It was a terrible time to be thinking about hors d'oeuvres.

Still, I came to find solace in all the details of wedding planning. A hopeless food lover, the reception menu was high on my list of Things to Do That Distract Me from Mom and Dad's Crumbling Marriage, and it was proving to be tricky. Because along with the neurologists and corporate officers who'd be attending the country club bash, there would also be cowboys . . . and handymen . . . and farmers . . . and large-animal vets—none of whom, I reckoned, would appreciate being rewarded for their long drive to my hometown with crudités and *brie en croûte*.

On the other hand, it was to be a formal affair, complete with engraved

Crane invitations and ethereal white tulle. I was fairly certain cocktail wieners in barbecue sauce wouldn't be enough. Plus, I'd always loved beautiful, elegant food, and thanks to a teenage fixation on the 1980s-era Martha Stewart, I knew precisely what kind of wedding food would satisfy me. Stuffed cherry tomatoes. Cucumbers with smoked salmon mousse. Caviar. Herbed cheeses and radishes. Stuffed snow peas. Marinated chicken skewers. Cold shrimp as far as the eye could see. The middle child in me had to find a way to satisfy both sides. The reception had to be a nod to both my and Marlboro Man's backgrounds . . . and not one of the six hundred guests could be left behind.

Marlboro Man was out of town, on a trip to the southern part of the state, looking at farm ground, the night I began conceiving of the best way to arrange the reception menu. I was splayed on my bed in sweats, staring at the ceiling, when suddenly I gave birth to The Idea: one area of the country club would be filled with gold bamboo chairs, architecturally arranged orchids and roses, and antique lace table linens. Violins would serenade the guests as they feasted on cold tenderloin and sipped champagne. Martha Stewart would be present in spirit and declare, "This is my daughter, whom I love. In her I am well pleased."

Martha's third cousin Mabel would prefer the ballroom on the other end of the club, however, which would be the scene of an authentic chuck wagon spread: barbecue, biscuits and gravy, fried chicken, Coors Light. Blue-checkered tablecloths would adorn the picnic tables, a country band would play "All My Exes Live in Texas," and wildflowers would fill pewter jugs throughout the room.

I smiled, imagining the fun. In one fell swoop, our two worlds—Marlboro Man's country and my country club—would collide, combine, and unite in a huge, harmonious feast, one that would officially usher in my permanent departure from city life, cappuccino, and size 6 clothes.

While I was deep in my fantasy, in yet another episode of perfect timing, Marlboro Man called from the road.

"Hey," he said, the mid-1990s spotty cell phone service only emphasizing the raspy charm of his voice.

"Oh! Just the person I want to talk to," I said, grabbing paper and a pen. "I have a question for you—"

"I bought your wedding present today," Marlboro Man interrupted.

"Huh?" I said, caught off guard. "Wedding present?" For someone steeped in the proper way of doing things, I was ashamed that a wedding gift for Marlboro Man had never crossed my mind.

"Yep," he said. "And you need to hurry up and marry me so I can give it to you."

I giggled. "So . . . what is it?" I asked. I couldn't even imagine. I hoped it wasn't a tennis bracelet.

"You have to marry me to find out," he answered.

Yikes. What was it? Wasn't the wedding ring itself supposed to be the present? That's what I'd been banking on. What would I ever get him? Cuff links? An Italian leather briefcase? A Montblanc pen? What do you give a man who rides a horse to work every day?

"So, woman," Marlboro Man said, changing the subject, "what did you want to ask me?"

"Oh!" I said, focusing my thoughts back to the reception. "Okay, I need you to name your absolute favorite foods in the entire world."

He paused. "Why?"

"I'm just taking a survey," I answered.

"Hmmm . . ." He thought for a minute. "Probably steak."

Duh. "Well, besides steak," I said.

"Steak," he repeated.

"And what else?" I asked.

"Well . . . steak is pretty good," he answered.

"Okay," I responded. "I understand that you like steak. But I need a little more to work with here."

"But why?" he asked.

"Because I'm taking a survey," I repeated.

Marlboro Man chuckled. "Okay, but I'm really hungry right now, and I'm three hours from home."

"I'll factor that in," I said.

"Biscuits and gravy . . . tenderloin . . . chocolate cake . . . barbecue ribs . . . scrambled eggs," he said, rattling off his favorite comfort foods.

Bingo, I thought, smiling.

"Now, hurry up and marry me," he commanded. "I'm tired of waiting on you."

I loved it when he was bossy.

I lay there on my bed, giddy over the new direction the reception had taken—it would be the perfect bridge between the old life and the new, the perfect symbol of the best of both our worlds. It might be hokey. It might be a raging success. Either way, it didn't matter. I pictured the laughter of the guests in attendance, the band playing their banjos, the champagne. I closed my eyes and saw the gold bamboo chairs and the tall, stalky flower arrangements . . . and I licked my lips when I imagined the stuffed snow peas. I'd always loved stuffed snow peas. Martha had done that to me.

Filled with energy, I hopped off the bed and headed downstairs to share the new ideas with my mom, who'd been toggling between *enthusiastically involved* and *hopelessly distracted* when it came to my wedding plans. I knew she'd get excited about this tweak in the plans, though; for all my mom's current angst, she was, at her core, fun-loving and adventurous. But as usual, when I arrived at the bottom of the stairs I saw that the door leading to the den was closed. I could hear the hushed tones of my parents' strained conversation—the subject of which, obviously, had to do with the state of their crumbling marriage. And who was responsible for what.

The stuffed snow peas would have to wait.

Not wanting any part of it, I turned on my heels and headed back up to my bedroom—the only drama-free zone in the entire house. It was too late for me to leave the house to see a movie or go get coffee or visit a bookstore, and my regular safe haven—my cowboy—was driving a long stretch of highway in the middle of Oklahoma. Lacking any other appealing option, I drew myself a deep, hot bath and filled it with an excessive amount of aromatherapy bubbles. Climbing in, I rested my head against the back of the tub, closed my eyes, inhaled the rosemary and lavender, and did everything within my power to shake the oppressive feeling that my parents' situation was going to get a lot worse. It hadn't improved at all in the months since Marlboro Man had proposed, and the only question remaining was whether disaster would strike before, during, or after the wedding ceremony.

I sat there in the warm, bubbly bathtub that night, trying to massage the building knots out of my stiff shoulders and doing my best to keep myself from completely losing my mind.

*M*ARLBORO MAN picked me up the next evening, exactly one month before our wedding day. Our evening apart had made the heart grow fonder, and we greeted each other with a magnificently tight embrace. It filled my soul, the way his arms gripped me . . . how he almost always used his superior strength to lift me off the ground. A wannabe strong, independent woman, I was continually surprised by how much I loved being swept, quite literally, off my feet.

We drove straight into the sunset, arriving on his ranch just as the sky was changing from salmon to crimson, and I gasped. I'd never seen anything so brilliant and beautiful. The inside of Marlboro Man's pickup glowed with color, and the tallgrass prairie danced in the evening breeze. Things were just different in the country. The earth was no longer a mere place where I lived—it was alive. It had a heartbeat. The sight of the country absolutely took my breath away—the vast expanse of the flat pastures, the endless view of clouds. Being there was a spiritual experience.

I looked around and realized we were headed down a different road than Marlboro Man would normally take. "I have to give you your wedding present," Marlboro Man said before I could ask where we were going. "I can't wait a month before I give it to you."

Butterflies fluttered in my stomach. "But . . . ," I stammered. "I haven't gotten *yours* yet."

Marlboro Man clasped my hand, continuing to look forward at the road. "Yes you have," he said, bringing my hand to his lips and turning me to a pool of melted butter right in his big Ford truck.

We wound through several curves in the road, and I tried to discern whether I'd been there before. My sense of direction was lousy; everything looked the same to me. Finally, just as the sun was dipping below the horizon, we came upon an old barn. Marlboro Man pulled up beside it and parked.

Confused, I looked around. He got me a barn? "What . . . what are we *doing* here?" I asked.

Marlboro Man didn't answer. Instead, he just turned off the pickup, turned to me . . . and smiled.

"What *is* it?" I asked as Marlboro Man and I exited the pickup and walked toward the barn.

"You'll see," he replied. He definitely had something up his sleeve.

I was nervous. I always hated opening gifts in front of the person who gave them to me. It made me uncomfortable, as if I were sitting in a dark room with a huge spotlight shining on my head. I squirmed with discomfort. I wanted to turn and run away. Hide in his pickup. Hide in the pasture. Lie low for a few weeks. I didn't want a wedding present. I was weird that way.

"But . . . but . . . ," I said, trying to back out. "But I don't have *your* wedding present yet." As if anything would have derailed him at that point.

"Don't worry about that," Marlboro Man replied, hugging me around the waist as we walked. He smelled so good, and I inhaled deeply. "Besides, we can share this one."

That's strange, I thought. Any fleeting ideas I'd had that he'd be giving me a shiny bracelet or sparkly necklace or other bauble suddenly seemed far-fetched. How could he and I share the same tennis bracelet? *Maybe he got me one of those two-necklace sets, the ones with the halved hearts,* I thought, *and he'll wear one half and I'll wear the other.* I couldn't exactly picture it, but Marlboro Man had never been above surprising me.

Then again, we were walking toward a barn.

Maybe it was a piece of furniture for the house we'd been working on—a love seat, perhaps. Oh, wouldn't that be the most darling of wedding gifts? A love seat? I'll bet it's upholstered in cowhide, I thought, or maybe some old western brocade fabric. I'd always loved those fabrics in the old John Wayne movies. Maybe its legs are made of horns! It just *had* to be furniture. Maybe it was a new bed. A bed on which all the magic of the world would take place, where our children—whether one or six—would be conceived, where the prairie would ignite in an explosion of passion and lust, where. . . .

Or maybe it's a puppy.

Oh, yes! That has to be it, I told myself. It's probably a puppy—a *pug,* even, in tribute to the first time I broke down and cried in front of him! *Oh my gosh—he's replacing Puggy Sue,* I thought. He waited until we were close enough to the wedding, but he doesn't want the pup to get any bigger before he gives it to me. Oh, Marlboro Man . . . you may have just zeroed in on what could possibly be the single most romantic thing you ever could have done for me. In my wildest dreams, I couldn't have imagined a more perfect love gift. A pug would be the perfect bridge between my old world and my new, a permanent and furry reminder of my old life on the golf course. As Marlboro Man slid open the huge barn doors and flipped on the enormous lights mounted to the beams, my heart began beating quickly. I couldn't wait to smell its puppy breath.

"Happy wedding," he said sweetly, leaning against the wall of the barn and motioning toward the center with his eyes. My eyes adjusted to the light . . . and slowly focused on what was before me.

It wasn't a pug. It wasn't a diamond or a horse or a shiny gold bangle . . . or even a blender. It wasn't a love seat. It wasn't a lamp. Sitting before me, surrounded by scattered bunches of hay, was a bright green John Deere riding lawn mower—a very large, very green, very mechanical, and very diesel-fueled John Deere riding lawn mower. Literally and figuratively, crickets chirped in the background of the night. And for the hundredth time since our engagement, the reality of the future for which I'd signed up flashed in front of me. I felt a twinge of panic as I saw the tennis bracelet I thought I didn't want go poof, disappearing completely into the ether. Would this be how presents on the ranch would always be? Does the world of agriculture have a different chart of wedding anniversary presents? Would the first anniversary be paper . . . or motor oil? Would the second be cotton or Weed Eater string?

I would add this to the growing list of things I still needed to figure out.

Chapter Nineteen

A FISTFUL OF ELMER'S

ONCE THE wedding gift was out of the way, Marlboro Man and I had to check one last item off our list before we entered the Wedding Zone: premarital counseling. It was a requirement of the Episcopal church, these one-hour sessions with the semiretired interim priest who led our church at the time. Logically, I understood the reasoning behind the practice of premarital discussions with a man of the cloth. Before a church sanctions a marriage union, it wants to ensure the couple grasps the significance and gravity of the (hopefully) eternal commitment they're making. It wants to give the couple things to think about, ideas to ponder, matters to get straight. It wants to make sure it's not sending two young lovers into what could be an avoidable domestic catastrophe. Logically, I grasped the concept.

Practically, however, it was an uncomfortable hour of sitting across from a sweet minister who meant well and asked the right questions, but who had clearly run out of juice in the zest-for-marriage department. It was emotional drudgery for me; not only did I have to rethink obvious things I'd already thought about a thousand times, but I also had to watch Marlboro Man, a quiet, shy country boy, assimilate and answer questions put to him by a minister he'd only recently met on the subject of love, romance, and commitment, no less. Though he was polite and reverent, I felt for him. These were things cowboys rarely talked about with a third party.

"What would you do if Ree became gravely ill?" Father Johnson asked Marlboro Man.

"Well, sir," Marlboro Man replied, "I'd take care of her."

"Who's going to do the cooking in your household?"

Marlboro Man smiled. "Ree's a great cook," he answered. I sat up proudly in my chair, trying not to remember the Linguine with Clam Sauce and the Marinated Flank Steak and whatever other well-intentioned meals I'd massacred early in our relationship.

"What about the dishes?" Father Johnson continued, channeling Gloria Steinem. "See yourself helping out there?"

Marlboro Man scratched his chin and paused. "Sure," he said. "Honestly, these aren't really things we've sat down and talked about." His voice was kind. Polite.

I wanted to crawl in a hole. I wanted to have my gums scraped. I wanted to go fight that huge prairie fire from a while back. Anything would be better than this.

"Have you talked about how many children you'd like to have?"

"Yes, sir," Marlboro Man said.

"And?" Father Johnson prodded.

"I'd like to have six or so," Marlboro Man answered, a virile smile spreading across his face.

"And what about Ree?" Father Johnson asked.

"Well, she says she'd like to have one," Marlboro Man said, looking at me and touching my knee. "But I'm workin' on her."

Father Johnson wrinkled his brow.

"How do you and Ree resolve conflict?"

"Well . . . ," Marlboro Man replied. "To tell you the truth, we haven't really had much conflict to speak of. We get along pretty darn well."

Father Johnson looked over his glasses. "I'm sure you can think of something." He wanted some dirt.

Marlboro Man tapped his boot on the sterile floor of Father Johnson's study and looked His Excellence straight in the eye. "Well, she fell off her horse once when we went riding together," he began. "And that upset her a little bit. And a while back, I dragged her to a fire with me and it got a little dicey. . . ." Marlboro Man and I looked at each other. It was the largest "conflict" we'd had, and it had lasted fewer than twelve hours.

Father Johnson looked at me. "How did you deal with that, Ree?"

I froze. "Uh . . . uh . . ." I tapped my Donald Pliner mule on the floor. "I told him how I felt. And after that it was fine."

I hated every minute of this. I didn't want to be examined. I didn't want my relationship with Marlboro Man to be dissected with generic, one-size-fits-all questions. I just wanted to drive around in his pickup and look at pastures and curl up on the couch with him and watch movies. That had been going just fine for us—that was the nature of our relationship. But Father Johnson's questioning was making me feel defensive, as if we were somehow neglecting our responsibility to each other if we weren't spending every day in deep, contemplative thought about the minutiae of a future together. Didn't a lot of that stuff just come naturally over time? Did it really serve a purpose to figure it out now?

But Father Johnson's interrogation continued:

"What do you want for your children?"

"Have you talked about budgetary matters?"

"What role do your parents play in your life?"

"Have you discussed your political preferences? Your stances on important issues? Your faith? Your religion?"

And my personal favorite:

"What are you both going to do, long term, to nurture each other's creativity?"

I didn't have an answer for him there. But deep down, I knew that, somehow, gravy would come into play.

I had nothing against Father Johnson's questions. And they were good questions—for a late-night game of quarters with a room full of friends looking for deep conversation, they were great. But there was just something about them that didn't seem applicable to Marlboro Man and me, or any couple who loved each other and was willing to jump into a life together and take a chance. Some of the questions seemed obvious—things we already knew and really didn't need to formally discuss. Some of them seemed premature—things we shouldn't necessarily already know but would figure out as we go along. Some of them were painfully vague.

"How much do you know about each other?" was Father Johnson's final question of the day.

Marlboro Man and I looked at each other. We didn't know everything yet; we couldn't possibly. We just knew we wanted to be together. Was that not enough?

"Well, I'll speak for myself," Marlboro Man said. "I feel like I know all I need to know in order to be sure I want to marry Ree." He rested his hand on my knee, and my heart leapt. "And the rest . . . I figure we'll just handle it as we go along." His quiet confidence calmed me, and all I could think about anyway was how long it would take me to learn how to drive my new lawn mower. I'd never mowed a lawn before in my life. Did Marlboro Man know this? Maybe he should have started me out with a cheaper model.

Just then Father Johnson stood up to bid us farewell until our session the following week. I picked up my purse from its spot next to my chair.

"Thank you, Father Johnson," I said, standing up.

"Wait just a second," he said, holding up his hands. "I need to give you a little assignment." I'd almost made a clean getaway.

"I want you both to show me how much you know about each other," he began. "I want you both to make me a collage."

I looked at him for a moment. "A collage?" I asked. "Like, with magazine pictures and glue?"

"That's exactly right," Father Johnson replied. "And it doesn't have to be large or elaborate; just use a piece of legal-size paper as the backdrop. I want you to fill it with pictures that represent all the things you know about the other person. Bring it to your session next week, and we'll look at them together."

This was an unexpected development.

I made the mistake of glancing at Marlboro Man, who I imagined had never felt more uncomfortable in his life than he did once he faced the prospect of sitting down and working with paper and glue in an effort to prove to someone else how much he knew about the woman he was going to marry. He tried to keep a straight face, to remain respectful, but I'd studied his beautiful features enough to know when things were going on under the surface. Marlboro Man had been such a good sport through our series of premarital training. And this—a collage assignment—was his reward.

I put on a happy face. "Well, that'll be fun!" I said, enthusiastically. "We can sit down and do it together sometime this week. . . ."

"No, no, no . . . ," Father Johnson scolded, waving his hands at me. "You can't do it together. The whole point is to independently sit down and make the collage without the other person present."

Father Johnson was awfully bossy.

We shook hands, promised to bring our assignments to the following week's appointment, and made our way to the parking lot. Once out of the church doors, Marlboro Man swatted me.

"Ow!" I shrieked, feeling the sting. "What was *that* for?"

"Just your Tuesday spanking," Marlboro Man answered.

I smiled. I'd always loved Tuesday.

We hopped in the pickup, and Marlboro Man started the engine. "Hey," he said, turning to me. "Got any magazines I can borrow?" I giggled as

Marlboro Man pulled away from the church. "I could use some glue, too," he added. "I don't think I have any at my house."

*W*EDDING PLANS moved ahead at a rapid pace. I decided on the cake, bought my wedding shoes, firmed up the reception menu, sent the country band its deposit, and pulled my mom away from her marital crisis long enough for the two of us to meet with the flower people so we could firm up the orchids and the daisies. I attended showers thrown by friends of my parents—none of whom had any idea that their longtime buddies' marriage was a shambles. I began packing my belongings in preparation for my move to my new home on the ranch, much as I'd packed to move—permanently, I thought at the time—to Chicago. It felt surreal, knowing I'd soon be living with the man of my dreams, and that I'd soon be leaving my childhood home for the last time.

I resumed Tuesday-night dinners with Ga-Ga, Delphia, Dorothy, and Ruthie, soaking up their small-town conversation as if my life—and my eventual survival in my new locale—depended on it.

I loved those dinners.

Chicken-fried steak had never tasted so good.

In the meantime, Marlboro Man was working his fingers to the bone. To prepare for our three-week honeymoon to Australia, he'd rearranged the schedule of many goings-on at the ranch, compressing a normally much longer shipping season into a two-week window. I could sense a difference in his work; his phone calls to me were fewer and farther between, and he was getting up much earlier than he normally did. And at night, when he did call to whisper a sweet "good night" to me before his head hit the pillow, his voice was scratchy, more weary than normal. He was working like a dog.

In the midst of all of this, the deadline for our collage assignment loomed. It was Monday evening before our Tuesday get-together with Father Johnson, and I knew neither Marlboro Man nor I had gotten around to our respective collages. There was just too much going on—too many cows, too many wedding decisions, too many cozy movies on Marlboro Man's tufted leather couch. We had way too much romance to take care of when we were together, and besides that, Father Johnson had explicitly told us we couldn't work on the collages in each other's presence. This was fine with me: sitting upright at a table and cutting out magazine photos was the last thing I wanted to do with such a fine specimen of a human. It would have been a criminal misuse of our time together.

Still, I didn't want to show up for the meeting empty-handed, so that night at my parents' house I holed up in my room, resolving not to come out until I completed my Father Johnson "How Well Do You Know Your Fiancé?" collage. I dug around in the upstairs storage room of my parents' house and grabbed the only old magazines I could find: *Vogue*. *Golf Digest*. The Phoebe Cates issue of *Seventeen*.

Perfect. I was sure to find a wealth of applicable material. *This is so dumb*, I thought just as my bedroom phone rang loudly. It had to be Marlboro Man.

"Hello?" I answered.

"Hey," he said. "What're you doing?" He sounded pooped.

"Oh . . . not much," I answered. "What about you?"

"Well . . . ," he began, his voice sounding heavy . . . serious. "I've got a little bit of a problem."

I didn't know everything about Marlboro Man. But I knew enough to know that something was wrong.

*W*HAT IS IT?" I asked, pasting a magazine photo of a football—found in an old *Seventeen* magazine spread—on my beloved's collage.

"Well, a bunch of cattle trucks just showed up," he said, trying to talk over the symphonic mooing of cows all around him. "They were supposed to get here tomorrow night, but they showed up early. . . ."

"Oh, no . . . that's a bummer," I said, not quite sure what he was getting at.

"So now I've got to work all these cattle tonight and get 'em shipped . . . and by the time I get done, the store in town will be closed," he began. Our appointment with Father Johnson was at ten the next morning. "So I think I'm just going to have to come over there really early tomorrow morning and do the thing at your house," Marlboro Man said. I could hardly hear him through the cattle.

"Are you sure?" I asked. "What time were you thinking of coming over?" I braced myself for the worst.

"I was thinking around six or so," he said. "That would give me plenty of time to get it done before we go."

Six? In the morning? *Ugh*, I thought. *I have only one more week of sleeping in. After we're married, there's no telling what time I'll have to get out of bed.*

"Okay," I said, my voice dripping with trepidation. "I'll see you in the morning. Oh, and hey . . . if I don't answer the door right away it probably means I'm doing some weight training or something."

"Gotcha," Marlboro Man answered, humoring me. "And hey—don't pull any muscles or strain yourself. We're getting married in less than a week."

My stomach fluttered as I hung up the phone and resumed work on my collage. I decided to really go for it and pretend I was back in sixth grade, when I'd been given a similar "About Me" collage assignment by my teacher, Mrs. Stinson. Back then I'd spent over a week cutting the guts out of old ballet magazines, painstakingly gluing pictures of Gelsey Kirkland,

Mikhail Baryshnikov, and so many of the other ballet greats I idolized at that time, and adorning the cracks and borders of the collage with images of pointe shoes, tutus, tiaras, ballet bags, and leg warmers. Ballet had been my life then, just as it had remained all the way through school. It had been my one and only focus until boys came into the picture, and even they'd had to fight ballet for my time, energy, and attention.

I worked into the night, reminiscing about my past while constructing a collage about the man of my future, and felt pangs of bittersweet nostalgia for the way I'd felt in the sixth grade when I was making that ballet collage, and in seventh, and in eighth, when my only thought of tomorrow was which color comb I'd stick into the back pocket of my Lee jeans, back when my parents were together and in love. When I was so blissfully unaware that a splintering family could hurt so very much.

I worked and worked, and before I knew it, my collage was finished. Still damp from Elmer's glue, the masterpiece included images of horses—courtesy, coincidentally, of Marlboro cigarette ads—and footballs. There were pictures of Ford pickups and green grass—anything I could find in my old magazines that even remotely hinted at country life. There was a rattlesnake: Marlboro Man hated snakes. And a photo of a dark, starry night: Marlboro Man was afraid of the dark as a child. There were Dr Pepper cans, a chocolate cake, and John Wayne, whose likeness did me a great favor by appearing in some ad in *Golf Digest* in the early 1980s.

My collage would have to do, even though it was missing any images depicting the less tangible things—the real things—I knew about Marlboro Man. That he missed his brother Todd every day of his life. That he was shy in social settings. That he knew off-the-beaten-path Bible stories—not the typical Samson-and-Delilah and David-and-Goliath tales, but obscure, lesser-known stories that I, in a lifetime of skimming, would never have hoped to read. That he hid in an empty trash barrel during a game of hide-and-seek at the Fairgrounds when he was seven . . . and that he'd gotten stuck and had to be extricated by firefighters. That he hated long pasta noodles because they were too difficult to eat. That he was sweet. Caring. Serious. Strong. The collage was incomplete—sorely lacking vital information. But it would have to do for now. I was tired.

My phone rang at midnight, just as I was clearing my bed of the scissors and magazines and glue. It was Marlboro Man, who'd just returned to his home after processing 250 head of cattle in the dark of night. He just wanted to say good night. I would forever love that about him.

"What've you been doing tonight?" he asked. His voice was scratchy. He sounded spent.

"Oh, I just finished up my homework assignment," I answered, rubbing my eyes and glancing at the collage on my bed.

"Oh . . . good job," he said. "I've got to go get some sleep so I can get over there and get after it in the morning. . . ." His voice drifted off. Poor Marlboro Man—I felt so sorry for him. He had cows on one side, Father Johnson on the other, a wedding in less than a week, and a three-week vacation in another continent. The last thing he needed to do was flip through old issues of *Seventeen* magazine for pictures of lip gloss and Sun-In. The last thing he needed to deal with was Elmer's glue.

My mind raced, and my heart spoke up. "Hey, listen . . . ," I said, suddenly thinking of a brilliant idea. "I have an idea. Just sleep in tomorrow morning—you're so tired. . . ."

"Nah, that's okay," he said. "I need to do the—"

"I'll do your collage for you!" I interrupted. It seemed like the perfect solution.

Marlboro Man chuckled. "Ha—no way. I do my own homework around here."

"No, seriously!" I insisted. "I'll do it—I have all the stuff here and I'm totally in the zone right now. I can whip it out in less than an hour, then we can both sleep till at least eight."

As if he'd ever slept till eight in his life.

"Nah . . . I'll be fine," he said. "I'll see you in the morning. . . ."

"But . . . but . . . ," I tried again. "Then *I* can sleep till at least eight."

"Good night . . ." Marlboro Man trailed off, probably asleep with his ear to the receiver.

I made the command decision to ignore his protest and spent the next hour making his collage. I poured my whole heart and soul into it, delving deep and pulling out all the stops, marveling as I worked at how well I actually knew myself, and occasionally cracking up at the fact that I was doing Marlboro Man's premarital homework for him—homework that was mandatory if we were to be married by this Episcopal priest. But on the outside chance Marlboro Man's tired body was to accidentally oversleep, at least he wouldn't have to walk in the door of Father Johnson's study empty-handed.

I WAS AWAKENED at dawn to the sound of Marlboro Man knocking on the front door. A rancher through and through, he'd made good on his promise to show up at six. I should have known. He'd probably gotten fewer than five hours of sleep.

I stumbled down the stairs, trying in vain to steady myself so I'd look like I'd been awake for longer than seven seconds. When I opened the door he was there, in his Wranglers, looking impossibly appealing for someone so profoundly sleep-deprived. The sweetness of his gentle grin was matched only by his adorably puffy eyes, which made him look like a little boy despite the steel gray hair on his head. My stomach fluttered; I wondered if there'd ever be a time when it would stop.

"Good morning," he said, stepping inside the door and nuzzling his face into my neck. A thousand tiny feathers tickled my skin.

Marlboro Man announced that he was ready to get to work on the collage; I smiled as we headed upstairs. I immediately made a beeline for the bathroom, where I manically brushed my teeth with Close-Up. Twice. I was wearing pajamas. My eyes were puffy. I looked like a woman twice my age. When I finally walked out into the bedroom, primped as I could hope to be at six in the morning, Marlboro Man was standing near my bed, holding the two collages in his hands and looking them over.

"Oh, you're in big trouble," he said, holding up the collage I'd made on his behalf.

"In trouble?" I smiled. "With you or Father Johnson?"

"Both," he said, lunging at me and tackling me onto the bed. "You were *not* supposed to do that." I laughed and tried to wriggle loose. He tickled my ribs. I screamed.

Three seconds later, when he felt I'd been adequately punished, we sat up and propped our heads against the pillows of my bed. "You did not do my homework assignment for me," he said, grabbing the collage again and looking it over.

"I had insomnia," I said. "I needed a creative activity." Marlboro Man looked at me, seemingly unsure of whether to kiss me, thank me . . . or just tickle me some more.

I didn't give him a chance. Instead I picked up the collage and took Marlboro Man on a tour so he'd be prepared for our appointment.

"Here's a pack of cigarettes," I said. "Because I used to smoke in college."

"Uh-huh," he answered. "I knew that."

"And here's a glass of white wine," I continued. "Because . . . I love white wine."

"Yes, I've noticed," Marlboro Man answered. "But . . . won't Father Johnson have a problem with that being on there?"

"Nah . . . ," I said. "He's Episcopalian."

"Got it," he said.

I continued with my collage orientation, pointing out the swatch of my favorite shade of turquoise . . . the pug . . . the ballet shoe . . . the Hershey's Kiss. He watched and listened intently, prepping himself for Father Johnson's upcoming grilling. Gradually the earliness of the morning and the cozy warmth of my bedroom got the better of us, and before we knew it we'd sunk into the irresistible softness of my bed, our arms and legs caught in a tangled maze.

"I think I love you," his raspy voice whispered, his lips nearly touching my ear. His arms wrapped even more tightly around my body, swallowing me almost completely.

We woke up just in time to make our 10:00 A.M. appointment. Ironically, after all the last-minute cramming, Father Johnson barely asked us about the specifics of the collages. Instead we spent most of our time walking around the sanctuary and preparing for the upcoming rehearsal. As much as I loved Father Johnson, I was more than excited that this would be our last official meeting together before he finally got down to business and married us. We wound up passing our Father Johnson test with flying colors . . . feeling only slightly guilty that we'd cheated on our homework.

There wasn't much time for guilt, anyway; the wedding was five days away.

Chapter Twenty

A FACEFUL OF DYNAMITE

*J*HAD A list of wedding tasks a mile long: bridesmaid gifts, lun-
cheons, catering decisions . . . and trying to keep everything
happy and peaceful between my parents, who'd lost the ability to conceal
the fact that the tension between them had reached an all-time high. Their
marriage was hemorrhaging, getting worse every day. Any childlike notion
I'd had that the hope and optimism of my impending wedding would somehow transform and rescue their marriage, would turn everything around,
had turned out to be a foolish pipe dream. The plane had lost power; it was
going down fast. I just hoped it wouldn't hit the ground before I walked
down the aisle.

Marlboro Man's wedding preparations were equally complicated. Not
only did he have to prepare for our three-week honeymoon by wrapping
up a long list of ranch duties, he also had to finalize the honeymoon plans,
which he'd handled entirely himself. He was also making regular trips to
my parents' house, picking up bags and boxes of my belongings and moving them to the house on the ranch that we'd soon share as a newly married
couple. It was a small bunkhouse, a little less than a thousand square feet,
situated just behind the large yellow brick home we'd begun renovating
a few months earlier. Since the little house hadn't been occupied in over
twenty years, we'd spent our spare time over the past several weeks clean-

ing it from top to bottom, replacing the tile floor, and redoing the tiny bathroom and kitchen so we could move right in after the honeymoon. The house was in a more centralized location on the ranch than the house where Marlboro Man lived when we met, and living there would allow us to closely monitor progress on the main house. Then, when we eventually moved into the main house, we'd have a nice little guesthouse out back—perfect for visiting grandmothers or siblings. Perfect for slumber parties for the kids.

This would be our new homestead—the thousand-square-foot bunkhouse and the larger, half-remodeled two-story home built next to it. The rusty, paint-chipped cattle pens out back. The old, but structurally sound, barn. The overgrown brush. The dead branches in the yard. The place needed work—constant work. It would be up to us to get it back to the way it needed to be.

But it was ours, and I loved it. Not having had any real experiences with a rural lifestyle, I looked at that homestead of ours as a little piece of paradise on earth—a place where Marlboro Man and I would live out our days in romantic, bucolic bliss. Where I'd milk cows every morning in my tiered prairie skirt, like the one I'd bought at The Limited back in 1983. Where the birds would chirp happily and visit me on the kitchen windowsill as I washed dishes. Where the sun would always rise in the east and set in the west. Where nothing disappointing or sad or scary or tragic would ever, ever happen.

At least I was right about the sun.

*I*T WAS wedding week—to date, the most important week of my life, miles above winning Miss Congeniality in the one and only pageant I ever entered. This would be the week where everything would really change. Gone would be the life I knew. Gone would be golf course living, high-rise apartments, or city lofts. Gone would be parties. And cappuccino. And bookstores. But blinding love made it impossible for me to care.

I'd been reborn since Marlboro Man had entered my life; his wild abandon and unabashed passion had freed me from the shackles of cynicism, from thinking that love had to be something to labor over or agonize about. He'd ridden into my life on a speckled gray horse and had saved my heart from hardness. He'd taught me that when you love someone, you say it—and that when it comes to matters of the heart, games are for pimply sixteen-year-olds.

Up until then that's all I'd been: a child masquerading as a disillusioned adult, looking at love much as I'd looked at a round of Marco Polo in the pool at the country club: when they swam after me, I'd swim away. And there are accusations of peeking and cheating, and you always wind up sunburned and pruney and pooped. And no one ever wins.

It was Marlboro Man who'd helped me out of the pool, wrapped a towel around my blistering shoulders, and carried me to a world where love has nothing to do with competition or sport or strategy. He told me he loved me when he felt like it, when he thought of it. He never saw any reason not to.

It was wedding week. My mom, happy to grab any opportunity to avoid the strife and stress in her own marriage, occupied herself in the last days by helping me tie up the final loose ends of a country club reception. Betsy came home from college for a whole week so that she and my mom could cut squares of red and blue bandana fabric, fill them with birdseed, and tie them into parcels with twine. They retrieved beautifully wrapped gifts from the local gift shops and helped me open them one by one. And they helped me coordinate gifts for my three bridesmaids, one of whom was my sister, of course, and they kept Mike—who, due to the rush of activity, was well on his way to a manic episode—entertained. They made sure hotel rooms were in place for out-of-town guests. And they did my laundry.

Meanwhile I decided to get a facial. I needed a little pick-me-up. I

needed to lie in a dark room away from the doorbell and the telephone and the flowers, away from red bandana squares and twine. Even then, in my midtwenties, I knew when I was in danger of becoming overwhelmed. I knew when I needed to decompress. A treatment room at a day spa had always been the answer.

I scheduled an hour-long exfoliating facial, more for the length of the treatment than the treatment type itself, and I loved every second of it. The aroma of essential oils filled the room, and soft African spiritual music played overhead. With ten minutes remaining, Cindy the Aesthetician whipped out a special bottle of fluid. "Now this," she said softly, opening the lid of the bottle and reaching for a large cotton swab. "This . . . is *magic*."

"What is it?" I asked, not really caring about the answer as long as I could stay in that chair a little longer. The African music was working for me.

"Oh, it'll just give you the slightest little healthy glow," she answered. "People won't even know what you've done, but they'll ask you why you look so great. *Perfect* for your wedding week."

"Ooooh," I said. "Sounds great!" I settled farther into the comfortably padded vinyl chair.

The cotton swab softly moved across my face, leaving a pleasant coolness behind. It swept over my forehead, down my nose, on the sides of my cheeks, and across my chin. It relaxed me and I melted. And slowly, I began to fall asleep. I considered reupping for another hour.

But then I felt the burning.

"Oooh," I said, opening my eyes. "Cindy, this doesn't feel right."

"Oh, good," Cindy said, sounding unconcerned. "You're starting to feel it now?"

Seconds later, I was in severe pain. "Oh, I'm *more* than feeling it," I answered, gripping the arms of the chair until my knuckles turned white.

"Well, it should stop here in a second . . . ," she insisted. "It's just working its magic—"

My face was melting off. *"Ouch! Ow! Seriously, Cindy! Take this stuff off my face! It's killing me!"*

"Oh, dear . . . okay, okay," Cindy answered, quickly grabbing a soaked washcloth and quickly wiping the nuclear solution from my skin. Finally, the intense burning began to subside.

"Gosh," I said, trying to be nice. "I don't think that's something I want to try again." I swallowed hard, trying to will the pain receptors to stop firing.

"Hmmm," Cindy said, perplexed. "I'm sorry it stung a little. But you'll love it tomorrow morning when you wake up! Your skin will look so fresh and dewy."

It better, I thought as I paid Cindy for the torture and left the tiny salon. My face tingled, and not at all in a good way. And as I walked to my car, the floodgates of wedding worry opened once again:

What if my dress doesn't zip?
What if the band doesn't show up?
What if the shrimp taste fishy?
I don't know how to two-step.
How long is the flight to Australia?
Are there tarantulas in the country?
What if there are scorpions in the bed?

The facial had done little to decompress me.

That night, Marlboro Man and I had a date. It was the Thursday night before our wedding, and the rehearsal dinner was the following night. It would be our last night alone together before we'd say *I do*. I couldn't wait to see him; it had been two whole days. *Forty-eight excruciating hours.* I missed him fiercely.

When he arrived on my parents' doorstep, I opened the door and smiled. He looked gorgeous. Solid. Irresistible.

Grinning, he stepped forward and kissed me. "You look good," he said softly, stepping back. "You got some sun today."

I gulped, flashing back to the agony of my facial that afternoon and fearing for the future of my face. I should have just stayed home and packed all day.

We went to a movie, Marlboro Man and me, longing for the quiet time in the dark. We couldn't find it anywhere else—my parents' house was bustling with people and plans and presents, and Marlboro Man had some visiting cousins staying with him on the ranch. A dim movie theater was our only haven, and we took full advantage of being only one of two couples in the entire place. We reverted back to adolescence, unashamed, cuddling closer and closer as the movie picked up steam. I took it even further, draping my leg over his and resting my hand on his tan bicep. Marlboro Man's arm reached across my waist as the temperature rose between us. Two days before our wedding, we were making out in a dark, hazy movie theater. It was one of the most romantic moments of my life.

Until Marlboro Man's whiskers scratched my sensitive face, and I winced in pain.

When we returned to my parents' house, Marlboro Man walked me to the door, his arm tightly around my waist. "You'd better get some sleep," he said.

My stomach jumped inside my body. "I know," I said, stopping and holding him close. "I can't believe it's almost here."

"I'm glad you didn't move to Chicago," Marlboro Man whispered, chuckling the soft chuckle that started all this trouble in the first place. I remember being in that same spot, in that same position, the night Marlboro Man had asked me not to go. To stay and give us a chance. I still couldn't believe we were here.

I went straight upstairs to my bedroom after Marlboro Man and I said good night. I had to finish packing . . . and I had to tend to my face, which was causing me more discomfort by the minute. I looked in the bathroom mirror; my face was sunburn red. Irritated. Inflamed. Oh no. What had Prison Matron Cindy done to me? What should I do? I washed my face with cool water and a gentle cleaner and looked in the mirror. It was worse. I looked like a freako lobster face. It would be a great match for the cherry red suit I planned to wear to the rehearsal dinner the next night.

But my white dress for Saturday? That was another story.

I slept like a log and woke up early the next morning, opening my eyes and forgetting for a blissful four seconds about the facial trauma I'd endured the day before. I quickly brought my hands to my face; it felt tight and rough. I leaped out of bed and ran to the bathroom, flipping on the light and looking in the mirror to survey the state of my face.

The redness had subsided; I noticed that immediately. This was a good development. Encouraging. But upon closer examination, I could see the beginning stages of pruney lines around my chin and nose. My stomach lurched; it was the day of the rehearsal. It was the day I'd see not just my friends and family who, I was certain, would love me no matter what grotesque skin condition I'd contracted since the last time we saw one another, but also many, many people I'd never met before—ranching neighbors, cousins, business associates, and college friends of Marlboro Man's. I wasn't thrilled at the possibility that their first impression of me might be something that involved scales. I wanted to be fresh. Dewy. Resplendent. Not rough and dry and irritated. Not now. Not this weekend.

I examined the damage in the mirror and deduced that the plutonium Cindy the Prison Matron had swabbed on my face the day before had actually been some kind of acid peel. The burn came first. Logic would follow that what my face would want to do next would be to, well, peel. This could be bad. This could be real, real bad. What if I could speed along that process? Maybe if I could feed the beast's desire to slough, it would leave me alone—at least for the next forty-eight hours.

All I wanted was forty-eight hours. I didn't think it was too much to ask.

I grabbed my favorite exfoliating facial scrub, the same one I'd used all the way through college. Not quite as abrasive as drugstore-brand apricot scrubs, but grainy enough to get serious and do the trick. It had to be the magic bullet. It had to work. I started by washing my unfortunate face with a mild cleanser, then I squirted a small amount of the scrub on my fingers . . . and began facilitating the peeling process.

I held my breath. It hurt. My face was in a world of pain.

I scrubbed and scrubbed, wondering why facials even existed in the first place if they involved such torture. *I'm a nice person*, I thought. *I go to church. Why is my skin staging a revolt?* The week of a girl's wedding was supposed to be a happy time. I should have been leaping gleefully around my parents' house, using a glitter-infused feather duster to sparkle up my wedding gifts, which adorned every flat surface in the house. I should have been eating melon balls and laughing in the kitchen with my mom and sister about how it's almost here! Don't you love this Waterford vase? Oooh, the cake is going to be *soooooo* pretty.

Instead, I was in my bathroom holding my face at gunpoint, forcing it to exfoliate on command.

I rinsed my face and looked in the mirror. The results were encouraging. The pruniness appeared to have subsided; my skin was a little rosy from the robust scrubbing, but at least flakes of dead epidermis weren't falling from my face like tragic confetti. To ward off any drying, I slathered my face with moisturizing cream. It stung—the effect of the isopropyl alcohol in the cream—but after the agony of the day before, I could take it. When it came to my facial nerve endings, I'd been toughened to a whole new level of pain.

THE NEXT DAY, I started getting dressed at three for the rehearsal. The beautiful cherry red suit had black stitching, and I had taken the skirt to a seamstress to have it shortened to a sexy upper-midthigh length—an unfortunate habit I'd picked up while watching too much *Knots Landing* in the late 1980s. I was relatively slender and not the least bit stacked on top, and my bottom was somewhat fit but wildly unremarkable. If I was going to highlight any feature of my anatomy, it would have to be my legs.

When I arrived at the rehearsal at the church, my grandmother kissed me, then looked down and said, "Did you forget the other half of your suit?"

The seamstress had gotten a little overzealous.

Friends and family arrived at the church: Becky and Connell, my two lifelong friends and bridesmaids. Marlboro Man's cousins and college friends. And Mike. My dear brother Mike, who hugged everyone who entered the church, from the little old ladies to the strapping former college football players. And just as I was greeting my Uncle John, I saw Mike go in for the kill as Tony, Marlboro Man's good college friend, entered the door.

"Wh-wh-wh-what is you name?" Mike's thundering voice echoed through the church.

"Hi, I'm Tony," Marlboro Man's friend said, extending his hand.

"It's n-n-n-nice to meet you, Tony," Mike shouted back, not letting go of Tony's hand.

"Nice to meet you too, Mike," Tony said, likely wondering when he would get his hand back.

"You so handsome," Mike said.

Oh, Lord. Please, no, I thought.

"Why . . . thank you, Mike," Tony replied, smiling uncomfortably. If it hadn't been my wedding rehearsal, I might have popped some popcorn, sat back, and enjoyed the show. But I just couldn't watch. Mike's affection had never been any respecter of persons.

The wedding rehearsal itself was uneventful until Father Johnson decided it was time to show Marlboro Man and me the proper way to walk to the marriage altar. Evidently, all of Father Johnson's theological studies and work was destined to culminate in whether or not Marlboro Man and I approached the altar in the perfectly correct and proper way, because he was intent on driving the point home.

"At this point," Father Johnson instructed, "you'll start to turn and Ree will take your arm." He lightly pushed Marlboro Man in the proper direction, and the two of us began walking forward.

"Nope, nope, nope," Father Johnson said authoritatively. "Come back, come back."

Marlboro Man's college friends snickered.

"Oh . . . what did we do wrong?" I asked Father Johnson humbly. Maybe he'd discovered the truth about the collages.

He showed us again. Marlboro Man was to turn and begin walking, then wait for me briefly. Then, as I took his arm, he was to lead me to the altar.

Wait. Wasn't that what we just did?

We tried again, and Father Johnson corrected us . . . again. "Nope, nope, nope," he said, pulling us both by the arm until we were back in our starting position. Marlboro Man's friends chuckled. My stomach growled. And Marlboro Man kept quietly restrained, despite the fact that he was being repeatedly corrected by his fiancée's interim minister for something that arguably wasn't all that relevant to the commitment we were making to spend the rest of our lives together.

We went through no fewer than seven more takes, and with each redo I began to realize that this was Father Johnson's final test for us. Forget the collage assignment—that was small potatoes. Whether we could keep our cool and take instruction when a nice steak dinner and drinks awaited us at the country club was Father Johnson's real decider of whether or not Marlboro Man and I were mature, composed, and levelheaded enough to proceed with the wedding. And while I knew Marlboro Man would grit his teeth and bear it, I wasn't entirely sure I could.

But I didn't have to. On the beginning of the eighth run, just after Father Johnson gave us another "Nope. You're not getting it right, kids . . ." Mike's loud voice echoed throughout the wood-and-marble sanctuary.

"Oh, c-c-c-c-come on, Father Johnson!"

The chuckles turned into laughter. And out of the corner of my eye I saw Tony giving Mike a subtle high five.

Thank goodness for Mike. He was hungry. He wanted to get on to the party.

WE FINALLY adjourned to the country club for the elegant rehearsal dinner hosted by Marlboro Man's parents. It was a large gathering of every close friend and family member in both of our lives. The sit-down dinner was filled with choruses of laughter and clinking of glasses . . . and my brother Doug calling my future mother-in-law "Ann" repeatedly.

Ann isn't my mother-in-law's name.

Once dinner was served, it was time for the official toasts: my childhood friend Becky, citing inside jokes that only the two of us, to this day, understand; Marlboro Man's uncle, who'd written a funny poem for the occasion, and whose commanding voice silenced the entire party; my sister, whose sweet sentiments elicited an "Awwww" from everyone in attendance; my dad, who choked up and couldn't continue . . . and left all the women sobbing at his display of fatherly emotion.

It left me with a lump in my throat. I knew my dad's tears were coming from a much deeper place than a father merely wishing his first daughter well. The hustle and bustle of the previous week had, until that moment, pushed the turmoil between my parents comfortably under the surface. That my parents' marriage was dangling by a delicate thread during a time when I was beginning my life with the greatest love of my life was a terrible joke. If I stopped and allowed myself to think about it for very long, I'd crumble.

I rescued my dad from the microphone, hurrying up to where he stood and giving him a supportive, upbeat hug just as one of Marlboro Man's closest childhood friends, Tom, made his way to the toasting station.

Tom carried with him a glass full of wine, which clearly hadn't been his first of the evening. He swaggered and swayed as he started to speak, and his eyes, while not quite at half mast, were certainly well on their way.

"In my mind," Tom began, "this is what love is all about."

Sounded good. A little slurred, but it was nice and simple.

"And . . . and . . . and in my mind," Tom continued, "in my mind, I know this is all about . . . this is all love here."

Oh dear. Oh no.

"And all I can say is that in my mind," he went on, "it's just so great to know that true love is possible right now in this time."

Crickets. Tap-tap. Is this thing on?

"I've known this guy for a long, long time," he resumed, pointing to Marlboro Man, who was sitting and listening respectfully. "And . . . in my mind, all I have to say is that's a long . . . long time."

Tom was dead serious. This was not a joke toast. This was not a ribbing toast. This was what was "in his mind." He made that clear over and over.

"I just want to finish by saying . . . that in my mind, love is . . . love is . . . everything," he continued.

People around the room began to snicker. At the large table where Marlboro Man and I sat with our friends, people began to crack up.

Everyone except Marlboro Man. Instead of snickering and laughing at his friend—whom he'd known since they were boys and who, he knew, had recently gone through a rough couple of years—Marlboro Man quietly motioned to everyone at our table with a tactful "Shhhh," followed by a quietly whispered "Don't laugh at him."

Then Marlboro Man did what I should have known he'd do. He stood up, walked up to his friend, who was rapidly entering into embarrassing territory . . . and gave him a friendly handshake, patting him on the shoulder. And the dinner crowd, rather than bursting into the uproarious laughter that had been imminent moments before, clapped instead.

I watched the man I was about to marry, who'd always demonstrated a tenderness and compassion for people—whether in movies or in real life—who were subject to being teased or ridiculed. He'd never shown a spot of discomfort in front of my handicapped brother Mike, for all the times Mike had sat on his lap or begged him for rides to the mall. He'd never mocked or ridiculed another person as long as I'd known him. And while his good friend Tom wasn't exactly developmentally disabled, he'd just gotten perilously close to being voted Class Clown by a room full of people at our rehearsal dinner. But Marlboro Man had swept in and ensured that didn't happen. My heart swelled with emotion.

Later, when the party had thinned out and Betsy and I ran to the ladies' room to primp, she remarked on Marlboro Man's chivalry, sighing over his sweet display of kindness.

Then she moved closer to me, zeroing in and focusing on the general area of my chin.

"Oh . . . my . . . God," she said, covering her mouth with her hand. "What's wrong with your face?"

My stomach fell to the floor. I found a bottle of Jergens on the bathroom counter and began rubbing it in, determined to beat the flaking skin into submission.

MOST OF the guests left the rehearsal dinner at the country club; the remaining group—a varied collection of important figures in both of our lives—had skittered away to the downtown hotel where all of the out-of-town guests were staying. Marlboro Man and I, not ready to bid each other good night yet, had joined them in the small, dimly lit (lucky for me, given the deteriorating condition of my epidermis) hotel bar. We gathered at a collection of tiny tables butted up together and wound up talking and laughing into the night, toasting one another and spouting various late-night versions of "I'm so glad I know you" and *"I love you, man!"* In the midst of all the wedding planning and craziness, hanging out in a basement bar with uncles, college friends, and siblings was a relaxing, calming elixir. I wanted to bottle the feeling and store it up forever.

It was late, though; I saw Marlboro Man looking at the clock in the bar.

"I think I'll head back to the ranch," he whispered as his brother told another joke to the group. Marlboro Man had a long drive ahead, not to mention an entire lifetime with me. I couldn't blame him for wanting a good night's sleep.

"I'm tired, too," I said, grabbing my purse from under the table. And I was; the long day had finally set in.

The two of us stood up and said our good-byes to all the people who loved us so much. Men stood up, some stumbling, and shook hands with Marlboro Man. Women blew kisses and mouthed *Love you guys!* to us as we walked out of the room and waved good-bye. But no one left the bar. Nobody loved us that much.

Marlboro Man and I walked together to our vehicles—symbolically parked side by side in the hotel lot under a cluster of redbud trees. Sleepiness had definitely set in; my head fell on his shoulder as we walked. His ample arms gripped my waist reassuringly. And the second we reached my silver Camry, the temperature began to rise.

"I can't wait till tomorrow," he said, backing me against the door of my car, his lips moving toward my neck. Every nerve receptor in my body simultaneously fired as his strong hands gripped the small of my back; my hands pulled him closer and closer.

We kissed and kissed some more in the hotel parking lot, flirting dangerously with taking it a step—or five—further. Out-of-control prairie fires were breaking out inside my body; even my knees felt hot. I couldn't believe this man, this Adonis who held me so completely and passionately in his arms, was actually mine. That in a mere twenty-four hours, I'd have him all to myself. *It's too good to be true,* I thought as my right leg wrapped around his left and my fingers squeezed his chiseled bicep. It was as if I'd been locked inside a chocolate shop that also sold delicious chardonnay and french fries . . . and played *Gone With the Wind* and Joan Crawford movies all day long—and had been told "Have fun." He was going to be my own private playground for the rest of my life. I almost felt guilty, like I was taking something away from the world.

It was so dark outside, I forgot where I was. I had no sense of geography or time or space, not even when he took my face in his hands and touched his forehead to mine, closing his eyes, as if to savor the powerful moment.

"I love you," he whispered as I died right there on the spot. It wasn't convenient, my dying the night before my wedding. I didn't know how my mom was going to explain it to the florist. But she'd have to; I was totally done for.

I'd had half a glass of wine all evening but felt completely inebriated. When I finally arrived home, I had no idea how I'd gotten there. I was intoxicated—drunk on a cowboy. A cowboy who, in less than twenty-four hours, would become my husband.

Chapter Twenty-one
SHE WORE A LILY WHITE VERA

I OPENED MY EYES. It was morning. I could hear the whirring of a passing electric golf cart on the seventh fairway outside, and the smell of coffee wafted up from downstairs. Gevalia coffee, the mail-order beans my mom had used since she first heard of the brand on the beach in Hilton Head one summer in the early 1980s. "Ghuh-*vahl*-ya," my mom's voice would sing when her monthly order arrived on her doorstep. "I just love my Ghuh-*vahl*-ya."

I just loved her Gevalia, too.

Mike's booming voice was downstairs. He was on the phone, as usual.

"M-m-m-my sister is gettin' married," I heard him announce to the person on the other end of the line. "And I am gonna s-s-s-sing at duh reception."

A long pause followed. I braced myself.

"Oh, p-p-p-prolly 'Elvira,' " Mike said.

Perfect, I thought, pulling myself out of bed. Mike singing "Elvira" at my reception. As if my scaly chin wasn't enough, I needed one more thought to terrorize me for the rest of my wedding day. Brushing my teeth, I left on my pajamas and stumbled downstairs. I needed some Gevalia in order to face the challenges ahead.

"Ooooh, pretty woman!" Mike ogled as I walked into the kitchen.

Mike clearly didn't have one speck of taste. With all my pretty night-gowns and PJs packed away in my honeymoon suitcase, I'd been reduced to my trusty old gray satin sleepwear. Victoria's Secret, circa 1986—back when model Jill Goodacre reigned supreme. Soft and worn and faded, they were as cozy and comfortable as they could be. They were decidedly not pretty, no matter what my brother Mike said.

"Good morning, Mike," I mumbled, making a beeline for the coffeepot.

"Oooooh!" he teased again. "Someone is getting *married* tonight! Woooooooo . . ."

"Yep," I said, taking that first glorious sip of java. "Hard to believe, isn't it?"

Mike put his hand over his mouth and snickered. Then he asked, "So . . . are you guys gonna do some . . . some *kissin*'?"

"I certainly hope so," I said. This only served to make Mike laugh harder.

"Ooooooh!" he squealed. "Are you gonna have a *baby*?"

Oh, Lord.

I took another hit of Gevalia and answered, "Not today." Mike cracked up again. He was clearly on a roll.

"What's so funny this morning, Mike?" I asked.

"Your s-s-s-stomach is gonna get so fat," he answered. Mike was quickly approaching manic stage—the result of a large, busy weekend and his routine being disrupted. Soon the inevitable crash would come. I just hoped I was on the plane to Australia when it happened. It wasn't going to be pretty.

"Oh, *whatever*, Mike," I answered, feigning indignation.

With that he stood up, my special, wonderful brother named Mike, and made his way across the kitchen to the place where I stood near the coffee-pot. Seven inches shorter than me, Mike wrapped his short arms around my waist and clung to me in a sweet bear hug. Resting his balding head on my chest, he patted my back affectionately.

"You so lovely," he said.

I wrapped my arms around his shoulders and rested my chin on his shiny noggin. I tried to respond, but my throat suddenly felt tight. I bit my lip and felt my nose sting.

"You my lovely, lovely sister," Mike repeated, not budging from our embrace.

It was just what I needed that Saturday morning: an anchoring hug from my brother Mike. "I love you, Mikey," I managed. And a bittersweet tear rolled slowly down my cheek.

THE WEDDING day moved forward with a long, invigorating bubble bath, another vigorous exfoliation of my increasingly scaly face, phone calls from friends, a slightly nervous stomach. The bridesmaids' luncheon was at noon: asparagus sandwiches, chatting, laughing, and talk of the honeymoon, plans, excitement. And a lot of talk of the country, and how on earth I was going to handle living there.

Nervous stomach.

Once home from the luncheon, I tried in vain to take a nap. There was no way; the adrenaline had officially kicked in. I checked my honeymoon packing one last time; it was all there, just as it had been the previous ten times I'd checked. I lay on my bed and stared at the wallpaper, realizing it might be the last time.

Before I knew it, four o'clock had rolled around; it was time to shower. The wedding was in exactly three hours.

Violently nervous stomach: I might not survive.

I headed to the church at five-thirty, wearing jeans, flip-flops, and brick red lipstick. My mom, calm and cool as a mountain lake, carried my white dress—plain and romantic, with a bodice that laced up corset-style in the back and delicate sheer sleeves. I carted in my shoes . . . my earrings . . .

my makeup . . . and my exfoliating scrub, in case my face decided to pull a last-minute sloughing. I wasn't about to roll over and take a last-minute sloughing without a fight. Not on *my* wedding day.

I walked up the stairs of the church of my youth—the beautiful gray stone Episcopal church with the beautiful red door and the comforting smell of Sunday school and coffee and incense and wine. It had baptized me and confirmed me and taught me the Nicene Creed . . . and shown me the transcendent beauty of the bright morning sun shining through stained-glass windows. It had cradled me through a mischievous childhood and an angst-filled adolescence, and had been the site of many a teenage crush—on Donnie, the much older youth group friend of my brother's, who was brooding and dangerous and probably didn't even know my name; on Stevo, two years ahead of me, who consumed my seventh-grade year and broke my heart when he fell in love with my good friend Carrie. And later on Bruce, the widower and father of two young children, whom I briefly thought I could rescue . . . but who only saw me as a silly schoolgirl who knew nothing about real life, or loss, or grief.

And he was right.

They rang through my head as I ascended the stairs of my church—all of the important milestones and theologies and boys that had shaped my spiritual experience. And now, the most important one of all: my marriage to the one man on earth with whom I could ever imagine spending my life. It was definitely my favorite sacrament to date.

Eric, my German hairdresser, was waiting for me in the large dressing room upstairs. He'd cut my auburn hair since I was six and had seen it through tragic self-trimmings of my bangs, unfortunate summers of excessive Sun-In use, and horrible home perms gone terribly wrong. He'd never shrunk from haughtily chastising me through my follicular antics and had thrown in plenty of Teutonic life coaching along the way, on every subject from pimply high school boys to current events and politics. And he'd pretty much made me feel equal parts stupid and uncultured on more than

one occasion with his superior knowledge of theater and art and opera.

But I loved him. He was important to me. So when I asked him to come to my wedding to transform my hair into an elegant and sexy and uncontrived but polished updo, Eric had answered, simply, "Yes."

And the moment I sat down in the chair, he chastised me for washing my hair right before I arrived.

"Ees juss too smooz," Eric scolded.

"I'm sorry," I begged. "Please don't ground me, Eric. I didn't want my head to stink on my wedding night."

And for the first time ever, I saw Eric crack a relaxed, mellow smile.

I loved it that Eric was there.

The clock ticked away toward seven; news circulated that the tuxedo-clad Marlboro Man had arrived. He'd spent the day with his groomsmen and guests, driving them to the big city and treating them all to black cowboy boots to match their tuxes. Black patent slip-ons—and monogrammed Dopp kits—weren't exactly his style. Even Mike got his own pair of shitkickers, which he proudly displayed to guests walking into the church.

My sister zipped me into my dress and laced up the delicate bodice; Eric attached my simple tulle veil as I slipped on my white satin Mary Jane pumps. I inhaled, trying my best to fill my lungs with air . . . but no matter what I did, they would only partially inflate. My size 6 dress—straddling the line between the perfect fit and one size too small—wasn't helping my respiration.

"We need to head downstairs in five minutes," the altar guild worker announced at the door.

My chest began to tighten as my wedding party—and Mike, who'd abandoned his usher post to make his way up to the dressing room—squealed. I immediately thought of my parents. Were they enjoying themselves? Or were they just going through the motions? Was my dad downstairs greeting guests, thinking to himself, *This is all a joke,* as his own marriage was crumbling before his eyes? I looked at my mom as she walked out of the room to head downstairs. She was resplendent, glowing. Was her mind elsewhere? My stomach began to throb as I watched my three bridesmaids grasp their bouquets and help one another with their makeup. My overactive mind continued to race.

What if Mike pitches a fit at the reception? What if he causes a scene? Did I pack enough shoes for the honeymoon? What if I don't like living in the country? Am I supposed to plant a garden? I don't know how to saddle a horse. What if I feel out of place? I never learned how to square dance. Is it do-si-do or allemande left? Wait . . . is it square dancing? Or two-stepping? I don't even know the dances. I don't belong out there. What if I want to get a job? There IS no job. Does J know I'm getting married today? Does Collin? Does Kev? What if I pass out during the ceremony? I've seen it on America's Funniest Home Videos *dozens of times. Someone always passes out. What if the food's cold when we get to the reception? Wait . . . it's supposed to be cold. Wait . . . some of it is, some of it isn't. What if I'm not what Marlboro Man's looking for? What if my face flakes off as I'm saying "I do"? What if my dress gets caught inside my panty hose? I'm so shaky all of a sudden. My hands feel so wet and clammy. . . .*

I'd never had a panic attack before. But as I would soon find out, there's a first time for everything.

Oh, Ree . . . don't do this now.

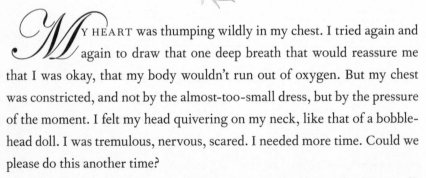

MY HEART was thumping wildly in my chest. I tried again and again to draw that one deep breath that would reassure me that I was okay, that my body wouldn't run out of oxygen. But my chest was constricted, and not by the almost-too-small dress, but by the pressure of the moment. I felt my head quivering on my neck, like that of a bobble-head doll. I was tremulous, nervous, scared. I needed more time. Could we please do this another time?

Despite my shakiness, my bridal party and I began the long walk toward the sanctuary downstairs. My knees shook with each step. Porcupine needles attacked my rosy cheeks.

My sister, Betsy, looked in my direction. "Uh," she said, concerned. "Are you okay?"

"Yeah, why?" I quickly answered, trying to will my nervous system into latency, at least for the next forty minutes or so.

"Oh . . . nothing," she said, delicately, trying not to alarm me further.

That's when my bridesmaid and childhood friend Becky chimed in, "Oh my *gosh*," she exclaimed. "You're so pale! Your face is as white as your dress!" Becky had always come right out with it.

"Oh, God . . . ," I muttered, and I meant it literally. "Please, God, help me. . . ." I felt the sweat forming on my upper lip, my brow, the back of my neck. If ever I needed God's help with a superficial matter, this was it. This was absolutely, undoubtedly, it.

"Get some Kleenex!" I gasped. *"Hurry!"* My three-woman wedding party obeyed my frantic demands. The altar guild lady stood politely by, checking her watch as Betsy, Becky, and Connell set their pale lavender rose bouquets onto the floor and began wiping, dabbing, and fanning me within an inch of my life.

"Stick them in my armpits!" I ordered, holding up my arms. Becky obliged, howling with laughter as she stuffed lavender Kleenex into my Vera Wang wherever she could find a centimeter of space. The Kleenex matched the bouquets, I noticed. What a beautiful coincidence.

I heard the organ playing Bach as flashbacks of my sweat attack at Marlboro Man's cousin's August wedding the year before flooded my consciousness; this only served to make me sweat more. Betsy grabbed magazines from a hall table, and the three of them attempted to fan me out of my sudden bout of diaphoresis. What was the matter with me? I was a young, fit, healthy woman. I imagined that Vera, if she knew me, would probably give my money back and reclaim the gown once she saw what my sweat glands were doing to her beautiful creation. I made a note to myself never to get married again. Way too much pressure. Way too much sweat-inducing pressure.

"It's time to go," Ms. Altar Guild sternly announced. I darted into the bathroom to check myself one last time. I was flushed. I hoped it would translate to "healthy and glowing." But without any powder, mascara, or a mask at my disposal, I had no choice but to give my bangs a quick finger-comb, take one more measly half-breath, and head downstairs so I could take my rightful place at the entrance of the gauntlet. In all the craziness of the previous months, elopement had never, ever sounded so appealing. I ordered my bridesmaid slaves to yank all the damp Kleenexes from my dress, then we began our march down the stairs. Becky howled the entire time. She'd always been a very supportive friend.

As soon as I reached the narthex, all my worries and sweat-related concerns disappeared when I locked eyes with my dad, whose turmoil over his problems with my mom bled through the temporary joy he'd painted on his face for the day. I knew this was terrible for him; not even a joyful family event could lessen the sadness of the wife of his youth slipping away—and, in fact, it probably made it worse. Though he couldn't have known that day just how fast it would come, I know he was well aware that his relationship with my mother was in imminent danger. Looking around at all the black ties, the pearls, the smiling faces, he must have sensed that it would be the last time we would all be together as a whole, cohesive family. That things would never, ever be the same again. And despite the brief distraction of my near-panic attack—and the clammy moistness of my wedding gown—I sensed it, too.

"You look beautiful," my dad said as he walked over to me and offered his arm. His voice was quiet—even quieter than his normal quiet—and it broke, trailed off, died. I took his arm, and together we walked forward, toward the large wooden doors that led to the beautiful sanctuary where I'd been baptized as a young child just after our family joined the Episcopal church. Where I'd been confirmed by the bishop at the age of twelve. I'd

worn a Black Watch plaid Gunne Sax dress that day. It had delicate ribbon trim and a lace-up tie in the back—a corset-style tie, which, I realized, foreshadowed the style of my wedding gown. I looked through the windows and down the aisle and could see myself kneeling there, the bishop's wrinkled, weathered hands on my auburn hair. I shivered with emotion, feeling the sting in my nose . . . and the warm beginnings of nostalgia-driven tears.

Biting my bottom lip, I stepped forward with my father. Connell had started walking down the aisle as the organist began playing "Jesu, Joy of Man's Desiring." I could close my eyes and hear the same music playing on the eight-track tape player in my mom's Oldsmobile station wagon. Was it the London Symphony Orchestra or the Mormon Tabernacle Choir? I suddenly couldn't remember. But that's why I'd chosen it for the processional—not because it appeared on *Modern Bride*'s list of acceptable wedding processionals, but because it reminded me of childhood . . . of Bach . . . of home. I watched as Becky followed Connell, and then my sister, Betsy, her almost jet-black hair shining in the beautiful light of the church. I was so glad to have a sister.

Ms. Altar Guild gently coaxed my father and me toward the door. "It's time," she whispered. My stomach fell. What was happening? Where was I? *Who* was I? At that very moment, my worlds were colliding—the old world with the new, the past life with the future. I felt my dad inhale deeply, and I followed his lead. He was nervous; I could feel it. I was nervous, too. As we took our place in the doorway, I squeezed his arm and whispered, "I love thee." It was our little line.

"I love thee, too," he whispered back. And as I turned my head toward the front of the church, my eyes went straight to him—to Marlboro Man, who was standing dead ahead, looking straight at me.

𝒞LOUDS CARRIED me forward from there. Others were in the church—I knew that logically—but I saw no one. No one but Marlboro Man and his black tuxedo and his white formal tie, and the new black cowboy boots he'd bought especially for the occasion. His short hair, which was the color of pewter. His gentle smile. He was a vision—strong, solid, perfect. But it was the smile that propelled me forward, the reassuring look on his face. It wasn't a smug, overconfident smile. It was a smile loaded with emotion—thoughts of our history, perhaps. Of the story that brought us to that moment. Relief that we'd finally reached our destined end, which was actually a beautiful beginning. Gratefulness that we'd met by chance and had wound up finding love.

And suddenly, I was beside him. My arm in his. My heart entirely in his hands.

Dearly beloved: We have come together in the presence of God to witness and bless the joining together of this man and this woman in Holy Matrimony. The bond and covenant of marriage was established by God in creation, and our Lord Jesus Christ adorned this manner of life by his presence and first miracle at a wedding in Cana of Galilee. It signifies to us the mystery of the union between Christ and his Church, and Holy Scripture commends it to be honored among all people.

The union of husband and wife in heart, body, and mind is intended by God for their mutual joy; for the help and comfort given one another in prosperity and adversity; and, when it is God's will, for the procreation of children and their nurture in the knowledge and love of the Lord. Therefore marriage is not to be entered into unadvisedly or lightly, but reverently, deliberately, and in accordance with the purposes for which it was instituted by God.

I glanced at Marlboro Man, who was listening intently, taking in every word. I held his bicep in my hand, squeezing it lightly and trying to listen to Father Johnson despite the distraction of Marlboro Man's work-honed muscles. Everything else was a blur: iron candlesticks attached to the end of each pew . . . my mother's olive green silk jacket with the mandarin collar . . . Mike's tuxedo . . . Mike's bald head. . . .

Will you have this man to be your husband; to live together in the covenant of marriage? Will you love him, comfort him, honor and keep him, in sickness and in health; and, forsaking all others, be faithful to him as long as you both shall live?

"I will." I breathed in.

The scent of roses . . . the evening light coming through the stained-glass window.

Will you have this woman to be your wife; to live together in the covenant of marriage? Will you love her, comfort her, honor and keep her, in sickness and in health; and, forsaking all others, be faithful to her as long as you both shall live?

"I will." That voice. The voice from all the phone calls. I was marrying that voice. I couldn't believe it.

We faced each other, our hands intertwined.

In the Name of God, I take you to be my wife, to have and to hold from this day forward, for better for worse, for richer for poorer, in sickness and in health, to love and to cherish, until we are parted by death. This is my solemn vow.

He stood before me, his face serious. My heart leaped in my chest. Then I spoke the words myself.

In the Name of God, I take you to be my husband, to have and to hold from this day forward, for better for worse, for richer for poorer, in sickness and in health, to love and to cherish, until we are parted by death. This is my solemn vow.

Marlboro Man watched me as I spoke, and he listened. My voice broke; emotion moved in. It was a beautiful moment—the most beautiful moment since we'd met.

Bless, O Lord, these rings to be a sign of the vows by which this man and this woman have bound themselves to each other.

We kneeled, and Father Johnson administered the blessing.

Most Gracious God . . . Let their love for each other be a seal upon their hearts, a mantle about their shoulders, and a crown upon their foreheads. . . . Bless them in their work and in their companionship; in their sleeping and in their

waking; in their joys and in their sorrows; in their life and in their death. . . . Send
therefore your blessing upon these your servants, that they may so love, honor,
and cherish each other in faithfulness and patience, in wisdom and true godli-
ness, that their home may be a haven of blessing and peace.

My heart pounded in my chest. This was real, it was not a dream. His hand held mine.

I now pronounce you husband and wife.

I hadn't considered the kiss. Not once. I suppose I'd assumed it would be the way a wedding kiss should be. Restrained. Appropriate. Mild. A nice peck. Save the real kisses for later, when you're deliciously alone. Country club girls don't make out in front of others. Like gum chewing, it should always be done in private, where no one else can see.

But Marlboro Man wasn't a country club boy. He'd missed the memo outlining the rules and regulations of proper ways to kiss in public. I found this out when the kiss began—when he wrapped his loving, protective arms around me and kissed me like he meant it right there in my Episcopal church. Right there in front of my family, and his, in front of Father Johnson and Ms. Altar Guild and our wedding party and the entire congregation, half of whom were meeting me for the first time that night. But Marlboro Man didn't seem to care. He kissed me exactly the way he'd kissed me the night of our first date—the night my high-heeled boot had gotten wedged in a crack in my parents' sidewalk and had caused me to stumble. The night he'd caught me with his lips.

We were making out in church—there was no way around it. And I felt every bit as swept away as I had that first night. The kiss lasted hours, days, weeks . . . probably ten to twelve seconds in real time, which, in a wedding ceremony setting, is a pretty long kiss. And it might have been longer had the passionate moment not been interrupted by the sudden sound of a person clapping his hands.

"Woohoo! All right!" the person shouted. *"Yes!"*

It was Mike. The congregation broke out in laughter as Marlboro Man and I touched our foreheads together, cementing the moment forever in our memory. We were one; this was tangible to me now. It wasn't just an empty word, a theological concept, wishful thinking. It was an official, you-and-me-against-the-world designation. We'd both left our separateness behind. From that moment forward, nothing either of us did or said or planned would be in a vacuum apart from the other. No holiday would involve our celebrating separately at our respective family homes. No last-minute trips to Mexico with friends, not that either of us was prone to last-minute trips to Mexico with friends. But still.

The kiss had sealed the deal in so many ways.

I walked proudly out of the church, the new wife of Marlboro Man. When we exited the same doors through which my dad and I had walked thirty minutes earlier, Marlboro Man's arm wriggled loose from my grasp and instinctively wrapped around my waist, where it belonged. The other arm followed, and before I knew it we were locked in a sweet, solidifying embrace, relishing the instant of solitude before our wedding party— sisters, cousins, brothers, friends—followed closely behind.

We were married. I drew a deep, life-giving breath and exhaled. The sweating had finally stopped. And the robust air-conditioning of the church had almost completely dried my lily-white Vera.

AFTER A few formal snapshots in the courtyard of the church, we headed for the reception at the country club. It became a party in no time: enough people to fill a small island nation, and enough food to feed them for days. Enough champagne to fill an Olympic-size swimming pool, and plenty of happiness and good cheer to last for a long time. Ranchers had finished shipping. Farmers had completed their harvest. Two families had joined together. There was good reason to celebrate.

I was hugged by everyone in Marlboro Man's family, including his grandma Ruth, his cousin Matthew, and Matthew's beautiful, vibrant mother, Marie, who was suffering from stage 4 breast cancer but couldn't miss the opportunity to see her son serve as one of Marlboro Man's groomsmen. She looked happy.

We danced to John Michael Montgomery's "I Swear." We cut the seven-tiered cake, electing not to take the smear-it-on-our-faces route. We visited and laughed and toasted. We held hands and mingled. But after a while, I began to notice that I hadn't seen any of the tuxedo-clad groomsmen—particularly Marlboro Man's friends from college—for quite some time.

"What happened to all the guys?" I asked.

"Oh," he said. "They're down in the men's locker room."

"Oh, really?" I asked. "Are they smoking cigars or something?"

"Well . . ." He hesitated, grinning. "They're watching a football game."

I laughed. "What game are they watching?" It had to be a good one.

"It's . . . ASU is playing Nebraska," he answered.

ASU? His alma mater? Playing Nebraska? Defending national champions? How had I missed this? Marlboro Man hadn't said a word. He was such a rabid college football fan, I couldn't believe such a monumental game hadn't been cause to reschedule the wedding date. Aside from ranching, football had always been Marlboro Man's primary interest in life. He'd played in high school and part of college. He watched every televised ASU game religiously—for the nontelevised games, he relied on live reporting from Tony, his best friend, who attended every game in person.

"I didn't even know they were playing!" I said. I don't know why I shouldn't have known. It was September, after all. But it just hadn't crossed my mind. I'd been a little on the busy side, I guess, getting ready to change my entire life and all. "How come you're not down there watching it?" I asked.

"I didn't want to leave you," he said. "You might get hit on." He chuckled his sweet, sexy chuckle.

I laughed. I could just see it—a drunk old guest scooting down the bar, eyeing my poufy white dress and spouting off pickup lines:

You live around here?

I sure like what you're wearing. . . .

So . . . you married?

Marlboro Man wasn't in any immediate danger. Of that I was absolutely certain. "Go watch the game!" I insisted, motioning downstairs.

"Nah," he said. "I don't need to." He wanted to watch the game so badly I could see it in the air.

"No, seriously!" I said. "I need to go hang with the girls anyway. Go. Now." I turned my back and walked away, refusing even to look back. I wanted to make it easy on him.

I wouldn't see him for over an hour. Poor Marlboro Man. Unsure of the protocol for grooms watching college football during their wedding receptions, he'd darted in and out of the locker room for the entire first half. The agony he must have felt. The deep, sustained agony. I was so glad he'd finally joined the guys.

I returned to the party just in time to hear Mike start in on his fourth round of "Elvira." His voice echoed through the entire town. *"Giddyuppa oompah-pah oompah-pah mow mow . . ."* The song was made for Mike to sing it. Every person in attendance boogied to the music: my new brother-in-law, Tim, who danced with my cousin Julie . . . Marlboro Man's cousin Thatcher, who twirled Betsy all over the dance floor . . . my parents' neighbor, Dr. Burris, who danced with everyone.

I crossed my arms and leaned back against the wall of the ballroom, enjoying a moment alone in the dark. Marlboro Man was happy, watching football with his closest college friends. The guests were happy—they danced and laughed and slurped biscuits and gravy with wild abandon. My mom sipped wine in the formal ballroom area, catching up with old friends. Finally I caught a glimpse of my dad, who was dancing with Beth and Barbara, the sisters of my bridesmaid Becky and lifelong family friends. Our dads had gone to high school together, and we'd all known one another since we were embryos. They were laughing—my dad and Beth and Barbara. He spun them and dipped them and twirled them as they giggled and smiled. He was happy, too. For that brief moment in time, he was happy.

I breathed in and closed my eyes, making sure to remember the moment.

Just then, the music stopped. The band needed a break from Mike's requests. As they were exiting the stage, a sudden uproar—an explosion— erupted from the first floor of the country club.

ASU had shocked the world by beating Nebraska. The final score: 19–0.

September twenty-first was about to go down in history as the most memorable date of Marlboro Man's life.

$\mathcal{S}$OON IT was time for us to leave; the clock had struck midnight, and we had miles to go before we slept. After throwing my bouquet and saying good-byes, Marlboro Man and I ran through the doors of the club and climbed into the back of a smoky black limousine—the vehicle that would take us to the big city sixty miles away, where we'd stay before flying to Australia the next day. As we pulled away from the waving, birdseed-throwing crowd at the front door of the club, we immediately settled into each other's arms, melting into a puddle of white silk and black boots and sleepy, unbridled romance.

It was all so new. New dress . . . new love . . . a new country— Australia—that neither of us had ever seen. A new life together. A new life for me. New crystal, silver, china. A newly renovated, tiny cowboy house that would be our little house on the prairie when we returned from our honeymoon.

A new husband. *My* husband. I wanted to repeat it over and over again, wanted to shout it to the heavens. But I couldn't speak. I was busy. Passion had taken over—a beast had been unleashed. Sleep deprived and exhausted from the celebration of the previous week, once inside the sanctity of the limousine, we were utterly powerless to stop it . . . and we let it fly. It was this same passion that had gotten us through the early stages of our relationship, and, ultimately, through the choice to wave good-bye to any life I'd ever imagined for myself. To become a part of Marlboro Man's life instead. It was this same passion that assured me that everything was exactly as it should be. It was the passion that made it all make sense.

*I*N THE coming year, real life would come crashing in around us. Within days of our wedding, we would receive unexpected, startling news that would cause us to cut our honeymoon short. Within weeks, we would endure the jarring turmoil of death . . . divorce . . . and disappointment. In the first year of our life together, we would be faced with difficult decisions, painful conflict, and drastic changes in plans.

And through every step of the way, it would be the passion that sustained us.

Part Three

Chapter Twenty-two
THE SICK AND THE DREAD

*A*S OUR plane touched down in Sydney I rubbed my eyes, which were so puffy and encrusted with fourteen hours' worth of postwedding airplane sleep that I couldn't see more than six inches in front of me. Aside from a viewing of the Aussie movie *Cosi* with Toni Collette and a couple of under-the-felt-blanket snuggles with Marlboro Man, I'd slept almost the entire flight—a result of the exhaustion, not just from having endured a six-hundred-plus-guests wedding, but also an almost year-long roller coaster with my parents. It was the deepest I'd slept in months.

Having crossed the international date line, it was Tuesday morning when Marlboro Man and I finally checked into the Park Hyatt, nestled right on the Sydney Harbor. Starving, we feasted on a big plate of scrambled eggs from the lobby buffet before heading up to our room, which overlooked the harbor and had remote control–operated drapes and a marble bathtub just big enough for two newlyweds hell-bent on discovering every single thing about each other's bodies that they could, as soon as humanly possible. We didn't come up for air till Wednesday afternoon.

"Let's just stay here for the whole three weeks," Marlboro Man said, tracing his finger along my scapula as we lay dreamily in our honeymoon bed.

"I'm game," I said, gazing at his whiskered face. Sydney was my new favorite place on earth.

MECHANICS' INSTITUTE LIBRARY
57 Post Street
San Francisco, CA 94104
(415) 393-0101

Marlboro Man pulled me closer, our heads nestling in each other's necks . . . our legs wrapping as tightly around each other as was orthopedically possible. We were as one flesh as two people could be. There were no two ways about it.

It didn't take long for us to realize, though, that we hadn't eaten since the eggs twenty-four hours earlier. Eating was the one desire of the flesh we hadn't fulfilled.

I remembered seeing a McDonald's near the entrance of our hotel, and since I needed a little exercise I offered to dart out for some safe and predictable American food, which would tide us over till the dinner we had reservations for that night. Our blood sugar was too low to comb the city, looking for a place to have a quick lunch.

I knew Marlboro Man was a ketchup-only guy when it comes to burgers, and that's what I ordered when I approached the counter: "Hamburger, ketchup only, please."

"Sar . . . you only want kitchipinmite?" the innocent clerk replied.

"Excuse me?"

"Kitchipinmite?"

"Uh . . . pardon?"

"You jist want a hamburger with kitchipinmite?"

"Uh . . . wha?" I had no idea what the poor girl was saying.

It took me about ten minutes to realize the poor Australian woman behind the counter was merely repeating and confirming my order: kitchip (ketchup) inmite (and meat). It was a traumatic ordering experience.

I returned to the hotel room, and Marlboro Man and I dug into our food like animals.

"This tastes a little funny," my new husband said.

I concurred. The mite was not right. It didn't taste like America.

*T*HAT NIGHT we got dressed up—Marlboro Man in his snug Wranglers and handsome black button-down shirt, me in a flowy taupe dress and black heels—and headed out for the restaurant that a tour booklet had told us was the most sublime dining experience in all of Sydney. We snuggled in the cab to the high-rise whose top floor housed the place.

"You're mine," Marlboro Man said, his strong hand caressing my knee in such a way that I considered asking the cab to return to the hotel. My hunger for a substantial meal was the only thing that propelled me onward to the restaurant.

The thirty-six-floor ride to the top of the building took seconds, it seemed, and when the elevator doors parted we were greeted by beautiful Aussie accents welcoming us to what appeared to be a gorgeous five-star restaurant. I inhaled deeply, smelling grilled meats . . . garlic . . . wine . . . freshly baked bread. It was a far cry from the peculiar McDonald's experience from earlier in the day, and after we were seated and began perusing the menu, I could see that we were home free. What an awesome joint.

But then, unexpectedly, the words on the menu began moving around the page; I blinked my eyes in an attempt to ward off the strange visual disturbance, but that only served to muddy them even more. I glanced at Marlboro Man, who was reading through the beef main courses, and immediately I felt an uncomfortable wave of nausea wash over my body. I grabbed the glass of water our waiter had just brought to the table; by the time I swallowed my first gulp, the situation was dire. Suddenly the aroma of the five-star establishment was a scourge, a predator drone following and firing suffering at me. I felt green.

"I'll be right back," I said, setting down the menu and making a beeline for the restrooms, which were at the top of a winding spiral staircase on the other side of the restaurant. By the time I reached the top of the stairs, I'd slapped my hand over my mouth, trying to ward off what I realized by then would certainly be vomit—and I barely made it to the bathroom in time to throw up everything I'd eaten in the past six months, it seemed.

What in the world? I thought to myself. I'd never experienced such a sudden attack of barf like this. *Could it be the mite from McDonald's? Maybe it was a kangaroo.*

I felt better immediately and stumbled to the sink area of the bathroom, where two hot young Aussie women were brushing their sexy blond hair and adjusting their short skirts so that they hit at just the perfect place on their bronze thighs—no doubt made such a beautiful shade of golden brown by the strong Australian sun. I, by contrast, looked in the mirror to find a mascara-smeared face and bulging eyes caused by my heaving episode a minute earlier. In my haste to leave the table, I'd left my purse, too, and had no makeup to save me. So I did my best, using the scented hand soap to lightly wash the black from under my eyes . . . and availing myself of the complimentary combs to give myself a quick hair touch-up. I hoped there weren't any vomit chunks in my wavy auburn locks. That would be sure to ruin Marlboro Man's dinner.

"You okay?" Marlboro Man asked when I returned to our table. He'd ordered a Coke, and his bread plate was covered with crusts. I'd been gone over ten minutes.

"Yes," I said. "I'm sorry; I just . . . I just got a little sick all of a sudden."

"What's wrong?" he said, by then probably alarmed by the green tinge of his new wife.

"I have no idea—it just hit me like a ton of bricks," I explained. "I'm fine now, though!"

"Maybe you're pregnant," he said with a sly grin.

I knew enough about the timing of conception and morning sickness to know that pregnancy likely wasn't the problem. "I don't think that's it—," I began. Then it hit me again even more violently than before, and I ran back to the bathroom, where I lost it again—this time in a different stall.

Sydney, we have a problem.

Immediately feeling better again, I tended to my appearance, resigning myself to skipping the whole "food part" of this dinner and instead plunging straight into survival mode. I wasn't going to let this ruin the first official meal of our honeymoon. Marlboro Man needed food. *Please, Lord, please. Let this be the last time.*

I combed my bangs again, which were starting to look a little sweaty.

When I exited the bathroom this time, Marlboro Man was standing right outside the door—just as he'd been at his grandmother's house when I'd had my flop sweat episode at his cousin's wedding. He put his arm around me as I dabbed the corners of my eyes with a Kleenex. The gagging had sent my tear ducts into overdrive.

"What's wrong, honey?"

It was the first time he'd called me that. I felt married.

"I have no idea!" I said. "I must have picked up a stomach bug or something. I'm so sorry!"

"It's okay—we can just head back to the hotel."

"No! I want you to eat. . . ."

"I'm fine—I just ate a whole basket of bread and had two Cokes. I'm good to go."

The nausea hit again, and I ran back into the bathroom.

After vomiting again, I decided to take him up on his offer.

Exiting the cab back at the hotel, I found walking to be difficult. I hadn't ingested a single drop of liquor, but I suddenly couldn't walk in a straight line. Grabbing Marlboro Man's arm, I used him to steady myself until we got to the room, where I immediately fell on the bed and wrapped myself in the comforter.

"I feel so sorry for you," Marlboro Man said, sitting down on the bed beside me and gently playing with my hair, a gesture that proved to be too much for me.

"Could you please not do that?" I said. "The motion kinda makes me sick."

I was a complete and utter mess.

I was a nauseated loser.

It was Marlboro Man who deserved the sympathy.

I FELL ASLEEP at nine that night and didn't move until nine the next morning, waking up still dressed and wrapped like a pupa in the Park Hyatt's comforter. Marlboro Man wasn't in the room; I was disoriented and dizzy, stumbling to the bathroom like a drunk sorority girl after a long night of partying. But I didn't look like a sorority girl. I looked like hell, pale and green and drawn; Marlboro Man was probably on a flight back to the States, I imagined, after having woken up and seen what he'd been sleeping next to all night. I made myself take a warm shower, even though the beautiful marble bathroom was spinning like a top. The water hitting my back made me feel better.

When I came out of the bathroom, refreshed and wearing the Park Hyatt robe, Marlboro Man was sitting on the bed, reading an Australian paper, which he'd picked up down the street along with some orange juice and a cinnamon roll for me in hopes it would make me feel better.

"C'mere," he said, patting the empty spot on the bed next to him. I obliged.

I curled up next to him. Like clockwork our arms and legs began to wrap around each other until we were nothing but a mass of flesh again. We stayed there for almost an hour—him rubbing my back and asking me if I was okay . . . me, dying from bliss with each passing minute and trying to will away the nausea, which was still very much hovering over our happiness.

I made myself get up and get dressed; I was determined to be a young, vibrant bride and spectacular honeymoon companion. We went out for lunch and tried a museum, but the dizziness became worse. I had to do something.

"I'm going to go back to the hotel and find a doctor," I said. "I've just got to do something to get rid of this. It's going to ruin our honeymoon."

"I think you're pregnant," Marlboro Man suggested again. But I knew that wasn't it.

We found a family clinic near the hotel and were able to get in to see Dr. Salisbury, a beautiful, tall physician with a strong, comforting voice and naturally blond hair. After a battery of neurological tests and a litany of standard diagnostic questions, she finally asked, "Did you recently take a long flight?"

I told her we'd flown from Oklahoma to Los Angeles, then from Los Angeles to Sydney.

"Did you sleep a lot of that time?" she continued.

"Pretty much the entire time," I answered. My concern grew. Could it be something terrible and communicable? TB, perhaps? The flu? A terrible strain of airborne malaria? "What's wrong, Doctor? Give it to me straight; I can take it."

"I believe what you have," she said, "is an inner ear disturbance—most likely brought on by the long flight and the sleep."

An inner ear disturbance? How boring. How embarrassing.

"What would sleeping a lot have to do with it?" I asked. As the daughter of a physician, I needed a little more data.

She explained that since I hadn't been awake much during the flight, I hadn't yawned or naturally taken other steps to alleviate the ear popping that comes from a change in cabin pressure, and that my ears simply filled with fluid and were causing this current attack of vertigo.

Fabulous, I thought. *I'm a complete wimp.* It was a real high point.

"Is there anything she can do to make it better?" Marlboro Man asked, looking for a concrete solution.

The doctor prescribed some decongestant and some antinausea medication, and I crawled out of her office in shame.

*T*HE NEXT morning, hallelujah, I was worlds better—a good thing, since it was time for us to retrieve our rental car for our drive up the coast of Australia.

Marlboro Man had planned the entire trip, right down to the rental car we'd use to drive from Sydney all the way up the eastern coast. He'd been especially excited about traveling to the Land Down Under. He'd always wanted to see how Australian ranches—known as cattle stations—compared with those in America.

This was the mid-1990s, a few years before the SUV revolution had taken full root in the world. Still, because we were planning to be in Oz for three weeks and would have lots of luggage, and because he had grown up driving only large vehicles and could never be comfortable in a regular car, Marlboro Man had decided renting an SUV for our Australian honeymoon was the way to go.

Britz Rentals of Australia was a large enough car rental firm that they *did* have SUVs for rent. And not just any SUVs—*Toyota Land Cruisers*, which, at that time in history, were considered a luxury vehicle. Marlboro Man was thrilled to the core to have booked and prepaid for the Land Cruiser in order to lock in a good rate. We checked out of our beautiful hotel room and loaded all our bags in a cab, directing the driver to take us to Britz, where we'd pick up our sleek Toyota Land Cruiser and begin our journey of love up the eastern Australian coast.

When the attendant at Britz Rentals of Australia whipped around in our prepaid-in-full honeymoon car, my eyes grew wide and I knew we were in trouble. It was an SUV, yes, and a Toyota Land Cruiser at that—just as Marlboro Man had ordered. It was white and clean and very shiny. And painted in huge bright orange and royal blue lettering across the hood, the roof, all four doors, and the tailgate of the vehicle, were scrawled the enormous words: BRITZ RENTALS OF AUSTRALIA.

I could see Marlboro Man's jaw muscles flex as he beheld his worst nightmare playing out in front of his eyes. He could hardly even bear to

gaze upon such an attention-grabbing abomination, let alone conceive of driving it all over an entire continent. Unfortunately, our last-minute attempts to trade to another vehicle proved to be futile; even if Britz hadn't been completely booked that week, it wouldn't have mattered anyway. Every single car in their fleet was smeared with the exact same orange and blue promotional graffiti.

Having no other transportational alternative, we set off on our drive, a black cloud of conspicuousness and, in Marlboro Man's case, dread following us everywhere we went. Being an attention-seeking middle child, I didn't really mind it much. But for Marlboro Man, this was more than his makeup was programmed to handle. As far as he was concerned, we were the Griswolds, and the Land Cruiser was our Family Truckster.

It was a pox on what might have been the perfect honeymoon.

Except for my inner ear disturbance. And the vomiting. And the slightly marsupial undertone to the hamburgers.

Chapter Twenty-three
FOR A FEW DOLLARS LESS

WE MADE our way to the misty Blue Mountains north of Sydney and settled into a resort in the smoky hills. My nausea was still hanging around, but the quiet, isolated resort lent itself well to lying around in the hotel room, ordering room service, and avoiding going anywhere at all, lest we have to drive our Britz rental. But it was fine with us, lying around a hotel room on the other side of the world, absolutely gobbling each other up and wondering why we ever had to return to our home country if it meant unwrapping each other from our arms for more than ten seconds. We were fused together, inextricably locked in a permanent state of bodily oneness. It was everything a honeymoon should be. I felt better, too. The mountain air had helped my equilibrium.

But we *would* eventually have to go home. Marlboro Man had a ranch to run—it would soon be time to ship more cattle—and besides that, renovation on our yellow brick house was going strong. We'd have to go home eventually, away from the days spent in bed, and begin our new life together in the country.

It was the middle of the night in the Blue Mountains when the phone rang in our hotel room. Marlboro Man and I jumped, unaware of what time it was in Australia or any other part of the world, for that matter. I couldn't even open my eyes. The mist outside had proven itself an intoxicating elixir.

"Hello?" Marlboro Man said. I could hear a man's voice through the receiver.

Moments passed, and I drifted back to sleep . . . until Marlboro Man sat up in bed and swung his legs around so his feet touched the ground.

"Damn, Slim," he said. "That's sure not good."

I opened my eyes. I had no idea what he could be talking about.

I listened to Marlboro Man as he continued what appeared to be an intense discussion with his brother. It was business-related. And it didn't sound like good news.

"Okay, Slim," he said. "Call me when you find out more."

Marlboro Man settled back under the covers. I heard him sigh.

"Everything okay?" I said sleepily, wrapping my leg back around his.

"Oh . . . ," he said, rolling over and adjusting his pillow. "Grain markets took a big dive today."

I couldn't tell if he was tired or stressed . . . or a little of both. But I could tell from his voice alone that the news had been unexpected.

I tossed and turned for a while before finally drifting off to sleep and dreaming about our wedding, my parents, our yellow Indian house, and our Land Cruiser from hell.

Our drive to the Gold Coast the next day was quiet. Marlboro Man had had another phone call with Tim before we'd pulled away from the hotel, and the situation sounded pretty dire. Corn and wheat prices were plummeting, and Marlboro Man was a continent away, unable to keep track of the situation and manage his commodity account, which was a hedge against the wild swings of the cattle market. He wanted to talk, to enjoy our continued drive north. But he was simply too preoccupied to engage in small talk. He had a new wife, a new house, a new homestead . . . and a mere week after his wedding day, what he thought was a secure situation back home was becoming more precarious with each phone call from his brother, Tim. I had no idea what to say or do; I didn't want to put on a happy face and ignore the fact that something heavy was going down; on the other hand, I didn't want to make it worse by asking him about it every five minutes.

Of all the things that had happened, this was the most peculiar honeymoon development.

*W*E CHECKED into our beachfront hotel, putting the stresses back home aside long enough to walk down the beach and have an early lobster dinner at a casual seaside shack. Marlboro Man and I shared a lobster tail larger than most cows back on the ranch, and I took the liberty of ordering a warm lobster casserole as a side dish. We'd be heading back to Oklahoma soon; I wasn't leaving Australia without ingesting all the lobster I could.

I burped quietly as we walked back to our resort. There was a lot of lobster in my belly.

By the time we returned to the hotel room, we were laughing again. Marlboro Man was teasing me about how many clothes I'd brought on the honeymoon, and I'd punched him in the arm; he, in turn, had trapped me in the corner of the elevator and tickled me, and I'd threatened to wet my pants if he didn't stop. And I wasn't kidding; I'd had a glass of wine at dinner, as well as two Diet Cokes. Tickling me in an elevator wouldn't be a good idea for very long.

The blinking message light on the phone screamed at us when we walked into the bedroom of our suite. Marlboro Man audibly exhaled, clearly wishing the world—and his brother and the grain markets and the uncertainties of agriculture—would leave us alone already. I wished they'd leave us alone, too.

In light of the recent developments, though, Marlboro Man picked up the phone and dialed Tim to get an update. I excused myself to the bathroom to freshen up and put on a champagne satin negligee in an effort to

thwart the external forces that were trying to rob me of my husband's attention. I brushed my teeth and spritzed myself with Jil Sander perfume before opening the door to the bedroom, where I would seduce my Marlboro Man away from his worries. I knew I could win if only I applied myself.

He was just getting off the phone when I entered the room.

"Dammit," I heard him mumble as he plopped down onto the enormous king-size bed.

Oh no. Jil Sander had her work cut out for her.

I climbed on the bed and lay beside him, resting my head on his arm. He draped his arm across my waist. I draped my leg around his.

He sighed. "The markets are totally in the shitter."

I didn't know the details, but I did know the shitter wasn't a good place.

I wanted to throw out the usual platitudes. *Don't worry about it, try not to think about it, we'll figure it out, everything will be okay.* But I didn't know enough about it. I knew he and his brother owned a lot of land. I knew they worked hard to pay for it. I knew they weren't lawyers or physicians by profession and didn't have a whole separate income to supplement their ranching operation. As full-time ranchers, their livelihoods were completely reliant on so many things outside of their control—weather, market fluctuations, supply, demand, luck. I knew they weren't home free in terms of finances—Marlboro Man and I had talked about it. But I didn't understand enough about the ramifications of this current wrinkle to reassure him that everything would be okay, businesswise. And he probably didn't want me to.

So I did the only thing I could think of to do. I assured my new husband everything would be okay between us by leaning over, turning off the lamp, and letting the love between us—which had zero to do with markets or grains—take over.

*W*E WOKE up two hours later vomiting, violently ill with what had to be food poisoning, the lobster exacting a violent revenge. The only saving grace was that the hotel suite also had a half bath; I elected to hole up in there while Marlboro Man splayed out in the master bath, both of us wondering all the while how a perfectly wonderful honeymoon could have gone so horribly south.

If I hadn't been so busy staring at the ceiling and wishing death would rescue me, I would have laughed hysterically. This had to be one of the most hilariously tragic honeymoons on record.

Not that it was the least bit funny.

Thirty-six hours later, we were on a plane back to the States. After an entire day of vomiting, diarrhea, and profuse sweating—not to mention my inner ear disturbance, the Griswold Family car rental, and the disintegrating nest egg back home—I'd told Marlboro Man I thought we should cut the trip short and head home, where we could decompress and unpack and rest . . . and think clearly. I didn't want my new husband to have the added stress of having to put on a happy face all the way up the coast to the Great Barrier Reef; three whole weeks in Australia weren't a prerequisite to our starting our life together.

"We'll come back sometime," I said during our layover in Auckland. And I meant it. For all the ridiculous developments of the previous week, I'd seen enough of Australia to know that I wanted to come back, albeit under less psychotic circumstances.

When we touched down back home Marlboro Man inhaled and exhaled deeply, as if deep down he knew the extent of the struggle awaiting him two hours from the airport, at the ranch where he'd grown up . . . on the land that he and his family loved so very much.

I exhaled, too, realizing at that very moment that we'd just officially crossed the line into the big, fat, real world.

Chapter Twenty-four
HOME ON THE RANGE

TIM WAS waiting for us at baggage claim; he greeted us with a semi-forced smile, shaking Marlboro Man's hand and patting him on the arm reassuringly. My new brother-in-law hugged me warmly and said welcome home, but I could see his worry in the air; it was thick and murky and charcoal gray, like an erupting ash cloud. The ride back to the ranch was mostly quiet, peppered with occasional anecdotes of our vomit-filled honeymoon and debriefings from Tim as to the gravity of the situation with the markets. They stayed in the moment, purposely avoiding the what-ifs and what-will-we-dos—concentrating instead on trying to get a grasp on how everything could have taken such a plunge in such a tiny breath of a moment. And—considering it came on the heels of such a celebratory, blessed event—how funny the timing was.

The sun was just dipping below the western horizon when we pulled up to our little house on the prairie. Despite the obvious turmoil I knew was swarming in the periphery, I couldn't help but instantly smile when I saw our little home. *Home,* I thought to myself—a strange response, considering I'd never spent a night there. But, being back there, I felt the heartbeat of our love affair that had started on that very ranch, the drives we'd taken, the dinners we'd cooked, the nights we'd spent watching submarine movies on his old leather couch, which Marlboro Man had already moved to our new little house so we'd be able to enjoy it immediately.

Poor couch. It must have been awfully lonely without us.

Tim bid us good-bye after helping us carry in my three-hundred-pound suitcase, and Marlboro Man and I looked around our quiet house, which was spick-and-span and smelled of fresh paint and leather cowboy boots, which lined the wall near the front door. The entry glowed with the light of the setting sun coming in the window, and I reached down to grab one of my bags so I could carry it to the bedroom. But before my hand made it to the handle, Marlboro Man grabbed me tightly around the waist and carried me over to the leather sofa, where we fell together in a tired heap of jet lag, emotional exhaustion, and—ironically, given the week we'd just endured—a sudden burst of lust.

"Welcome home," he said, nuzzling his face into my neck. Mmmm. This was a familiar feeling.

"Thank you," I said, closing my eyes and savoring every second. As his lips made their way across my neck, I could hear the sweet and reassuring sound of cows in the pasture east of our house. We were home.

"You feel so good," he said, moving his hands to the zipper of my casual black jacket.

"You do, too," I said, stroking the back of his closely cut hair as his arms wrapped more and more tightly around my waist. "But . . . uh . . ." I paused.

My black jacket was by now on the floor.

"I . . . uh . . . ," I continued. "I think I need to take a shower." And I did. I couldn't do the precise calculation of what it had meant for my hygiene to cross back over the international date line, but as far as I was concerned, I hadn't showered in a decade. I couldn't imagine christening our house in such a state. I needed to smell like lilac and lavender and Dove soap on the first night in our little house together. Not airline fuel. Not airports. Not clothes I'd worn for two days straight.

Marlboro Man chuckled—the first one I'd heard in many days—and

as he'd done so many times during our months of courtship, he touched his forehead to mine. "I need one, too," he said, a hint of mischief in his voice.

And with that, we accompanied each other to the shower, where, with a mix of herbal potions, rural water, and determination, we washed our honeymoon down the drain.

"I'M SORRY about our honeymoon," Marlboro Man said when we woke up the next morning. It was 4:30, still dark outside, and we were wired, our internal clocks in a state of utter confusion. He caressed my side as I stretched and sighed. Our bed was so warm and cozy and dreamy.

"It's okay," I said, smiling. "I'm so glad we came home . . . I love it here." Our bedroom was tiny, about nine feet by nine feet. It cradled us like a protective cocoon.

"I love *you* here," he replied.

We stayed in bed the entire morning, purposely denying that a world beyond our cocoon even existed.

MARLBORO MAN and I settled in together, soaking up the first days of married life on the ranch that was my new home. He spent his days working cattle; his evenings figuring out the business ramifications of the imploding financial situation in which he and Tim now found themselves. I, on the other hand, spent my days getting organized and washing his muddy clothes, failing miserably in my attempts to remove the greenish brown manure stains and making plans instead to order a hundred pairs of the jeans he wore so I could just replace them every day. I saw no other alternative.

I unpacked my clothes gradually, hanging them in the tiny closet that

Marlboro Man and I now shared and folding what wouldn't fit in under-the-bed storage boxes. The myriad skin scrubs and facial creams and lotions I'd collected over the previous few years now filled my half of the large wooden medicine cabinet that hung on the bathroom wall over the single pedestal sink; my cookbooks—old and new—took their place on the shelves above the kitchen pantry.

We had no place to put the stacks of wedding gifts we'd received—the silver trays and crystal goblets and pewter meat platters. Marlboro Man's mother came over to help me pack and consolidate it all for storage in the separate garage apartment adjacent to the yellow brick house—whose renovation plowed along daily.

In the evening time, I'd try to acclimate myself to the new kitchen setup: a four-burner portable gas range, a single-bowl stainless sink, a sparkly new economy-size fridge. I'd picked out a charming tile with watercolor cows sectioned off according to the cuts of beef, and all the words were in French—a last-ditch effort on my part to be worldly. The word *BOEUF* peppered our countertops. It made Marlboro Man laugh.

On our sixth night home, after subsisting mostly on cold sandwiches and hard-boiled eggs, I boiled a chicken in the new Calphalon stockpot I'd received as a gift from my old college roommate, Jill, removing it with stainless tongs given to me by the mother of a childhood friend. When it was cool enough to handle, I meticulously picked the meat off the bone, unsure of how much fat and gristle to leave behind. I'd decided to inaugurate our kitchen with my mom's Chicken Spaghetti, a comfort food I thought would hit the spot in our first week home. Cooking the spaghetti, I combined it with the chicken and added onions, green peppers, and pimientos from a jar. And to seal the deal as a domestic goddess, I added cream of mushroom soup, holding the two open cans over the mixing bowl for a good minute before the solidified soup finally plopped out, both in a cylindrical mass. Adding a splash of broth and a bunch of grated sharp cheddar, I stirred it to mix it up, seasoned it with salt and cayenne, then baked it in an earthenware

pottery dish, courtesy of my mother-in-law's first cousin. As it baked, the blessed casserole smelled just like it did when I was a child, which was likely the last time I'd eaten it. I marveled that the scent of a specific dish could remain in one's consciousness for over two decades. Except for the dark brown hair and the crumbling marriage, I'd officially become my mother.

Marlboro Man, happy to have something warm to eat, declared it the best thing he'd ever eaten. I looked at the mess in the kitchen and felt like moving.

Marlboro Man and I watched movies that night. Our TV satellite hadn't been hooked up yet, so he'd transported his movie collection and VCR from his old house. And I didn't have to get up and drive home when they were over, because I already was home.

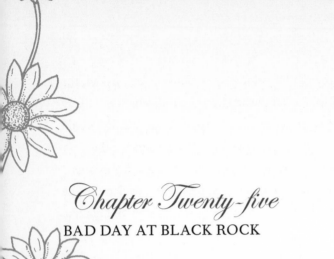

Chapter Twenty-five
BAD DAY AT BLACK ROCK

FIVE WEEKS to the day after our wedding, we drove to my home-town to have dinner with my parents, who wanted to welcome us back from the honeymoon with a nice dinner at the country club. I hugged my mom and dad, and shuddered; the familiar tension between them was present and palpable. Clearly nothing had improved since I'd said good-bye to them at the wedding reception.

Somehow, during the course of the previous several weeks, amid the honeymoon and the settling in and the fizzy first days of matrimony, I'd allowed myself to assume that since I was no longer a daily witness to the unraveling of my parents' marriage, it must not actually be happening.

Thirty seconds in their presence blew that completely out of the water.

We ordered steak and baked potatoes and salads and desserts, but, strangely, by the second bite of steak, I knew I couldn't go on any longer. The thought of the piece of meat in front of me suddenly repelled me, and I was instantly transported to the nausea spell I'd experienced at the best restaurant in all of Sydney. *Oh no,* I thought. *It's back.* I didn't say anything, continuing to pick at the food in front of me as Marlboro Man and I shared the more pleasant aspects of our Australian honeymoon.

When we hugged good-bye and I watched my parents climb into their car—my mother immediately staring out the window as my father shifted into drive and stared straight ahead—I knew in my heart things had gotten worse. The pit of my stomach ached in more ways than one.

As Marlboro Man and I walked to our car, his arm around my shoulders and my head resting on his chest, I held him tightly, promising myself I'd never let that coldness take root between us. I couldn't even bear the thought, couldn't even imagine it. I loved Marlboro Man so much. Had my parents ever felt that way? I know they had. I'd seen it. I clutched Marlboro Man even tighter as we continued our walk through the parking lot.

We drove home slowly, almost in utter silence. I knew Marlboro Man was preoccupied; the business of the ranch weighed heavily on his mind. As for me, all I could think about were my parents and my stupid inner ear disturbance, which had clearly chosen to pay me a visit that night. I was sick again, just like I'd been for most of our Australian honeymoon.

And then it really hit me.

"Stop the car," I said suddenly, just before we crossed the county line. Before the pickup even came to a complete stop, I opened my door and hopped out, throwing up my dinner, completely splattering the shoulder of the highway.

On the growing list of Undignified Moments of My Life, it assumed a very high position.

THE NAUSEA was so bad when I awoke the next morning, I could hardly get out of bed. Marlboro Man had already left the house; I hadn't even heard him get up. I lifted my head off the pillow and immediately plopped it back down. I felt as green as I imagined I looked, and I was so afraid of throwing up again after the side-of-the-road upchuck the night before that I simply curled into a fetal position and lay there for another hour. I wished I had a nurse button so someone could bring me Froot Loops.

It was, curiously, the only food on Earth that sounded remotely palatable.

I managed to work my way to a standing position by midmorning, shuffling my feet to the fridge in our tiny kitchen and sipping some cold orange juice. The blood sugar surge seemed to help immediately. I rifled through the cabinets for something, anything that would fill the gaping hole of nauseating hunger in my gut, but all options looked and sounded awful. I couldn't bear the thought of a ham sandwich. Imagining milk trickling down my esophagus almost sent me over the edge. Even the saltines might as well have been covered in hair. This was bad. Really, really bad. I had to somehow make it to the shower, then see about getting a doctor's appointment. I couldn't go on like this.

The shower turned out to be glorious once I adjusted the water to a cool enough temperature so as not to produce any steam. I washed my hair, noticing that my favorite shampoo suddenly smelled like Hades—as did my trusty facial scrub, which had so loyally saved my face from looking like the back of a lizard on the day of my wedding. Just as I was rinsing the last of the suds from my hair, Marlboro Man suddenly burst through the door of the bathroom and yelled, *"Hey!"*

I screamed bloody murder from the startle, then screamed again because I was naked and feeling queasy and unattractive. Then I felt sick from the excitement. *"Hi,"* I managed, grabbing a towel from the rack and wrapping it around myself as quickly as I could.

"Gotcha," he said, smiling the sexiest smile I'd ever seen while in such a sick state. Then he stopped and looked at me. "Are you okay?" He must have noticed the verdant glow of my skin.

"I'll be honest," I said, making my way back to our bedroom. "It's pretty bad. I'm going to try to get in to the doctor today and see if there's anything he can do about it." I fell backward onto the bed. "My ears must have been permanently damaged or something."

Marlboro Man moved toward me, looking like the cat that had just eaten the canary. "Scared you, didn't I?" he chuckled as he wrapped his

arms around my towel-cloaked body. I breathed him in, wrapping my arms around him, too.

Then I shot up and raced back to the bathroom so I could throw up again.

ARLBORO MAN went back to work—he and Tim were receiving a load of steers—and I drove over to my hometown to see the only doctor that could work me in on such short notice. I'd wanted to see an ear-nose-throat physician, since I already knew it was an inner ear issue, but they were all booked at least two weeks out. I couldn't bear the thought of throwing up that long. After a battery of questions, a few palpations of my lymph nodes, and a peek inside my ears, the doctor leaned back against the counter, crossed his arms, and said, "Any chance you might be pregnant?"

I knew that wasn't it. "Well, it wouldn't be impossible," I humored him. "But I know that's not what it is. I got this same thing on our honeymoon, just as soon as we got to Australia. It's definitely some kind of vertigo/inner ear thing." I swallowed hard, wishing I'd brought along some Froot Loops.

"When was your wedding?" he asked, looking at the calendar on the wall of the exam room.

"September twenty-first," I answered. "But again . . . I know it's my ears."

"Well, let's just rule it out," the doctor said. "I'll send the nurse in here in a minute, okay?"

Waste of time, I thought. "Okay, but . . . do you think there's anything we can do about my ears?" I really didn't want to feel this way anymore.

"Marcy will be in here in just a second," he repeated. He wasn't acknowledging my self-diagnosis at all. *What kind of doctor is this?*

Marcy soon entered the room with a plastic cup with a bright green lid—the perfect reflection of my skin tone. "Do you think you can give us a urine sample, hon?" she asked.

I can give you a vomit sample, I thought. "Sure," I said, taking the cup and following Marcy to the restroom like a good little patient. *And don't call me hon,* I thought. I was cranky. I needed something to eat, and I felt like bursting into tears.

A minute later, I exited the bathroom and handed Marcy the sample cup, which I'd wiped clean with a paper towel.

"Okay, hon," she said. "You can just head back to the room and I'll be back in a sec."

Stop calling me hon.

I felt awful. Tingly and flushed and awful. If I moved my head too quickly in any direction, I'd gag. I suddenly felt a surge of sympathy for people who felt this way all the time, from chemotherapy treatments or gastrointestinal problems or other medical reasons. There's no way I could function in this state for any length of time. I just prayed an effective treatment existed. I couldn't predict what they'd need to do to my ears, but I was willing to try anything to achieve relief. I had things to do, after all. I needed to go be a wife.

My legs swung back and forth as I sat on the exam table and waited for Marcy or the doctor to return. A Wendy's Frosty suddenly sounded delicious. *At last,* I thought. *Something other than Froot Loops. Hurry up, Marcy! I've got to get to the drive-thru.*

Moments later, Marcy and the doctor entered the room together. Marcy was smiling.

"You're pregnant, my dear," the doctor said.

My stomach lurched. "What?" I exclaimed. "But that can't be why I'm sick . . . can it?"

After a series of uncomfortable questions from the doctor as to the various dates of this and that, Marcy giggled as the doctor walked me through—with his pencil—the dates on the wall calendar, dates that explained when I could have gotten pregnant and why now, over five weeks after our wedding day, I was barfing my ever-loving guts out and craving Froot Loops and Frosties.

Pregnant.

Pregnant?

What should I do?

Should I tell Marlboro Man?

Should I go lie down and put my feet up on pillows?

What will this mean for my figure?

I suddenly had a lot of things to figure out.

$\mathcal{D}$RIVING BACK to the ranch, sucking down the last of the most delicious Wendy's Frosty I'd ever ingested in my life, I instinctively clutched my abdomen, which felt flat as a pancake because of the lack of food I'd been able to eat over the previous forty-eight hours. Pregnant? Already? I knew it could happen. I knew it was possible. But I didn't think it would happen this quickly.

Then my mind began to race. What had I had to drink over the past few weeks? What medications had I taken? What food? What did this mean for Marlboro Man and me? Was he ready? He said he wanted children, but did he really mean it? What would it mean for my body? My soul? My heart? Could I share myself with a baby? Did labor hurt?

I pulled up at home and saw Marlboro Man's truck next to the house. When I walked in the door of our little white house, he was there, sitting on the bench, taking off his boots.

"Hey," he said, leaning back against the wall. "How're you doing?"

"Better," I replied. "I had a Frosty."

He pulled off his left boot. "What'd you find out?"

"Well," I started. My lip began to quiver.

Marlboro Man stood up. "What's wrong?" he said.

"I'm p . . ." My lip quivered even more, making it difficult to speak. "I'm pregnant!" I cried. The tears started rolling.

"What?" he exclaimed, moving toward me. "Really?"

All I could do was nod. The lump in my throat was too big for me to talk.

"Oh, wow." He moved in, hugging me close. I guess he hadn't expected it either.

I just stood there and cried silently. For our past . . . for our future. For my nausea and my fatigue. For receiving a diagnosis.

As for Marlboro Man, he just stood there and held me as he always had when I'd broken into unanticipated crying attacks, all the while trying his best not to explode with excitement over the fact that his baby was growing in my belly.

THAT NIGHT, after having lived with the news for mere hours, Marlboro Man couldn't stand it anymore. He wanted to tell our families. Forget waiting until the end of the first trimester; forget sleeping on it a couple of nights. Something important had happened. He saw no need to keep it a secret.

"Hey," he said when his mom answered the phone. I could hear her bright voice in the receiver. "Ree's pregnant," he blurted out, as open as he'd been in the first weeks of our relationship.

"Yep," he continued, answering his mom's questions. "We're pretty excited." He and his mom continued chatting. I could hear her excitement, too.

When the call ended, he handed me the portable phone. "Do you want to call your folks?" he asked. He would have called the newspaper if it had been open.

More focused on my growing nausea than on making phone calls, I took the phone anyway and dialed my parents' house. After several rings, my dad finally answered. "Hello," the voice said quietly.

"Hi, Dad," I announced.

"Hi, sweetie," my dad said. His voice sounded strange. Something was wrong.

"What's wrong, Dad?" I asked.

"Your mom . . . your mom left tonight," he said. "She said she has an apartment and she's leaving. She's gone. . . ." His voice trailed to a whisper.

My heart sank. I sat there on the sofa, unable to move.

I TOLD MARLBORO Man immediately—it was the second piece of stunning news we'd received that day—then headed back to my hometown by myself. I had to see my dad, to make sure he was okay, and I wanted to go by myself. I couldn't subject Marlboro Man to that level of in-law strife this early in the game, and I wasn't sure my dad would be comfortable talking freely in front of his new son-in-law.

"It won't be too late," I told him. "I just want to make sure he's okay."

"I'm sorry, honey," Marlboro Man said, hugging me before I left.

Man. What a day.

I called my mom the second I got in my car.

"Mom," I said. "What's going on?"

She was quiet for a moment. "Ree," she said. "It's been coming for a long time."

"What's been coming?" I countered. "Throwing away a thirty-year marriage?" My crankiness had returned.

She paused for a long time. I crossed the cattle guard as I made my way toward the main highway. "It's not that simple, Ree . . . ," she began. The line went quiet while we both tried to figure out something productive to say. I held back. Nothing could be gained by blurting out angrily what I was thinking: that my mom was about to demolish our family. That it was all so preventable . . . so unnecessary. That she was pulling the rug out from under us all.

That I was going to have a baby . . . that I needed her right now.

I hung up the phone. My mom—likely aware of the futility of trying to have a productive, meaningful conversation that night—didn't call back.

When I arrived at the house—the house where I'd grown up—my dad opened the door and we hugged and cried, my dad's cry more of a stunned whimper than a sob.

"I'm sorry, Dad," I said, hugging him tightly.

He couldn't answer.

I stayed with my dad for two hours, sitting and talking with him until his best friend, Jack, arrived. My brother Doug, in another city, had called Betsy and told her what was going on. Around town, I could already feel, the news was starting to spread.

On the ride back to the ranch that night, after I'd made sure my dad was psychologically stable, I called Mike.

"B-b-but where will Mom live?" Mike asked after I explained what was going on.

"Well . . . I think she has an apartment. But we don't really know what's going on yet," I explained. "We'll just wait and see, okay?"

"Wh-wh-wh-what is the apartment like?" he asked.

"Mikey, I just don't know," I answered. "I just . . . I don't know right now. But don't worry, okay? We'll figure it all out."

"Where will we have Christmas?" Mike asked.

I swallowed hard. "We'll have it here, I'm sure . . . ," I began. My eyes started welling with tears.

"But dey are n-n-n-not going to get a diforce . . . are dey?" Mike asked.

It would take him a while to grasp this.

We talked for a few more minutes, said our good nights, and I hung up the phone and sobbed. I needed this not to be happening—not now. *Please, please, please . . . not now.*

I arrived back home just before midnight, and Marlboro Man met me at the car. I could hear nothing but cows and crickets when I climbed out of my car and into his arms, which were strong and warm and comforting. I was a wreck—sick to my stomach and even more sick in my heart—and Marlboro Man helped me to the house, as if I were crippled by a terminal illness. I was completely beat, hardly able to finish my shower before I fell into bed with Marlboro Man, who rubbed my back as I tried with all my might to keep from throwing up, breaking down, and completely saturating my red floral pillowcase with tears.

Chapter Twenty-six
DARK CANYON

I WOKE UP the next morning feeling drained . . . but, magically, a bit better on the nausea front. Maybe, I reasoned, I'd have the shortest bout of morning sickness in the history of pregnancy. I stood up from my bed and waited for the nausea to kick in, but it didn't. Feeling hopeful, I washed my face and got dressed; Marlboro Man was gone, of course, having gotten up and gone to work while it was still dark. I put on my makeup, wondering if I'd ever get up at the same time as Marlboro Man. Wondering if anyone ever did.

Around eleven, after calling my dad to check on him, I scoured the kitchen for lunch ideas and finally settled on chili. It would be okay for several hours, I figured, so whenever Marlboro Man came home it would be ready. Wives made chili for lunch, right? I still hadn't figured out the flow of things. I diced up some onion and garlic, breathing through my mouth to avoid making myself sick again, and threw it into a pot with a two-pound package of ground beef, which I'd thawed in the fridge earlier in the week. I didn't have packets of chili seasoning in my pantry—I hadn't put that item into my grocery shopping loop yet—so I improvised, sprinkling in chili powder, paprika, cayenne, cumin . . . whatever spice smelled remotely like I always remembered chili smelling. By the time it really started bubbling, the smell of chili had taken over the universe and the queasiness had returned with a vengeance. It was the worst smell I'd ever experienced—pungent garlic, the horrible, overwhelming aroma of cumin . . . the stench of cooking flesh.

By the time Marlboro Man walked in the door, I was stirring in the canned kidney beans and minutes away from throwing up.

"Mmmm . . . smells good," he said. He walked over to the stove and wrapped his arms around my waist, resting his palms on my belly. "How are you, Mama?" he asked. Butterflies went crazy in my stomach. He did it for me, even when cumin was making me sick.

"I'm better today," I said, focusing on my physical condition. "How are you?"

"I'm good," he said. "I'm worried about you, though." His hands caressed my ribs, my arms, my sides.

He touched me all the time; physical indifference was never a problem with Marlboro Man.

The phone rang suddenly, and I continued stirring the chili as he walked into the living room and picked it up. He talked for a while as I added the last dash of salt, then came back into the kitchen.

"Marie's only got a few hours," he said. "They're telling all the family it's time to come down."

I turned off the stove. "Oh no," I said. "No." It was all I could say.

"If you're not feeling up to it, you don't have to come," Marlboro Man said. "Everyone will understand."

But I wanted to. Her fight was ending. Even though I was the newest member of the family, I couldn't possibly not go.

But when we walked through the door of Marie and Uncle Tom's house, I wanted to be anywhere in the world but there. Family was huddled around, hugging one another and crying. Food was being served, but no one was eating. I didn't know how to greet people. Whether to smile. Whether to hug. Whether to cry. I thought of my parents. I felt oppressed. I couldn't breathe.

Matthew met us at the door and tried to smile as he hugged us both, then led us to the back bedroom where his mother lay in her bed, unconscious and breathing laboriously. Marie's brother sat at her side and held her hand in his, bringing it to his face affectionately and speaking to her in a gentle voice. Her parents stood close by, consoling each other in an embrace. Matthew joined his sister, Jennifer, on the bed, touching their mother's legs . . . her arms . . . anything to maintain the physical connection they knew would soon no longer be possible. And her husband, Tom, sat on a chair, presiding sadly over the whole gathering of friends and family. It was so heavy with grief, so horribly sad—I couldn't bear to be in the room. My mother-in-law was in the kitchen helping with the food and dishes; I slipped backward out of the bedroom to be with her instead. Marlboro Man followed close behind me. After enduring the death of his brother Todd years earlier, he'd had about enough of this kind of mourning to last him a lifetime.

Just as we arrived in the kitchen, sobs came from the bedroom. Marie had taken her last breath. I heard Jennifer crying out loud for her mother; Marie's parents saying "No . . . no . . ." over and over. I heard the tears of Marie's closest friends, who were also huddled around her bedside. I felt myself breaking and excused myself to a guest bathroom on the other side of the house. I was crumbling.

I locked myself in the blue half bath and sunk to the floor, with my back against the tile wall. I felt like an intruder. It wasn't my place to be there. But maybe it was; I was Marlboro Man's wife. It was his family, so it was also mine. Meanwhile, my dad was at home alone, probably going crazy in his suddenly empty house. I needed to check on him, to help him through this. But I couldn't bear the thought of walking into our house again without my mom there. I felt a pang of nausea as my eyes welled up with tears—tears for Marie, tears for my dad, for my sister and brothers and my grandparents. Tears for Marlboro Man and his recent stress, for Marie's daughter, who was fresh out of college and would begin her adult life without her mother. I thought of every happy Christmas of my childhood and realized

I'd never have one again. And I thought of Mike, who thrived on routine and stability, and wondered how he would endure the upheaval. I thought of Marie, and how kind she'd been to me in the short time I'd known her. My tears turned into a wellspring, my sniffles into heaving sobs.

Stop it, I ordered myself. *You can't be hysterical here. You can't walk out among Marlboro Man's family with red, puffy eyes.*

It was their grief, not mine; I didn't want them to think I was just putting on emotion. But I couldn't control the tears, no matter how much I tried. I grabbed a washcloth and dabbed it on my face as I heard the plaintive wails of Marie's family from the other room. It was over; Marie was gone. My parents were over; they were splitting up. Knowing the rest of the house was otherwise occupied, I stayed there in the blue bathroom and buried my face in my hands, crying uncontrollably. *I'll have to stay in here, I imagined, until I can compose myself.*

I'll have to stay in here until I'm sixty.

I DIDN'T ATTEND Marie's funeral. By the time it rolled around days after her death, my morning sickness had turned into a debilitating all-day nausea that dictated every motion of my body for all the hours I was awake. What I'd experienced a couple of weeks prior was just a little tummy ache compared to the plague of queasiness I was now enduring.

I was miserable. I wanted to be a young, energetic new wife, full of vim and vigor. Instead I was olive green, plastered to my bed, and unable to raise my head from the pillow without munching a handful of sugared cereal. Every time Marlboro Man entered our bedroom to check on me, he'd step on an Apple Jack. I'd hear it crunch into the carpet and he'd look down at the crumbs on the sole of his boot . . . and all I could do was watch. When I could bear to stand erect, I'd taken to sniffing lemon halves to ward off the nausea. Spent lemon halves littered the house; I was afraid to let one out of my sight for more than ten seconds.

I was a vision of loveliness—charming in every way—and no help on the ranch at all. Marlboro Man was working hard—the many loads of cattle he'd bought in the month before our wedding were starting to come in, and I wanted to help him get through it. But the smell of manure was too much for me to take. The smell of air alone sent me into dry heaves, even with a lemon wedge shoved under my nose. I couldn't cook. Everything—from apples to bread, not to mention animal flesh in any form—would make me cry and hurl. I'd drive twenty-five minutes to town just to pick up a pizza, then stop halfway home and put it in the trunk because the smell was so horribly overpowering.

All the while, Marlboro Man tried his best to sympathize with me, his new hormone-poisoned and depressed wife. But there was no way he could possibly understand. "Maybe if you just hop up and jump in the shower," he'd say, stroking my back, "you'll feel better."

He didn't understand. "There's no hopping," I'd wail. "There's no jumping!" I wanted to go home to my mom and crawl in my old bed. I wanted her to bring me soup. But there wasn't a home to go to anymore.

I was in a new place, in a new world . . . and suddenly my life was completely unrecognizable. I didn't want to be pregnant. If I'd gone ahead and moved to Chicago, I wouldn't be. I'd be away from my parents' separation and nowhere near pregnancy hormones and maybe wearing a sleek black turtleneck and eating Italian food with friends.

Italian food . . .

Ugh. I feel sick.

Chapter Twenty-seven
THE MISFIT

THE NAUSEA lingered for weeks. In the meantime, I tried my best to acclimate to my new life in the middle of nowhere. I had to get used to the fact that I lived twenty miles from the nearest grocery store. That I couldn't just run next door when I ran out of eggs. That there was no such thing as sushi. Not that it would matter, anyway. No cowboy on the ranch would touch it. *That's bait,* they'd say, laughing at any city person who would convince themselves that such a food was tasty.

And the trash truck: there wasn't one. In this strange new land, there was no infrastructure for dealing with trash. There were cows in my yard, and they pooped everywhere—on the porch, in the yard, even on my car if they happened to be walking near it when they dropped a load. There wasn't a yard crew to clean it up. I wanted to hire people, but there were no people. The reality of my situation grew more crystal clear every day.

One morning, after I choked down a bowl of cereal, I looked outside the window and saw a mountain lion sitting on the hood of my car, licking his paws—likely, I imagined, after tearing a neighboring rancher's wife from limb to limb and eating her for breakfast. I darted to the phone and called Marlboro Man, telling him there was a mountain lion sitting on my car. My heart beat inside my chest. I had no idea mountain lions were indigenous to the area.

"It's probably just a bobcat," Marlboro Man reassured me.

I didn't believe him.

"No way—it's huge," I cried. "It's seriously got to be a mountain lion!"

"I've gotta go," he said. Cows mooed in the background.

I hung up the phone, incredulous at Marlboro Man's lack of concern, and banged on the window with the palm of my hand, hoping to scare the wild cat away. But it only looked up and stared at me through the window, imagining me on a plate with a side of pureed trout.

My courtship with Marlboro Man, filled with fizzy romance, hadn't prepared me for any of this; not the mice I heard scratching in the wall next to my bed, not the flat tires I got from driving my car up and down the jagged gravel roads. Before I got married, I didn't know how to use a jack or a crowbar . . . and I didn't want to have to learn now. I didn't want to know that the smell in the laundry room was a dead rodent. I'd never smelled a dead rodent in my life: why, when I was supposed to be a young, euphoric newlywed, was I being forced to smell one now?

During the day, I was cranky. At night, I was a mess. I hadn't slept through the night once since we returned from our honeymoon. Besides the nausea, whose second evil wave typically hit right at bedtime, I was downright spooked. As I lay next to Marlboro Man, who slept like a baby every night, I thought of monsters and serial killers: Freddy Krueger and Michael Myers, Ted Bundy and Charles Manson. In the utter silence of the country, every tiny sound was amplified; I was certain if I let myself go to sleep, the murderer outside our window would get me.

And if the prospect of serial killers wasn't enough, my thoughts would invariably turn to my parents . . . to my family. My mom, happily on her own in her new one-bedroom apartment. Would I ever be able to forgive her? My dad, deeply depressed in his empty house. What if he just lost it one day and ended it all? My sister, at college and floating. Will she ever want to come home again? My brother Doug, whose bitterness over my parents' divorce was tangible. And Mike, who was exactly the same as he'd always been. I wondered why the rest of us couldn't be so blissfully oblivious to all of the human complications around us.

I was exhausted, unable to make it through one day without crying or gagging or worrying. I'd fallen in love, married a cowboy, and moved to the peaceful, bucolic countryside. But it was peace that eluded me the most.

The honeymoon was over, almost before it ever began.

*A*MID THE stack of issues facing us as a newly married couple, one thing I decided we no longer needed to worry about was the big renovation of the house next door. Marlboro Man had been dead set on continuing the project—more, I suspected, for my sake than for his. But as the work crew arrived day after day and unloaded pallets and boxes and supplies, I couldn't reconcile it with the financial turmoil I knew the ranch was in. Marlboro Man wanted to plow through and get it done—he wanted us to have a real, grown-up home when our baby arrived. But even if we made it through the remodel itself, we'd still have to furnish and fill it. I couldn't imagine picking out hinges and doorknobs and sofas in the midst of all the other stress. I didn't like the feeling of contributing to the already heavy burden.

"Hey . . . ," I said as we climbed into bed one rainy night. "What if we just put the house on hold for a while?" I reached over to my bedside table, grabbed the lemon half, and took a big sniff. Lemon halves were my new narcotic.

Marlboro Man was quiet. He worked his leg under mine and locked it into what had become its official position. It was warm.

"I think maybe we should get to a stopping point," I said. "And just put it on hold for a while."

"I've thought about it," he answered quietly. He rubbed his leg slowly up and down mine.

Feeling better, I set the lemon back on the table and reached my arm toward him, rolling over and draping my other leg over his waist and resting my head on his chest. "Well, I was thinking it might be easier for me not to worry about it with my parents and the baby and everything else." Maybe it would be more effective, I thought, if I turned the focus on me.

"Well, that makes sense," he said. "But let's talk about it tomorrow." He wrapped his other arm around my waist, and within seconds we were in a totally different world, where parents and drywall—and crippling nausea—were no longer welcome.

AFTER A few days, I brought it up again. *Our little house will be fine*, I told him. *We should just wait . . . I'm only twenty-seven . . . I haven't earned a big, huge, fancy house yet . . . I'd feel like an impostor. I don't want to have to do all that cleaning. I'll get scared with all that space. I don't like furniture shopping. I'm not in the mood to decide on paint colors. We can finish it later, when things get back to normal.* Though I knew deep down that "normal" in agriculture was probably a relative term.

Marlboro Man agreed, and after a few days of boarding up and capping off and sealing, the last of the workmen pulled away from our half-finished yellow Indian home on the prairie. And what should have been a moment of disappointment or sadness actually had the opposite effect: I didn't care one bit. I smiled, realizing that all the best things I'd imagined about marriage actually were possible—that it transcends things and possessions and plans. That no matter how much I would have loved a dishwasher and a laundry room inside the house, what I wanted most was Marlboro Man. And I had him.

Not two months into my marriage, it was a delicious moment of affirmation and clarity.

Then I realized I'd be having a baby in a few months, and I wouldn't have a dishwasher.

My heart began to race with panic.

Chapter Twenty-eight

ST. NICK IN CHAPS

NOVEMBER ROLLED around and brought with it a new hope: I woke up one cold, windy morning, and just as suddenly as it had arrived, the evil spell of nausea was gone. I could raise my head without chomping on Cocoa Puffs first. The smell of air didn't make me hurl. I could move without shuddering; shower without gagging. Marlboro Man was still working his fingers to the bone, but I was suddenly more equipped to be there for him in a way I hadn't been in the weeks before. I took pride in sorting our laundry into piles, in working to remove the mud and manure and blood from his jeans, in folding his socks and underwear and placing them in the second drawer of our small pine dresser, which barely fit inside our tiny bedroom.

The small window of time—a mere month—had made all the difference in the world. My parents were still separated, but somehow, with my renewed physical strength, I was able to put it in a place where it didn't poke me in the heart over and over. Finally, I could get through an entire day without crying.

No longer repelled by the smell of onions or raw meat, I was able to cook dinner again. I taught myself how to make things like pot roast and Salisbury steak and stew. I slowly learned, through trial and error, that some cuts of meat are tough because of their higher concentration of connective tissues, and that those cuts must be slowly cooked for hours and hours before they become tender. I went crazy with this new knowledge, cooking briskets and short ribs and arm, shoulder, and rump roasts, convinced I'd uncovered some kind of holy grail of culinary knowledge. I slow-cooked meat practically every day, and with the nausea gone, I inhaled it. I was eating for two, after all. I owed it to our growing baby.

With the nausea gone, evenings with Marlboro Man slowly began resembling the way they'd been before. We watched movies on the couch together—his head on one end, my head on the other, our legs in a tangled mess of coziness. He'd play with my toes. I'd rub his calves, which were rock hard and tough from day after day on horseback. After the purgatory of the previous weeks, things were officially delicious again.

Marlboro Man was delicious again. After a love-drenched honeymoon in Australia, we'd returned home to a bitter reality that had put a screeching halt to what should have been the most romantic days of our lives together. Since my nausea had been so bad that the mere smell of skin made me sick, it had been difficult for me to lie in bed with him some nights—let alone entertain any other thoughts. It had been a cold, frigid autumn in more ways than one. If Marlboro Man hadn't been so happy about his child developing in my body, I imagined he might have taken me back for a refund. I was so glad that this time had finally passed.

THE AIR turned colder and Thanksgiving Day arrived, marked by an enormous, warm lunchtime feast at my in-laws' house . . . and a sad postdinner evening at my dad's. It was the first time my siblings and I had been together since my parents had split, and the absence of my mother from our home left a gaping hole that was visible. It was awful and uncomfortable, a searing pain you'd give anything not to feel. My dad's eyes were gray; his face drawn; his mood morose. Betsy and I tried our best to combine our efforts in order to create the illusion of having our mother there, but it was forced and futile. I wished I could fast-forward through Christmas; I didn't want to have to feel those feelings again anytime soon.

My brother Doug had completely estranged himself from our mom. He and my sister-in-law were expecting their first baby any day, and he was understandably irked that we all had to negotiate this new family development when we should be enjoying one another's company, talking about baby names, and passing out in a turkey-induced tryptophan coma. He didn't feel like playing happy family by spending Thanksgiving at separate homes of our mother and father . . . and frankly, neither did I. It was such an avoidable death that had transpired—what about all the families who'd lost their mother to a car accident or cancer? And we lost ours . . . to marital ambivalence? Our collective anger was a bitter side dish.

My mother, well aware of how raw all of our emotions were, spent a quiet Thanksgiving at Ga-Ga's house. She called me after Marlboro Man and I returned home that night.

"Happy Thanksgiving, Ree Ree," she said in her subdued—but still sing-songy—voice.

"Thank you," I said, polite and cold. I couldn't let myself go there. I was just feeling strong again.

"Did you have a good day?" she continued.

"Yes," I replied. "We had a good meal here on the ranch, then went over to . . . to Dad's." I felt like I was talking to a stranger.

"Well . . ." Her voice trailed off. "I really missed seeing you."

I tried to speak but couldn't. I couldn't purport to know everything about my parents' marriage, who did what to whom and when. But my parents had been happy. We'd been a family. My dad had worked hard, my mom had raised four children, and at a time when they should have been reveling in the good work they'd done and really enjoying each other, my mom decided she was through.

Deep down, I knew that nothing in life was black or white. I knew that

if you weighed one side against the other throughout the whole course of their marriage, it would probably come out a wash. But that first Thanksgiving, my emotions so close to the surface and raw, my mom was the villain who'd dropped a bomb on our family. And the rest of us were wandering around in the smoldering aftermath.

"Happy Thanksgiving, Mom," I said, before hanging up the phone.

I was so mad at her, I couldn't see straight.

I went to bed and sucked on Rolaids.

*M*ARLBORO MAN had to spend the rest of Thanksgiving weekend weaning the calves that had been born the previous spring, and since I was clearly feeling better, I no longer had a get-out-of-jail (or sleep-in-till-nine) card to use. He woke me up that Saturday morning by poking my ribs with his index finger.

A groan was all I could manage. I pulled the covers over my head.

"Time to make the doughnuts," he said, peeling back the covers.

I blinked my eyes. The room was still dark. The world was still dark. It wasn't time for me to get up yet. "Doughnuts . . . huh?" I groaned, trying to lie as still as I could so Marlboro Man would forget I was there. "I don't know how."

"It's a figure of speech," he said, lying down next to me. Make the doughnuts? What? Where was I? Who was I? I was disoriented. Confused.

"C'mon," he said. "Come wean calves with me."

I opened my eyes and looked at him. My strapping husband was fully clothed, wearing Wranglers and a lightly starched blue plaid shirt. He was rubbing my slightly chubby belly, something I'd gotten used to in the previous few weeks. He liked touching my belly.

"I can't," I said, sounding wimpy. "I'm . . . I'm pregnant." I was pulling out all the stops.

"Yep, I know," he said, his gentle rub turning back into a poke again.

I writhed and wriggled and squealed, then finally relented, getting dressed and heading out the door with my strapping cowboy.

We drove a couple of miles to a pasture near his parents' house and met up with the other early risers. I rode along with one of the older cowboys in the feed truck while the rest of the crew followed the herd on horseback, all the while enjoying the perfect view of Marlboro Man out the passenger-side window. I watched as he darted and weaved in the herd, shifting his body weight and posture to nonverbally communicate to his loyal horse, Blue, how far to move from the left or to the right. I breathed in slowly, feeling a sudden burst of inexplicable pride. There was something about watching my husband—the man I was crazy in love with—riding his horse across the tallgrass prairie. It was more than the physical appeal, more than the sexiness of his chaps-cloaked body in the saddle. It was seeing him do something he loved, something he was so good at doing.

I took a hundred photos in my mind. I never wanted to forget it as long as I lived.

Back in the pens, once the herd was gathered, the men gingerly and methodically guided the calves into a separate gated area. The cows mooed and their babies bawled once they realized the extent of the physical distance between them, and my bottom lip began to tremble in sympathy. Before that moment, I had no hands-on experience of the tug of motherhood and the tangible connection between the hearts of a mother and child, whether it be bovine, equine, or human. And while I knew that what I was witnessing was a rite of passage, a normal part of agriculture, I realized for the first time that this enormous thing that would be happening in a few short months—this motherhood thing—was serious business.

It took a morning among cows for me to understand.

I GREW STRONGER and more stable, and by Christmastime, I was Wonder Woman. Completely over any semblance of morning sickness, I felt like I could do anything. I bought a Christmas tree for our house, decorating it with crocheted snowflakes given to me years earlier, ironically, by my ex J's sweet mother. My jeans, which had been pretty tight by Thanksgiving weekend, could no longer be buttoned. Desperate for a solution, I'd rigged a Goody ponytail holder through the buttonhole and stretched it across the button. It worked like a charm. I figured I'd just keep adding more ponytail holder extensions as my belly grew larger and larger. I decided I could probably get away with just wearing my regular clothes if I minded my p's and q's and didn't gain too much weight.

After the crazy fall we'd had, Marlboro Man and I chose to spend Christmas Eve alone. I didn't want to subject myself to my parental turf wars, and Marlboro Man just wanted to stay home and relax, watch movies, and enjoy life on one of the few days of the year that markets and cattle can be put on the back burner. I played a Johnny Mathis CD and made dinner for us: steaks, foil-wrapped baked potatoes, and salad with Hidden Valley Ranch dressing. I poured Dr Pepper in wine goblets and lit two tapered candles on our small farm table in our tiny kitchen.

"It's so weird that it's Christmas Eve," I said, clinking my glass to his. It was the first time I'd spent the occasion apart from my parents.

"I know," he said. "I was just thinking that." We both dug into our steaks. I wished I'd made myself two. The meat was tender and flavorful, and perfectly medium-rare. I felt like Mia Farrow in *Rosemary's Baby,* when she barely seared a steak in the middle of the afternoon and devoured it like a wolf. Except I didn't have a pixie cut. And I wasn't harboring Satan's spawn.

"Hey," I began, looking into his eyes. "I'm sorry I've been so . . . so pathetic since, like, the day we got married."

He smiled and took a swig of Dr Pepper. "You haven't been pathetic," he said. He was a terrible liar.

"I haven't?" I asked, incredulous, savoring the scrumptious red meat.

"No," he answered, taking another bite of steak and looking me squarely in the eye. "You haven't."

I was feeling argumentative. "Have you forgotten about my inner ear disturbance, which caused me to vomit all across Australia?"

He paused, then countered, "Have you forgotten about the car I rented us?"

I laughed, then struck back. "Have you forgotten about the poisonous lobster I ordered us?"

Then he pulled out all the stops. "Have you forgotten all the money we lost?"

I refused to be thwarted.

"Have you forgotten that I found out I was pregnant after we got back from our honeymoon and I called my parents to tell them and I didn't get a chance because my mom left my dad and I went on to have a nervous breakdown and had morning sickness for six weeks and now my jeans don't fit?" I was the clear winner here.

"Have you forgotten that I got you pregnant?" he said, grinning.

I smiled and took the last bite of my steak.

Marlboro Man looked down at my plate. "Want some of mine?" he asked. He'd only eaten half of his.

"Sure," I said, ravenously and unabashedly sticking my fork into a big chunk of his rib eye. I was so grateful for so many things: Marlboro Man, his outward displays of love, the new life we shared together, the child growing inside my body. But at that moment, at that meal, I was so grateful to be a carnivore again.

I took a shower after dinner and changed into comfortable Christmas Eve pajamas, ready to settle in for a couple of movies on the couch. I remembered all the Christmas Eves throughout my life—the dinners and wrapping presents and midnight mass at my Episcopal church. It all seemed so very long ago.

Walking into the living room, I noticed a stack of beautifully wrapped rectangular boxes next to the tiny evergreen tree, which glowed with little white lights. Boxes that hadn't been there minutes before.

"What . . . ," I said. We'd promised we wouldn't get each other any gifts that year. *"What?"* I demanded.

Marlboro Man smiled, taking pleasure in the surprise.

"You're in trouble," I said, glaring at him as I sat down on the beige Berber carpet next to the tree. "I didn't get you anything . . . you told me not to."

"I know," he said, sitting down next to me. "But I don't really want anything . . . except a backhoe."

I cracked up. I didn't even know what a backhoe was.

I ran my hand over the box on the top of the stack. It was wrapped in brown paper and twine—so unadorned, so simple, I imagined that Marlboro Man could have wrapped it himself. Untying the twine, I opened the first package. Inside was a pair of boot-cut jeans. The wide navy elastic waistband was a dead giveaway: they were made especially for pregnancy.

"Oh my," I said, removing the jeans from the box and laying them out on the floor in front of me. "I love them."

"I didn't want you to have to rig your jeans for the next few months," Marlboro Man said.

I opened the second box, and then the third. By the seventh box, I was the proud owner of a complete maternity wardrobe, which Marlboro Man and his mother had secretly assembled together over the previous couple of weeks. There were maternity jeans and leggings, maternity T-shirts and darling jackets. Maternity pajamas. Maternity sweats. I caressed each garment, smiling as I imagined the time it must have taken for them to put the whole collection together.

"Thank you . . . ," I began. My nose stung as tears formed in my eyes. I couldn't imagine a more perfect gift.

Marlboro Man reached for my hand and pulled me over toward him.

Our arms enveloped each other as they had on his porch the first time he'd professed his love for me. In the grand scheme of things, so little time had passed since that first night under the stars. But so much had changed. My parents. My belly. My wardrobe. Nothing about my life on this Christmas Eve resembled my life on that night, when I was still blissfully unaware of the brewing thunderstorm in my childhood home and was packing for Chicago . . . nothing except Marlboro Man, who was the only thing, amidst all the conflict and upheaval, that made any sense to me anymore.

"Are you crying?" he asked.

"No," I said, my lip quivering.

"Yep, you're crying," he said, laughing. It was something he'd gotten used to.

"I'm not crying," I said, snorting and wiping snot from my nose. "I'm not."

We didn't watch movies that night. Instead, he picked me up and carried me to our cozy bedroom, where my tears—a mixture of happiness, melancholy, and holiday nostalgia—would disappear completely.

Chapter Twenty-nine

TERROR AT THE GOLDEN ARCHES

*T*HE FIRST winter on the ranch was long and bitter cold, and I
quickly discovered that on a working cattle ranch, heavy snow
and ice does not mean cuddling close to a warm fire, wrapping in fuzzy
blankets, and sipping hot chocolate. On the contrary. The more the ice
and snow fell, the more grueling Marlboro Man's daily work became. The
cattle on the ranch, I realized quickly, were completely dependent upon
us for their survival; if they weren't provided with daily feed and hay, I
learned, they'd have no source of food, no source of warmth, and wouldn't
last three days before succumbing to the cold. Water was another concern; several days of below-freezing weather meant the ponds across the
ranch were topped with an eight-inch crown of solid ice—too thick for the
animals to break through themselves in order to drink. So Marlboro Man
made his way around the ranch, stopping at each pond and using a heavy
ax to break holes along the edge of the water so the livestock would remain
adequately hydrated.

I went feeding with him a lot. I had no reason not to; our tiny house
was so easy to keep clean and neat, there was nothing else to be done after
8:00 A.M. Our television satellite was iced over and inoperable, anyway, and
if I stretched out on the couch and tried to read a book, my gestating body
would just fall asleep. So when my new husband awoke just after daylight

and began layering on his winter gear, I'd stretch, yawn, then roll out of bed and do the same.

My cold-weather gear left a lot to be desired: black maternity leggings under boot-cut maternity jeans, and a couple of Marlboro Man's white T-shirts under an extra-large ASU sweatshirt. I was so happy to have something warm to wear that I didn't even care that I was wearing the letters of my Pac-10 rival. Add Marlboro Man's old lumberjack cap and mud boots that were four sizes too big and I was on my way to being a complete beauty queen. I seriously didn't know how Marlboro Man would be able to keep his hands off of me. If I caught a glimpse of myself in the reflection of the feed truck, I'd shiver violently.

But really, when it came right down to it, I didn't care. No matter what I looked like, it just didn't feel right sending Marlboro Man into the cold, lonely world day after day. Even though I was new at marriage, I still sensed that somehow—whether because of biology or societal conditioning or religious mandate or the position of the moon—it was I who was to be the cushion between Marlboro Man and the cruel, hard world. That it was I who'd needed to dust off his shoulders every day. And though he didn't say it, I could tell that he felt better when I was bouncing along, chubby and carrying his child, in his feed truck next to him.

Occasionally I'd hop out of the pickup and open gates. Other times he'd hop out and open them. Sometimes I'd drive while he threw hay off the back of the vehicles. Sometimes I'd get stuck and he'd say shit. Sometimes we'd just sit in silence, shivering as the vehicle doors opened and closed. Other times we'd engage in serious conversation or stop and make out in the snow.

All the while, our gestating baby rested in the warmth of my body, blissfully unaware of all the work that awaited him on this ranch where his dad had grown up. As I accompanied Marlboro Man on those long, frigid mornings of work, I wondered if our child would ever know the fun of sledding on a golf course hill . . . or any hill, for that matter. I'd lived on the

ranch for five months and didn't remember ever hearing about anyone sledding . . . or playing golf . . . or participating in any recreational activities at all. I was just beginning to wrap my mind around the way daily life unfolded here: wake up early, get your work done, eat, relax, and go to bed. Repeat daily. There wasn't a calendar of events or dinner dates with friends in town or really much room for recreation—because that just meant double the work when you got back to work. It was hard for me not to wonder when any of these people ever went out and had a good time, or built a snowman.

Or slept past 5:00 A.M.

O N THE cusp of spring, the ice began to melt, the frigid cold passed, and my belly continued to expand. Calves began dropping to the ground, and the smell of burning grass filled the countryside.

As my girth increased, so did my vanity level, no doubt because I felt the need to overcompensate for the dreaded Frumpy-Barefoot-Pregnant stereotype that had somehow taken root in my mind. I spent more time primping, scrubbing, and polishing, all in an attempt to look sexy and vibrant at home. I tried with all my might to keep control of my weight gain, pushing away the Cheetos and sweets and walking a mile or two every evening. I needed to lighten up and embrace the miracle of the life growing inside of me. But whatever—I still wanted to look hot. And so I did what I had to do to survive.

For the few days preceding my monthly OB checkup, I was especially vigilant. I was keeping a pregnancy weight journal, and for my emotional well-being I grew to crave the nurse's *ooohs* and *aaahs* over my staying within the recommended weight range at each appointment. I needed to see my meticulous, weight-conscious doctor nod in approval as he reviewed the number. It was like lifeblood being pumped into my veins, and satisfied my ever-shallow ambition to be the Hot Pregnant Wife of the Century.

And frankly, it gave me a goal to strive for until the following month's appointment.

Plus, it meant that immediately following my monthly checkups, I got to splurge at McDonald's. I'd always schedule my doctor visits right at 9:00 A.M. and wouldn't allow myself to eat breakfast beforehand, lest the mere volume of the food skew the weigh-in result. So by the time I made the hour-long drive to the doctor's office in my hometown and endured the thirty-minute appointment, I was ravenous. Violently hungry. McDonald's was the only thing that could satisfy.

The second I exited the medical building, I'd sprint from the door to my car, breaking speed records to get to the Golden Arches because I knew that there, heaven awaited. It was there that I'd get to indulge in my Monthly Feast: two breakfast burritos, a bacon, egg, and cheese biscuit, hash browns, and—perfect for my growing baby—a large Dr Pepper. And I couldn't even wait till I exited the parking lot. Seconds after I'd pull away from the drive-thru, I'd rip into the first burrito and finish it off before even making it to the highway. I had one purpose and one purpose only: *I must ingest this breakfast burrito immediately or I will die of hunger.* So I'd insert the burrito as far into my mouth as it would go and bite off about half of it, then chew and swallow as quickly as I could so I could feel the immediate rush of satisfaction that comes from a gestating body finally getting the calories it deserves.

It was hunger like none I'd ever experienced.

This continued till Easter, when a good family friend invited my sister, Betsy, and me to attend a shower in honor of their daughter, who was getting married that summer. It was the first time I'd made an official appearance in my hometown since the wedding, and I made sure I was dressed and made up to the hilt. I'd likely be seeing many people from my premarriage life that I hadn't seen in a while, and I wanted everyone to see that I was happy and fulfilled and positively thriving in my new life as a rancher's pregnant wife.

When I arrived, I immediately saw the mother of an ex-boyfriend, the kind of ex-boyfriend that would make you want to look as good as possible if you ran into his mother at a shower when you were several months pregnant. She saw me, smiled politely, and made her way across the room to visit with me. We hugged, exchanged pleasantries, and caught up on what we'd both been doing. As we talked, I fantasized about her reporting to her son, my ex, the next day. *Oh, you should have seen Ree. She was positively glowing! You should have seen how wonderful she looked! Don't you wish you had married her?*

Deep into our small talk, I made mention of how long it had been since she and I had seen each other. "Well . . . I did see you recently," she replied. "But I don't think you saw me."

I couldn't imagine. "Oh really?" I asked. "Where?" I hardly ever came to my hometown.

"Well," she continued. "I saw you pulling out of McDonald's on Highway Seventy-five one morning a few weeks ago. I waved to you . . . but you didn't see me."

My insides suddenly shriveled, imagining myself violently shoving breakfast burritos into my mouth. "McDonald's? Really?" I said, trying my best to play dumb.

"Yes," my ex's mother replied, smiling. "You looked a little . . . hungry!"

"Hmmm," I said. "I don't think that was me."

I skulked away to the bathroom, vowing to eat granola for the rest of my pregnancy.

Chapter Thirty
THE PLAINSWOMAN

*S*PRING FLEW by and summer quickly arrived; my belly grew right alongside the daylilies, zinnias, and tomatoes Marlboro Man's mom had helped me plant in a small garden outside the house. For Marlboro Man, the coming of the baby proved to be an effective diversion from the aftermath of the previous fall's market woes. More and more, it looked like Marlboro Man might have to sell some of his land in order to keep the rest of the ranch afloat. As someone who didn't grow up on a ranch, I failed to feel the gravity of the situation. You have a problem, you have an asset, you sell the asset, you solve the problem. But for Marlboro Man, it could never be that simple or sterile. For a ranching family, putting together a ranch takes time—sometimes years, even generations of patiently waiting for this pasture or that to become available. For a rancher, the words of Pa in *Gone With the Wind* ring beautifully and painfully true: *Land is the only thing worth working for . . . worth fighting for, worth dying for. Because it's the only thing that lasts. . . .* The thought of parting with a part of the family's ranch was a painful prospect; Marlboro Man felt the sting daily. To me it seemed like an easy fix; to Marlboro Man, it was a personal failure. There was nothing I could do to make it better except to be there to catch him in my arms every night, which I willingly and eagerly did. I was a soft, lumpy pillow. With heartburn and swollen ankles.

"Your belly's getting *big,*" he said one night.

"I know," I answered, looking down. It was kind of hard to deny.

"I love it," he said, stroking it with the palm of his hand. I recoiled a little, remembering the black bikini I'd worn on our honeymoon and how comparatively concave my belly looked then, and hoping Marlboro Man had long since put the image out of his mind.

"Hey, what are we naming this thing?" he asked, even as the "thing" fluttered and kicked in my womb.

"Oh, man . . ." I sighed. "I have no idea. Zachary?" I pulled it out of my wazoo.

"Eh," he said, uninspired. "Shane?" Oh no. Here go the old movies.

"I went to my senior prom with a Shane," I answered, remembering dark and mysterious Shane Ballard.

"Okay, scratch that," he said. "How about . . . how about Ashley?" How far was he going to take this?

I remembered a movie we'd watched on our fifteenth date or so. "How about Rooster Cogburn?"

He chuckled. I loved it when he chuckled. It meant everything was okay and he wasn't worried or stressed or preoccupied. It meant we were dating and sitting on his old porch and my parents weren't divorcing. It meant my belly button wasn't bulbous and deformed. His chuckles were like a drug to me. I tried to elicit them daily.

"What if it's a girl?" I said.

"Oh, it's a boy," he said with confidence. "I'm positive."

I didn't respond. How could I argue with that?

*M*ORE AND more, I began helping around the homestead. I learned to operate my John Deere mower so I could keep the yard around our house—and our half-remodeled, boarded-up yellow brick house—neatly trimmed. Marlboro Man was working like a dog in the Oklahoma summer, and I wanted to make our homestead a haven for him. The heat was so stifling, though, all I could stand to wear was a loose-fitting maternity tank top and a pair of Marlboro Man's white Jockey boxers, which I gracefully pulled down below my enormous belly. As I rode on the bouncy green mower in my heavily pregnant state, my mind couldn't help but travel back to the long country drive I'd taken when I was engaged to Marlboro Man, when we'd stumbled upon the old homestead and found the half-naked woman mowing her yard. And here I was: *I had become that woman*. And it had happened in less than a year. I caught a glimpse of myself in the reflection of our bedroom window and couldn't believe what I was seeing. The Playtex bra was all I was missing.

I was nesting now, completely powerless to stop the urge to give our entire house, yard, and garage a daily scrubbing. Inexplicably, I began cleaning baseboards for the first time in my life. I wiped down the insides of cabinets and made lists of what to dust on what days of the week. Monday was the top of the fridge. Tuesday was the top of the cabinet in the bathroom. Every day I washed and dried Onesies, burp cloths, and tiny socks in an intoxicating potion of Dreft and Downy; our whole house smelled like a white, puffy cloud.

Marlboro Man was so excited for his son to be born. We'd elected not to have the gender-identifying sonogram, but he was convinced, as was I, that it was going to be a boy. Marlboro Man had grown up in a house with two brothers, on a ranch full of cowboys. A son would come first; it was simply predestined.

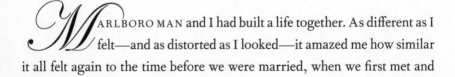

MARLBORO MAN and I had built a life together. As different as I felt—and as distorted as I looked—it amazed me how similar it all felt again to the time before we were married, when we first met and fell in love. We had been very much in our own little world then—spending 95 percent of our time together alone. Now, in our little house on the prairie, it was still just the two of us. In an effort to spin optimism out of the sorrow of my parents' split, I told myself that their separation, paradoxically, had actually brought Marlboro Man and me closer together. If I'd had a home to go to—one still thriving with a mother and a father and all of the warmth with which I'd been surrounded as a child—I might have been tempted to visit home more often. To fold laundry with my mom. To sit and visit and cook and bake and maybe spend slightly less time at home with my new husband who, it turned out, had needed me so much over the previous several months. So it was good, I told myself. In the long run, this whole divorce ordeal would all prove to be good.

But it really wasn't good at all. My dad was having a hard time, and in my growing concern, I'd taken to visiting him weekly to assess how he was doing. And seeing him still so despondent, I couldn't help but project my irritation onto my mother. Why was I having to bear the burden of worry over my father's emotional health when I should be spending all my time in anticipation over the birth of my baby?

And that really got me going. What was going to happen when I had the baby? Such a monumental event would surely warrant both my parents being present at the hospital, which was a scenario so horrifying to me that I began to lose sleep about it. My parents hadn't seen each other since the day my mother left our house; how would my sanity survive such a meeting occurring while I'm in labor or recovering? After stewing about it for several nights, I decided I had no choice but to call my mom and be honest about my dread.

"Hi, Mom," I said, my voice as far away from warm as I could muster. "Can I talk to you about something?"

"Sure, Ree Ree," she said, positive and chirpy.

I let it out, explaining that while I'd love for her to be present at the hospital, I just wasn't sure that was the best time for there to be a face-to-face

encounter with my dad. It wasn't that I didn't want her there, I explained—
it was really more about me. The day would be stressful enough without my
having to worry about everyone else's feelings.

She understood. Or, if she didn't, she wasn't about to argue with a nine-
months-pregnant woman.

I checked this item of worry off my to-do list, right along with the
sterilized refrigerator, sparkling baseboards, Q-tipped doorknobs, and
Cloroxed floors.

Everything was in place.

I was ready.

Chapter Thirty-one
THE HILLS RUN PINK

A WEEK BEFORE my due date, Marlboro Man had to preg-test a hundred cows. Preg-testing cows, I would learn in horror that warm June morning, does not involve the cow urinating on a test stick and waiting at least three minutes to read the result. Instead, a large animal vet inserts his entire arm into a long disposable glove, then inserts the gloved arm high into the rectum of a pregnant cow until the vet's arm is no longer visible. Once his arm is deep inside the cow's nether regions, the vet can feel the size and angle of the cow's cervix and determine two things:

1. Whether or not she is pregnant.
2. How far along she is.

With this information, Marlboro Man decides whether to rebreed the nonpregnant cows, and in which pasture to place the pregnant cows; cows that became bred at the same time will stay in the same pasture so that they'll all give birth in approximately the same time frame.

Of course, I understood none of this as I watched the doctor insert the entire length of his arm into a hundred different cows' bottoms. All I knew is that he'd insert his arm, the cow would moo, he would pull out his arm, and the cow would poop. Unintentionally, each time a new cow would pass through the chute, I'd instinctively bear down. I was just as pregnant as many of the cows. My nether regions were uncomfortable enough as it was. The thought of someone inserting their . . .

It was more than I probably should have signed up for that morning.

"God help me!" I yelped as Marlboro Man and I pulled away from the working area after the last cow was tested. "What in the name of all that is holy did I just witness?"

"How'd you like that?" Marlboro Man asked, smiling a satisfied smile. He loved introducing me to new ranching activities. The more shocking I found them, the better.

"Seriously," I mumbled, grasping my enormous belly as if to protect my baby from the reality of this bizarre, disturbing world. "That was just . . . that was like nothing I've ever seen before!" It made the rectal thermometer episode I'd endured many months earlier seem like a garden party.

Marlboro Man laughed and rested his hand on my knee. It stayed there the rest of the drive home.

At eleven that night, I woke up feeling strange. Marlboro Man and I had just drifted off to sleep, and my abdomen felt tight and weird. I stared at the ceiling, breathing deeply in an effort to will it away. But then I put two and two together: the whole trauma of what I'd seen earlier in the day must have finally caught up with me. In my sympathy for the preg-tested cows, I must have borne down a few too many times.

I sat up in bed. I was definitely in labor.

IMMEDIATELY, I kicked into gear and did what the plan dictated: I got out of bed and took a shower, washing every last inch of myself until I squeaked. I shaved my legs all the way up to my groin and dried my hair and curled it, and put on layers of shimmery makeup. By the time I gently tapped Marlboro Man on the shoulder and told him the news, I looked like I was ready for a night on the town . . . and the contractions were intense enough to make me stop in my tracks and wait until they passed.

"What?" Marlboro Man raised his head off the pillow and looked at me, disoriented.

"I'm in labor," I whispered. Why was I whispering?

"Seriously?" he replied, sitting up and looking at my belly, as if it would look any different.

Marlboro Man threw on his clothes and brushed his teeth, and within minutes we were in the car, driving to the hospital over sixty miles away. My labor was progressing; I could tell. I felt like something was inside my body and wanted to come out.

It was a normal sensation, given the circumstances.

AN HOUR later we were pulling into the hospital parking lot. Sparkly and shiny from my hair and makeup job, I had to stop and bend over six times between the car and the front door of the hospital. I literally couldn't take a step until each contraction ended. Within an hour after checking in, I was writhing on a hospital bed in all-encompassing pain and wishing once again that I'd gone ahead and moved to Chicago. It had become my default response when things got rough in my life: morning sickness? I should have moved to Chicago. Cow manure in my yard? Chicago would have been a better choice. Contractions less than a minute apart? Windy City, come and get me.

Finally, I reached my breaking point. It's an indescribable feeling, the throes of hard labor—that mind-numbing total body cramp whose origin you can't even begin to wrap your head around. After trying to be strong and tough in front of Marlboro Man, I finally gave up and gripped the bedsheet and clenched my teeth. I groaned and moaned and pushed the nurse button and whimpered to Marlboro Man, "I can't do this anymore." When the nurse came into the room moments later, I begged her to put me out of my misery. My salvation arrived five minutes later in the form of an eight-inch needle, and when the medicine hit I nearly began to cry. The relief was indescribably sweet.

I was so blissfully pain-free, I fell asleep. And when I woke up confused and disoriented an hour later, a nurse named Heidi was telling me it was time to push. Almost immediately, Dr. Oliver entered the room, fully scrubbed and wearing a mask.

"Are you ready, Mama?" Marlboro Man asked, standing near my shoulders as the nurse draped my legs and adjusted the fetal monitor, which was strapped around my middle. I felt like I'd woken up in the middle of a party. But the weirdest party ever—one where the hostess was putting my feet in stirrups.

I ordered Marlboro Man to remain north of my belly button as nurses scurried into place. I'd made it clear beforehand: *I didn't want him down there*. I wanted him to continue to get to know me the old-fashioned way—and besides, that's what we were paying the doctor for.

"Go ahead and push once for me," Dr. Oliver said.

I did, but only hard enough to ensure that nothing accidental or embarrassing would slip out. I could think of no greater humiliation.

"Okay, that's not going to work at all," Dr. Oliver scolded.

I pushed again.

"Ree," Dr. Oliver said, looking up at me through the space between my legs. "You can do way better than that."

He'd watched me grow up in the ballet company in our town. He'd watched me contort and leap and spin in everything from *The Nutcracker* to *Swan Lake* to *A Midsummer Night's Dream*. He knew I had the fortitude to will a baby from my loins.

That's when Marlboro Man grabbed my hand, as if to impart to me, his sweaty and slightly weary wife, a measure of his strength and endurance.

"Come on, honey," he said. "You can do it."

A few tense moments later, our baby was born.

Except it wasn't a baby boy. It was a seven-pound, twenty-one-inch baby girl.

It was the most important moment of my life.

And more ways than one, it was a pivotal moment for Marlboro Man.

Chapter Thirty-two
UNFORGIVEN

I LAY THERE, depleted and relieved that whatever used to be in my body was now out. Marlboro Man, on the other hand, was stunned. Patting me affectionately, he stared at our newborn baby girl with a shocked expression he couldn't have hidden if he'd tried. "Congratulations," Dr. Oliver had said moments before. "You have a daughter."

You have a daughter. In the previous several months of gestation, I'd been so indoctrinated with the notion that we were having a boy, it hadn't even occurred to me that things might go the other way. I couldn't even imagine Marlboro Man's surprise.

"Good job, Mama," he said, leaning down and kissing my forehead. The nurses immediately wrapped our little one in a white blanket and set her on my chest. Plop. There she was. Lying on top of me. Writhing and looking pink and pitiful and about as precious as anything I'd ever seen. Marlboro Man grasped my hand, squeezing it softly. "Wow," he said, almost in a whisper. He stared and stared. We were totally quiet. We could hardly move.

My throat began to tighten as I realized what had just happened. The being that had been growing inside of my abdomen, that had tapped and kicked and pummeled me in the ribs and bladder during those final weeks, that had brought me heartburn and exhaustion and weeks of debilitating nausea, was now lying on my chest, looking around this strange new world in which she found herself. It was the most surreal moment of my life—more surreal than any moment of surprise during my courtship with Marlboro Man, the father of this new human that had just arrived on the scene and changed absolutely everything. She had arms and legs and a nose and a tongue, which she slowly thrust in and out of her tiny mouth in an effort to familiarize herself with the sensation of air. She was a person—alive and moving around in a real world. I realized that tears were rolling down my face. I hadn't even noticed I was crying.

WHEN MARLBORO Man and I had gotten married, he had his sights set on starting a family *sooner* rather than *later.* I was slightly more ambivalent; I knew having a child would probably wind up somewhere in our future, but I hadn't exactly been chomping at the bit to procreate. When I'd "turned up" pregnant five weeks after our wedding day, no one had been more excited than Marlboro Man.

That's partly because he just *knew* we'd be having a son. Aside from the occasional visit from a female cousin, Marlboro Man and his brothers hadn't had much contact with or interaction with girls. His mother had been a positive female role model, but most all of the day-to-day ranching activity involved nothing but men.

I could feel his disappointment hovering thick in the air. Though he made every effort to appear supportive and pleased, I could tell that Marlboro Man was utterly shocked, just as anyone would be whose life had just—in one, single, amniotic fluid-drenched instant—metamorphosed into something completely different from what he had always imagined it would be.

Once the baby was assessed and declared healthy and the nurses went about the unenviable job of cleaning up my nether regions, Marlboro Man picked up the phone to call his parents, who had coincidentally taken a two-day trip, not expecting I'd go into labor when I did.

"It's a girl," I heard Marlboro Man tell his mom. Nurses dabbed my bottom with gauze. "Ree did great," he continued. "The baby's fine." The doctor opened up a suture kit.

I took a few deep breaths, staring at the baby's striped knit cap, placed on her head by one of the nurses. Marlboro Man spoke quietly to his parents, answering their questions and providing them with details about when we'd gone to the hospital and how it had all gone. I drifted in and out of listening to him talk; I was too busy trying to assimilate what had just happened to me. Then, toward the end of the conversation, I heard him ask his mother a question.

"So . . . what do you do with girls?" he said.

His mother knew the answer, of course. Though she hadn't had any girls of her own, she herself had been the oldest child of a rancher and had grown up being her father's primary ranch hand throughout her childhood years. She knew better than anyone "what you do with girls" on a working ranch.

"The same thing you do with boys," she answered.

I chuckled softly when Marlboro Man relayed his mom's sentiments. For the first time in our relationship, he was the one in a foreign land.

A LITTLE WHILE later, I found myself waking, groggy and nauseated, from a deep sleep in a regular hospital room. Disoriented, I glanced around the room and finally found Marlboro Man, who was quietly parked in a comfortable chair in the corner and holding our flannel-wrapped little bundle. He was wearing faded jeans and a white T-shirt—the best he could manage the night before, when my unexpected labor had yanked us both out of bed. His muscular arms holding our baby were almost too much for me to take. Just as I sat up to take a closer look, the baby stretched out her two arms and made a series of tiny gurgling sounds. I was not in Kansas anymore.

"Hey, Mama," Marlboro Man said, smiling.

I smiled back, unable to take my eyes off the sight in front of me. Those Hallmark commercials weren't kidding. A man holding a newborn baby was a beautiful thing to behold. My stomach growled, then gurgled.

"Wow," I said. "I'm really hungry." And just like that, out of the blue, it hit me. I glanced around the room frantically, knowing I was seconds away from losing it. Fortunately, I found a clean trash can parked right beside my bed and grabbed it just in time to absolutely fill it with projectile vomit. It was chartreuse and abundant, and splattered the lily white trash bag like a Pollock canvas. I snorted and sniffed and coughed. I felt like a demon.

I could hear Marlboro Man getting up. "You okay?" he said, clearly not knowing what the heck he was supposed to be doing. I grabbed a wad of Kleenexes and wiped the corners of my mouth. As mortified as I was, my stomach felt a hundred times better.

A nurse entered the room just after I set down the trash can. "How you doing?" she asked with a sweet smile. Little did she know the fun she'd just missed.

"Uh . . . I," I began.

"She just threw up," Marlboro Man, still holding the baby, reported. I got a whiff of the vomit and hoped Marlboro Man wasn't smelling it, too.

"Oh, you did?" the nurturing nurse said, looking around at the unmistakable evidence.

"Yeah," I said. "I think it was just all the medication. I feel better now." I hiccupped loudly and rested my head back on the pillow.

The nurse did some cleaning up and whisked away the trash can as I lay there staring at the ceiling. I felt better physically, but it shocked me just how far I'd fallen. Months earlier, I couldn't even bear the thought of sweating in front of Marlboro Man. Now I'd hurled a bright greenish yellow liquid all over the room as he held our peacefully sleeping baby. I could see the last of my dignity swirl down a big, nasty drain on the floor.

Before I could change the subject and begin talking to Marlboro Man about the weather, the chipper nurse returned to the room and sat down on the end of my bed with a clipboard.

"I need to check your vitals, hon," she explained. It had been several hours since I'd given birth. I guess this was the routine.

She felt my pulse, palpated my legs, asked if I had pain anywhere, and lightly pressed on my abdomen, the whole while making sure I wasn't showing signs of a blockage or a blood clot, a fever or a hemorrhage. I stared dreamily at Marlboro Man, who gave me a wink or two. I hoped he would, in time, be able to see past the vomit.

The nurse then began a battery of questions.

"So, no pain?"

"Nope. I feel fine now."

"No chills?"

"Not at all."

"Have you been able to pass gas in the past few hours?"

Insert awkward ten-second pause

I couldn't have heard her right. "What?" I asked, staring at her.

"Have you been able to pass gas lately?"

Another awkward pause

What kind of question is this? "Wait . . . ," I asked. *"What?"*

"Sweetie, have you been able to pass gas today?"

I stared at her blankly. "I don't . . ."

" . . . Pass gas? You? Today?" She was unrelenting. I continued my blank, desperate stare, completely incapable of registering her question.

Throughout the entire course of my pregnancy, I'd gone to great lengths to maintain a certain level of glamour and vanity. Even during labor, I'd attempted to remain the ever-fresh and vibrant new wife, going so far as to reapply tinted lip balm before the epidural so I wouldn't look pale. I'd also restrained myself during the pushing stage, afraid I'd lose control of my bowels, which would have been the kiss of death upon my pride and my marriage; I would have had to just divorce my husband and start fresh with someone else.

I had never once so much as passed gas in front of Marlboro Man. As far as he was concerned, my body lacked this function altogether.

So why was I being forced to answer these questions now? I hadn't done anything wrong.

"I'm sorry . . . ," I stammered. " I don't understand the question. . . ."

The nurse began again, seemingly unconcerned with my lack of comprehension skills. "Have you . . ."

Marlboro Man, lovingly holding our baby and patiently listening all this time from across the room, couldn't take it anymore. "Honey! She wants to know if you've been able to *fart* today!"

The nurse giggled. "Okay, well maybe that's a little more clear."

I pulled the covers over my head.

I was not having this discussion.

$\mathcal{L}$ATE THAT evening, I begged Marlboro Man to go back to the ranch to sleep. We'd had visits from my dad, our grandmothers, my best friend, Becky, and Mike. My mom had even peeked her head in once she'd determined the coast was clear, and I'd been poked and prodded and checked by nurses all day long. I felt tired and gross, not having been given permission to shower yet, and I didn't want him to sleep on a hard cot in the room. Plus, I couldn't risk being asked about my bodily functions in his presence again. "Go home and get some sleep," I said. "I'll still be here in the morning."

He didn't put up much of a fight. He was exhausted; I could tell. I was exhausted, too—but I was supposed to be. I needed Marlboro Man to stay strong.

"Good night, Mama," he said, kissing my head. I loved this new

"Mama" thing. He kissed our baby on the cheek. She grunted and twisted. I moved my face to hers and inhaled. Why hadn't anyone ever told me babies smelled so good?

After Marlboro Man left, the room was beautifully quiet. I nestled more deeply into the surprisingly comfortable hospital bed and cradled the baby like a football, unbuttoning my peach pajama top and hooking her on for the tenth time in the past several hours. She'd struggled on the previous tries, but this time—almost in an effort to comfort me now that Marlboro Man had left—she opened her tiny mouth and latched on. I closed my eyes, laid my head back on the pillow, and savored my first moments alone with my child.

Seconds later, the door to my room opened and my brother-in-law, Tim, walked in. He'd just finished working a huge load of cattle. Marlboro Man would have been, too, if I hadn't gone into labor the night before.

"Hey!" Tim said enthusiastically. "How's it going?"

I yanked the bedsheet far enough north to cover the baby's head and my exposed breast; as much as I loved my new brother-in-law, I just couldn't see myself being that open with him. He caught on immediately.

"Oops—did I come at a bad time?" Tim asked, a deer caught in the headlights.

"You just missed your brother," I said. The baby's lips fell off my nipple and she rooted around and tried to find it again. I tried to act like nothing was happening under the covers.

"No kidding?" Tim asked, looking nervously around the room. "Oh, I should have called first."

"Come on in," I said, sitting up in the bed as tall as I could. The epidural had definitely worn off. My bottom was beginning to throb.

"How's the baby?" he asked, wanting to look but unsure if he should look in her direction.

"She's great," I answered, pulling the little one out from under the covers. I prayed I could get my nipple quickly tucked away without incident.

Tim smiled as he regarded his new niece. "She's so cute," he said tenderly. "Can I hold her?" He reached out his arms like a child wanting to hold a puppy.

"Sure," I said, handing her over, my bottom stinging by now. All I could think about was getting in the shower and spraying it with the nozzle I'd noticed earlier in the day when the nurse escorted me to the bathroom. I'd started obsessing over it, in fact. The nozzle was all I could think about.

Tim seemed as surprised at the baby's gender as his brother had been. "I was shocked when I heard!" he said, looking at me with a smile. I laughed, imagining what Marlboro Man's dad might be thinking. That the first grandchild in such a male-dominated ranching family turned out to be a girl was becoming more humorous to me each minute. This was going to be an adventure.

As Tim held the baby, I rested my head back on the pillow; I was too tired to hold it together much longer.

"How's she eating?" Tim asked. A funny question. He seemed genuinely interested.

"Pretty good," I said, squirming a little bit at the subject matter. "I think she'll catch on after a while."

Catch on? Latch on? I was so confused.

"You're feeding her your own milk, right?" Tim asked awkwardly.

Feeding her your own milk?

Oh dear.

"Um, yes . . . ," I answered. "I'm br . . . I'm breast-feeding." Tim, could you please go now?

Then he let me have it. "You know, you need to be careful not to get a sour bag."

I sat there, staring blankly ahead. Little did I know it was but one of the many times my brother-in-law would draw a parallel between me and livestock.

Chapter Thirty-three

TOMBSTONE

TWO DAYS later, on a stifling hot midsummer afternoon, Marlboro Man packed my hospital bags into his pickup, buckled our seven-pounder into her comparatively huge car seat, and helped me into the backseat for our drive back home to the ranch. I should have been so happy—I had the guy and the baby and she was healthy and the sun was shining—but it didn't feel right to me, the whole leaving-the-hospital thing. I wasn't ready at all. I'd just gotten used to the beeping of the monitors and the coziness of the warm, secure hospital room. I'd grown accustomed to the nurses checking on me every couple of hours . . . and candy stripers bringing me warm meals of stew, mashed potatoes, and green beans. At the hospital, I knew what to expect. In two short days, I'd mastered it. I had no idea what would be waiting for me at home.

When Marlboro Man pulled away from the hospital, it hit me: instantly, I felt desperate and alone. Pressing my face against the window, I acted like I was asleep . . . and quietly sobbed the whole way home. I wanted my mom, but I'd pushed her away to the point where she was keeping her distance out of respect for my wishes. If only she were at the other end of this hour-long drive, everything would be okay.

We got home to find twenty cows in our yard. "Dammit," Marlboro Man muttered under his breath, as if this was the last thing he needed right then. That made me cry harder, and I could no longer shield Marlboro Man from the sounds of my wailing. As he got out of the car, he looked back at me and said, "What's *wrong?*" He moved toward me, more than likely concerned at the unexpected sight of my swollen, red, puffy face. "What happened?"

"I want to go back to the hospital!" I cried. A cow dropped a fresh green load on my daylilies.

"What's wrong?" Marlboro Man asked again. "Seriously . . . are you in pain?"

That only served to make me feel foolish, as if I would have no good excuse to lose it unless I was hemorrhaging out of my ears. I sobbed even harder, and the baby began to wriggle. "I just don't feel right," I cried again. "I feel . . . I don't know how to do anything!"

Marlboro Man wrapped me in his arms, completely clueless as to what to do. "Let's go inside," he said, rubbing my back. "It's hot out here." He unbuckled the baby's car seat and pulled her out of the car, and the three of us walked past the cows and toward the house. My echinacea blooms were all missing their petals. *Stupid rabbits,* I thought. I'll kill 'em with my bare hands if they go near my flowers again. Then I started crying harder that I'd even had such a thought.

We walked into our house, which was spotless and smelled of Clorox and lemon. A vase of fresh flowers sat on our dining table in the breakfast nook. Not a thing was out of place. I took a deep breath and exhaled . . . and suddenly everything felt better. The baby was fussing now—she'd been in the car seat since we'd left the hospital over an hour earlier—so I pulled her out, lay down on the bed with her, and started nursing. Almost immediately, the two of us fell into a deep sleep. When I woke up, it was almost dark. I hoped it was early the next morning, which would have meant we'd slept all night long . . . but, in fact, only an hour had passed since we'd dozed off.

After I woke up, splashed cold water on my face, and drank nearly a gallon of orange juice, our first evening home turned out to be dreamy: Marlboro Man and I ate pieces of a casserole his mom had left in our fridge earlier in the day. For dessert we feasted on a homemade angel food cake his grandmother, Edna Mae, had brought by. Edna Mae's angel food cakes were light . . . fluffy . . . perfect. She'd gone the extra mile with this one and coated it with a creamy white seven-minute frosting, then chilled the iced cake to perfection. I gobbled down three pieces without even knowing I'd taken a bite. It was lifeblood for my postpartum body.

After dinner Marlboro man and I sat on the sofa in our dimly lit house and marveled at the new little life before us. Her sweet little grunts . . . her impossibly tiny ears . . . how peacefully she slept, wrinkled and warm, in front of us. We unwrapped her from her tight swaddle, then wrapped her again. Then we unwrapped her and changed her diaper, then wrapped her again. Then we put her in the crib for the night, patted her sweet belly, and went to bed ourselves, where we fell dead asleep in each other's arms, blissful that the hard part was behind us. A full night's sleep was all I needed, I reckoned, before I felt like myself again. The sun would come out tomorrow . . . I was sure of it.

We were sleeping soundly when I heard the baby crying twenty minutes later. I shot out of bed and went to her room. *She must be hungry,* I thought, and fed her in the glider rocking chair before putting her in her crib and going back to bed myself. Forty-five minutes after my head hit the pillow, I was awakened again to the sound of crying. Looking at the clock, I was sure I was having a bad dream. Bleary-eyed, I stumbled to her room again and repeated the feeding ritual. *Hmmm,* I thought as I tried to keep from nodding off in the chair. *This is strange. She must have some sort of problem,* I imagined—*maybe that cowlick or colic I'd heard about in a movie somewhere? Goiter or gouter or gout?* Strange diagnoses pummeled my sleep-deprived brain. Before the sun came up, I'd gotten up six more times, each time thinking it had to be the last, and if it wasn't, it might actually kill me.

I woke up the next morning, the blinding sun shining in my eyes. Marl-

boro Man was walking in our room, holding our baby girl, who was crying hysterically in his arms.

"I tried to let you sleep," he said. "But she's not having it." He looked helpless, like a man completely out of options.

My eyes would hardly open. "Here." I reached out, motioning Marlboro Man to place the little suckling in the warm spot on the bed beside me. Eyes still closed, I went into autopilot mode, unbuttoning my pajama top and moving my breast toward her face, not caring one bit that Marlboro Man was standing there watching me. The baby found what she wanted and went to town.

Marlboro Man sat on the bed and played with my hair. "You didn't get much sleep," he said.

"Yeah," I said, completely unaware that what had happened the night before had been completely normal . . . and was going to happen again every night for the next month at least. "She must not have been feeling great."

"I've got to go meet a truck," Marlboro Man said. "But I'll be back around eleven."

I waved good-bye without even looking up. I couldn't take my eyes off my baby. As she lay there and sucked, I began to feel strange. My entire chest felt tight and warm to the touch, and my breasts, I noticed, were larger than I ever remembered them being—even in the last days of my pregnancy. Once the baby fell asleep again, I made my way to the shower. It was the only thing that could possibly pump some life into my sleep-deprived body. I let the warm water fall on my face and sting my eyes, hoping to somehow wash away the utter exhaustion that had taken over. Slowly, three minutes in, I began to feel better . . . just in time to notice that the tight, uncomfortable feeling in my chest had returned with a vengeance. I glanced down to find, to my horror, that my breasts had become spigots, both shooting milk eight inches in front of my body.

And they showed absolutely no signs of stopping. They sprayed and sprayed.

If I, the daughter of a physician, had been prepared for the medical side of pregnancy and childbirth, I was completely dumbfounded by this development. Nothing could have prepared me for the horror.

That night, Marlboro Man invited Tim over to our house. I hid in my bedroom the entire time, clutching towels to my bosom and trying desperately to get my now-fussy, squirming baby to relieve the building pressure in my breasts . . . while at the same time avoiding any kind of interaction with Marlboro Man and Tim. I was way too busy trying to assimilate what was happening with my body and my mind—not to mention my life—to hold any kind of coherent conversation.

They were invaders, anyway—those men in my living room. Invaders who didn't belong in my nest with my new baby bird. They were dodo birds . . . maybe grackles. I'd peck them if they got too close. *Why were they in my nest, anyway?*

Later that night, just as I was dozing off, I heard cries and yells from the other room as Marlboro Man and Tim watched Mike Tyson bite off Evander Holyfield's ear on live TV. The baby, who'd finally, at long last, gone to sleep moments earlier, woke up and began to cry again.

It was official: I was in hell.

Chapter Thirty-four
TEARS WON'T WATER STEERS

MY MILK had burst onto the scene with a vengeance, and eating became the baby's new vocation. The next two weeks of her life marked the end of my life as I knew it; I was up all night, a hag all day, and Marlboro Man was completely on his own. I wanted nothing to do with anyone on earth, my husband included.

"How are you doing today?" he'd ask. I'd resent that I had to expend the energy to answer.

"Want me to hold the baby while you get up and get dressed?" he'd offer. I'd crumble that he didn't like my robe.

"Hey, Mama—wanna take the baby for a drive?" Not no, but *hell* no. We'll die if we leave our cocoon. The rays from the sun will fry us and turn us to ashes. And I'd have to put on normal clothes. Forget it.

I'd kicked into survival mode in the most literal sense of the word— not only was laundry out of the question, but so was dinner, casual conversation, or any social interaction at all. I had become a shell of a person—no more human than the stainless steel milk machines in dairy farms in Wisconsin, and half as interesting. Any identity I'd previously had as a wife, daughter, friend, or productive member of the human race had melted away the second my ducts filled with milk. My mom dropped by to help once or twice, but I couldn't emotionally process her presence. I hid in my room with the door shut as she did the dishes and washed laundry without help or input from me. Marlboro Man's mom came to help, too, but I couldn't be myself around her and holed up in my room. I didn't even care enough to pray for help. Not that it would have helped; stainless steel milk machines have no soul.

*B*ETSY CAME to visit two weeks after I returned from the hospital, though I wasn't sure I cared. She picked up the house and kept laundry loads going and even held the baby for two-minute pockets in between her frequent feedings. With zero assistance or conversation from me, my kid sister cooked chicken noodle soup and tacos and our mother's delectable lasagna. She even learned how to chase the stray cows that made their way into our yard. I waddled into the kitchen to get a drink of water one morning to find her waving a broom and running around the yard. *Maybe she can just move in here and take my place,* I fantasized. *She'd like it out here. And she's cute and fun and thin . . . she and Marlboro Man should get along just great.*

Deep in the throes of postpartum desperation, I wanted no part of any of it anymore. Not the cows, not the yard, not the laundry. Not even the cowboy that came along with it, the one working his fingers to the bone day in and day out as he tried to negotiate the ever-changing markets and figure out the best course of action to take for his ranch and new baby and wife, who'd spiraled from the young, full-of-life woman he'd married ten months earlier to someone who hardly existed anymore.

Betsy, seventy-two hours into her visit, had picked up on all of this. She waited until Marlboro Man left to work cattle that morning before giving it to me straight.

"You kinda look like crap," she said, an ironically sweet tone in her voice.

"Shut up!" I barked. "You try doing this sometime!"

"I mean, I know it's hard and all . . . ," she began.

I held up my hand. "Don't even say it," I ordered. "You seriously have no idea." My eyes welled up with tears.

"Fine," she said, folding a pair of jeans. "But you need to at least take a shower and put on some cute clothes. It'll make you feel better."

"Clothes will not make me feel better!" I yelled, cradling the baby close.

"I promise, they will," she argued. "I'm convinced you cannot be happy if you wear that robe any longer."

I defied her suggestions and stayed in bed, and Betsy made her way out to the kitchen and threw together some sandwiches. I ate them, but only to keep my milk production going.

I ate four of her chocolate chip cookies for the same reason, then, still grimy and disheveled, climbed back into bed.

Marlboro Man returned home late that afternoon and came into the bedroom, eating a chocolate chip cookie along the way. The baby and I had just woken up from a two-hour nap, and he plopped down on the bed next to us. Without speaking, he stroked her little head with his index finger. I watched him the entire time; his eyes never left her. The room was quiet; the whole house was, in fact. Betsy must have gone out to the laundry room to switch loads. Without thinking, my arm found its way over to him and draped across his back. It was the first time I'd so much as touched him since I'd come home from the hospital. He glanced at me, flashed a faint smile, and draped his arm over my middle . . . and, magically, blessedly, the three of us fell back asleep—Marlboro Man in his mud-stained clothes, me in my milk-stained pajamas, and our perfect little child resting peacefully between our bodies.

*W*HEN I woke up an hour later, something had changed. Maybe it was the sleep . . . maybe it was the tender moment with Marlboro Man . . . maybe it was my sister's tough-love pep talk, or a combination of the three. I got out of bed quietly and made my way to the shower, where I washed and scrubbed and polished my body with every single bath product I could find. By the time I turned off the water, the bathroom smelled like lemongrass and lavender, wisteria and watermelon. The aromatherapy worked; while I didn't exactly feel beautiful again, I felt less like Jabba the Hut. I peeked out of the bathroom and through the bedroom door; Marlboro Man and the baby were still sound asleep. So I kept going, brushing on translucent powder and a little bit of pink blush, and adding some putty-colored eye shadow and a good coat or two of mascara. With each stroke of the brush, each wave of the wand, I felt more and more like myself. A light smudge of grape-colored lip gloss sealed the deal.

On a roll, I tiptoed into the bedroom and reached into the closet for my soft black maternity leggings, the ones that had been replaced by nasty plaid pajama bottoms fourteen days earlier. I ran my hands along the line of tops that hung on the rod, instinctively landing on a loose-fitting light blue top I'd been able to wear in the earlier months of pregnancy. It was pretty and light and feminine—a stark contrast to the dark green terry cloth robe that had been permanently affixed to my body in recent days. I sneaked back into the bathroom and changed into my new uniform, finishing it off with a pair of dangly mother-of-pearl earrings I'd picked up in a gift shop in Sydney, probably before I'd even conceived. Not wanting to turn on the noisy hair dryer, I scrunched my hair between my fingers to give it some body. Then I stood back and took a good, long look in the mirror.

I recognized myself again. The pale, spiritless ghost had been replaced by a slightly tired and moderately puffy version of my former normal self. I was no beauty queen, not by a long shot . . . but I was me again. The shower had been, if not an exorcism, a baptism. I'd been reborn. I shuddered, imagining what Marlboro Man had thought every time he'd seen me shuffle around in my dingy white terry cloth slippers, my hair on top of my head in a neon green scrunchie. I brushed my teeth, shook my hair, and walked out of the bathroom . . . just as Marlboro Man was waking up.

"Wow," he said, pausing midstretch. "You look good, Mama."

I smiled.

That night, Tim came over. Betsy made wings and brownies, and the five of us—Marlboro Man, Tim, Betsy, the baby, and I—sat and talked, laughed, and watched a John Wayne movie.

I was exhausted and depleted. And it was one of the best nights of my life.

I WOKE UP at nine the next morning, engorged but feeling alive. Almost as if she'd received some sort of office memo regarding the new optimism in the house, my new baby—wrinkled and skinny and helpless—had slept peacefully next to me all night, waking only twice to eat. I touched my finger to her tiny arm, still covered in soft translucent fuzz, and baby love washed over me in a rushing wave. Since the first night home from the hospital, desperation had moved in and rendered me incapable of savoring a single moment with her. Until now. I stared at her little ears, inhaled her indescribable scent, and placed my palm on her perfect head, closing my eyes and thanking God for such an undeserved gift. She was perfection.

When we finally surfaced from the bedroom, Betsy was stirring a pot on the stove. Marlboro Man was gone for the day, driving with Tim to check on some wheat pasture in the southern part of the state. It was Betsy's last day on the ranch; her summer school class would begin the following week, and she had to get back to the real world. And it was time. Her work here was done.

"What's that?" I asked, looking at the stove.

"Cinnamon rolls," she said, grabbing a packet of yeast from the pantry.

My mouth watered on the spot. Our mom's cinnamon rolls. They were beyond delicious, a fact confirmed not just by our immediate family, but also by the neighbors, church members, and friends who received them as Christmas gifts year after year during my childhood. It was a holiday ritual, one that lasted almost a full twenty-four hours. My mom would get out of bed early, scald milk, sugar, and oil in separate large pots, then use the mixture to make dough. The three of us would roll the dough into large rectangles, then douse them with obscene amounts of melted butter, cinnamon, and sugar before rolling them into logs and slicing them individually. Then, after baking, we'd drizzle a coffee-maple icing on the rolls and my mom would deliver them while they were still warm in the pan.

They were the best cinnamon rolls in existence. Why hadn't I made them yet?

Later, when the dough was ready and Betsy and I rolled and drizzled, the baby napped blissfully in the bouncer seat on the floor. I thought about my mom, and the countless times we'd made cinnamon rolls together . . . and all the beautiful memories that were cemented in my mind wherein these beautiful, gooey cinnamon rolls were front and center. And when I sunk my fork into a finished roll and took my first bite, I could swear I heard the comforting voice of my mom, who, I realized, had drenched my childhood with more love and affection and fun than any child should have.

I imagined her smile . . . and smiled, too.

Chapter Thirty-five
FAIR BLOWS THE WIND

ARLBORO MAN and Tim had buckled down and been able to push through the acute financial danger of the previous fall. The markets were improving, and the light at the end of the tunnel was becoming brighter. Still, it was going to be an uphill climb. The debt on the ranch was a continual reminder that sitting back and resting easy was never going to be a way of life for us. Marlboro Man didn't have a side profession he could use to supplement a ranching operation; he had to do it the old-fashioned way: through blood, sweat, and tears. And prayer.

We'd permanently boarded up the large Indian house next to the little white house we called home. I couldn't imagine anytime soon when we'd be able to bite off the financial commitment of remodeling and furnishing it, and we had to keep it sealed up to keep the critters away. In a way, the boarded-up house was a nice, daily reminder of what might be someday but also what didn't really matter all that much. Our blueprints were rolled up and neatly tucked in a closet—right next to my wedding veil and wedding shoes and prepregnancy Anne Klein jeans, which weren't really part of my life anymore.

*O*UR BABY was two months old on that warm September evening when the skies turned a disturbing shade of pink. I knew the color well; it's that of a sky whose oxygen is being sucked away by a distant, ominous force. I knew a storm was coming; I could smell it in the air. Marlboro Man was on a remote section of the ranch, helping Tim process steers. Much stronger now that the baby was sleeping through the night, I'd been catching up on laundry and housework all day. By late afternoon, I had a pot roast in the oven and the black clouds had started to move in.

"I'll be home in an hour," Marlboro Man said, calling me from his mobile phone.

"Is it raining there?" I asked. "It's eerie here at our house."

"The lightning is striking out here," he said. "It's kind of exciting." I laughed. Marlboro Man loved thunderstorms.

I hung up and kept folding but noticed the breeze outside—which had been picking up all afternoon—had completely stopped blowing. The trees were still. The sky was frightening. I shivered, even though it wasn't the least bit cold.

I flipped on the TV and immediately saw a radar map with a nicely dressed weatherman standing in front. I was able to determine, from the shape of our county and my general knowledge of our whereabouts therein, that the area on the map that was receiving the most finger pointing and frantic discussion was the one surrounding our immediate area—a swath of dark red in the shape of a hook wrapped perfectly around our county. *Yikes,* I said to myself. *That doesn't look good.*

Sound asleep in her swing, the baby didn't flinch when the phone rang a second time. It was Marlboro Man again.

"You need to take the baby to the cellar in the brick house," he said, a new urgency to his voice.

"What?" I said, my heart pounding in my chest. "What do you mean?"

"There's a tornado near Fairfax and it's moving east-southeast," he said quickly. "You need to head over there just in case."

"Just in case?" I scrambled around the room, looking for my shoes. "Wait—where do you fit into this scenario?"

"Look, just get on over there!" he said. "It'll take me twenty minutes to get there!" He wasn't kidding. And Marlboro Man loved storms. This was serious. I threw on a pair of Marlboro Man's mud boots. It was the closest thing I could find.

I hung up and grabbed a huge throw from the sofa. I had no idea why; I just knew I needed it. I also grabbed a pillow, three bottles of water, a flashlight, a handful of granola bars, and my baby . . . then opened the door and ran into the strange pink world, crossing the yard outside of our house and running up the porch steps of the yellow brick Indian house that, once upon a time, would have been our home. Tucking the bottles of water and blanket under my arm, I flung open the side door—the only entrance to the boarded-up building—then ran inside and slammed the door behind me. It was dark; there was no electricity. I used the flashlight to guide me to the door that led to the stairs of the basement, and without thinking, I descended into the dungeon. Not because I was deathly afraid of the tornado or because Marlboro Man had told me to . . . but because I was now a mother. It was the first time I'd ever experienced that level of protective instinct—the kind where no choice is involved. It was the only thing that allowed me to forget the fact that rattlesnakes had once built a nest down there.

I parked myself on a bench against the basement wall, completely unsure of what was going to happen. The baby was awake now, so I nursed her as I sat in the quiet, dark basement, listening for any signs of destruction overhead. I thought about Marlboro Man. The cowboys. Neighboring ranchers. Our horses and cattle. My in-laws. *Where are they, and are they safe? Will the storm get them before it gets me? Are houses and barns being leveled as I sit here, safe in this scary basement? What if the house blows off the foundation and sucks us into the sky?* I wrapped the baby tightly in the soft throw I'd brought along . . . and buried my face in the top of her bald head, breathing in her beautiful scent. The wind was howling now. I could hear it.

I sat there in the darkness—just a faint hint of early-evening sky visible through a rectangular basement window. Slowly rocking my child back and forth, I began to reflect on the months that had brought me here, the unbelievable experiences I'd had and transitions I'd made: From Los Angeles back to the middle of the country. From independent person fleeing a relationship to one madly in love with a cowboy. From autonomous human to wife . . . from *wife* to *wife and mother* . . . from vibrant, sexual being to baby-feeding machine . . . from depressed and desperate new mother to a slightly stronger and more fortified version of myself. From anxious, preoccupied daughter of now-divorced parents to an adult woman with her own family.

It wasn't about me anymore. I had a child. A husband who needed me to be there for him in the midst of what was turning out to be a terrible time to be making a living in agriculture. I didn't have time to get mired in the angst of my own circumstances anymore. I didn't have time for the past. My family—my new family—was all that mattered to me. My child. And always and forever, Marlboro Man.

And then he appeared—walking down the basement steps in his Wranglers and rain-drenched boots. He stepped into the basement, a warm, gentle smile on his face. It was Marlboro Man. He was there.

"Hey, Mama . . . ," he called. "It's all fine."

The storm had passed us by, the funnel cloud dissipating before it could do any damage.

"Hey, Daddy," I answered. It was the first time I'd ever called him that.

Looking on the ground at the water bottles and granola bars, he asked, "What's all this for?"

I shrugged. "I wasn't sure how long I'd be down here."

He laughed. "You're funny," he said as he scooped our sleeping baby from my arms and threw the blanket over his shoulder. "Let's go eat. I'm hungry." We walked across the yard to our cozy little white house, where we ate pot roast with mashed potatoes and watched *The Big Country* with Gregory Peck . . . and spent the night listening to a blessed September thunderstorm send rain falling from the sky.

THE NEXT morning, after the storm had passed and Marlboro Man had left with his horse, I sat and fed our baby on the rocking chair outside the front door. I watched the bountiful eastern sky change from black to cerulean to magenta to an impossible shade of reddish orange, and I breathed in the country air, relishing the new strength I'd felt building inside of me. I knew our problems weren't over. Only one year into our marriage, we'd been through enough that I knew the storm from the night before was but one of many we would face together in the coming years. I knew the last of the struggles weren't fully behind us.

But still . . . I couldn't shake the feeling.

I could see it. I knew.

The sun was getting ready to rise.

Recipes

Here are some of my favorite recipes from my
past, from my present . . . and from my heart.

PASTA PRIMAVERA
8 servings

Compliments of my vegetarian former life.

1 pound penne

4 tablespoons butter

2 tablespoons olive oil

½ onion, chopped

4 garlic cloves, minced

1 cup bite-size broccoli pieces

2 carrots, peeled and sliced thin

1 red bell pepper, cut into strips

1 yellow squash, sliced thin

2 zucchini, sliced thin

8 ounces crimini or button
    mushrooms, sliced thin

Salt to taste

¼ to ½ cup dry white wine

½ cup low-sodium vegetable or
    chicken broth (plus more as
    needed)

1 cup heavy cream

1 cup half-and-half (plus more as
    needed)

½ cup freshly grated Parmesan
    cheese (plus more for garnish)

Freshly ground black pepper to taste

½ cup frozen peas

8 basil leaves, cut into a chiffonade
    (plus more for garnish)

Cook the pasta according to the package directions.

Heat 2 tablespoons of the butter and the olive oil in a large skillet over medium-high heat. Add the onion and garlic and cook for 1 or 2 minutes, until they start to turn translucent. Throw in the broccoli, and stir. Add the carrots. Cook for 1 minute, then transfer the vegetables to a large plate.

Add the red pepper strips to the skillet. Stir them around for a minute, then transfer them to the plate.

Add 1 tablespoon butter to the skillet. Add the squash and zucchini, cook for less than a minute, and transfer to the plate. Cook the mushrooms for 1 or 2 minutes, add salt to taste, and transfer to the plate.

To make the sauce, pour ¼ to ½ cup wine into the skillet. Add the broth and the remaining 1 tablespoon of butter and scrape the bottom of the skillet. Cook for 2 to 3 minutes, or until the liquid starts to thicken.

Stir in the cream and half-and-half. Add the Parmesan and salt and pepper to taste.

Dump the veggies, peas, and basil into the sauce. Add the pasta and stir. If the sauce seems a little thick, or if there doesn't seem to be enough sauce, add a good splash of broth and a little more half-and-half.

Adjust the seasonings and garnish with additional Parmesan and basil as desired.

TIRAMISU
12 servings

My one true love . . . before I met Marlboro Man, anyway.

5 whole egg yolks

¼ cup plus 4 tablespoons sugar, divided

¾ cup Marsala wine, divided

1 pound mascarpone cheese, at room temperature

1 cup heavy cream

1½ cups brewed espresso or coffee

1 tablespoon vanilla

One 7-ounce package ladyfingers (savoiardi)

Cocoa powder, for dusting

Prepare a medium saucepan of simmering water. Place the egg yolks in a medium glass bowl. Add ¼ cup of the sugar and whisk until the eggs are pale yellow. Place the mixing bowl in the saucepan of simmering water. Gradually add ½ cup of the Marsala, whisking constantly.

Cook the mixture, scraping the sides and bottom of the bowl occasionally, for 5 minutes. Cover with plastic wrap and refrigerate for at least 45 minutes, or until cool. (This mixture is called zabaglione.)

Place the mascarpone cheese in a small bowl and stir until smooth. In a large mixing bowl, combine the heavy cream and the remaining 4 tablespoons sugar and whip until soft peaks form. Add the mascarpone cheese and the zabaglione. Fold the mixture gently. Cover with plastic wrap and refrigerate for 1 to 2 hours.

In a small mixing bowl, combine the espresso or coffee, the remaining ¼ cup Marsala, and the vanilla.

Arrange the ladyfingers in a single layer in a 9 x 13-inch pan. Spoon ½ to 1 tablespoon of the coffee mixture over each ladyfinger. Plop $^1/_3$ of the zabaglione mixture on top of the coffee mixture and spread smoothly. Sprinkle a thin layer of cocoa powder on top. Repeat the layering process two more times.

Cover and refrigerate the tiramisu for a few hours before serving. To serve, spoon helpings onto individual plates.

NOTE: Tiramisu does not last beyond 24 to 36 hours, as everything eventually starts to break down and become soupy.

LINGUINE WITH CLAM SAUCE
6 servings

Serve to cowboys with caution.

1 pound linguine

1 tablespoon olive oil

2 tablespoons butter

3 garlic cloves, minced

Two 10-ounce cans chopped clams, drained, juice reserved

¾ cup white wine

Juice of ½ lemon, plus lemon slices for garnish

2 tablespoons flat-leaf parsley

¾ cup heavy cream

Salt and freshly ground black pepper to taste

Freshly grated Parmesan cheese, for garnish

Cook the linguine al dente, according to the package directions.

In a large skillet over medium-high heat, add the olive oil and 1 tablespoon of the butter.

Add the garlic and clams. Stir and cook for 3 minutes.

Pour in the white wine, scraping the bottom of the pan with a spoon. Cook for 3 to 4 minutes, until the sauce has reduced. Add the remaining 1 tablespoon of butter and stir to melt.

Reduce the heat and squeeze in the lemon juice.

Sprinkle in the parsley and pour in the cream. Add salt and pepper to taste and more clam juice if needed. Cook over low heat for 3 minutes.

Pour the pasta into a heated serving bowl. Pour the contents of the skillet over the pasta. Toss to combine and top with the Parmesan. Garnish each bowl with a slice of lemon.

MARINATED FLANK STEAK
4 servings

Finished product should not resemble leather.

½ **cup soy sauce**

½ **cup sherry**

3 **tablespoons honey**

2 **tablespoons sesame oil**

2 **heaping tablespoons minced ginger**

5 **garlic cloves, minced**

½ **teaspoon crushed red pepper flakes**

1 **flank steak**

Combine all the ingredients except the flank steak in a glass or ceramic dish. Place the flank steak in the dish and flip it to coat both sides of the meat with the marinade. Cover with plastic wrap and refrigerate for at least 3 to 6 hours.

Heat a grill or grill pan over high heat. Grill the steak for 2 minutes on each side, rotating the meat 90 degrees once on each side to achieve nice grill marks.

Remove the meat to a cutting board and let it rest for a few minutes before slicing.

Cut the meat against the grain into strips and serve with potatoes or pasta.

TAGLIARINI QUATTRO FORMAGGI (FOUR-CHEESE PASTA)

6 servings

Slightly undercook the pasta so the dish won't look like grits.

1 cup heavy cream

1 pound tagliarini or angel hair pasta

2 tablespoons butter

½ cup grated Fontina cheese

½ cup grated Parmesan cheese

½ cup grated Romano cheese

4 ounces goat cheese

Salt and freshly ground pepper to taste

¼ teaspoon ground nutmeg

1 garlic clove, halved (for rubbing bowls)

Warm the cream in a small saucepan over low heat.

Prepare the pasta according to the package directions, but just until al dente; do not overcook!

Drain the pasta and return it to the pot. Add the butter, the warmed cream, and the cheeses. Stir gently, allowing the cheeses to melt and coat the pasta. Season with salt, pepper, and the nutmeg. Stir gently to combine.

Rub pasta bowls with the garlic. Serve the pasta in the bowls.

ROASTED BEEF TENDERLOIN
8 servings

Serve to any vegetarians that might need converting.

**One 6- to 7-pound whole beef
    tenderloin (or two 3-pound beef
    tenderloin butts)**

2 tablespoons kosher salt

3 teaspoons black pepper

1 tablespoon sugar

⅓ cup plus 1 tablespoon olive oil

2 tablespoons bacon grease

1 tablespoon butter

Preheat the oven to 450°F.

Trim all the fat and tough tissue from the tenderloin (or have the butcher do it!).

Combine the salt, pepper, sugar, ⅓ cup of the olive oil, and the bacon grease in a small bowl. Set aside.

Heat a heavy skillet over very high heat. Add the butter to the skillet with the remaining 1 tablespoon olive oil. When the pan is very hot, place the tenderloin in it. Sear each side for 1 to 1½ minutes, until it starts to turn brown.

Place the meat in a baking pan fitted with a roasting rack and pour the seasoning/bacon grease mixture over the top. Rub the seasoning mixture into the meat with your fingers, making sure it coats the surface evenly. Insert a meat thermometer sideways into the thickest part of the meat and roast for 15 to 20 minutes, until the thermometer registers 120°F to 125°F.

Remove the meat from the oven and allow it to rest on a cutting board for 10 minutes.

Slice and serve.

TOMATO-BASIL PIZZA
8 servings

Where's the beef?

CRUST

1 teaspoon or ½ packet active dry yeast

4 cups all-purpose flour

1 teaspoon kosher salt

½ cup extra virgin olive oil, plus more for drizzling

TOPPING

5 tablespoons prepared pesto

Kosher salt

1 pound fresh mozzarella, sliced thin

5 Roma tomatoes, sliced

½ cup grated Parmesan cheese

To make the crust, pour 1½ cups warm water into a bowl. Sprinkle the yeast over the water and set aside.

Combine the flour and salt in a mixing bowl.

Drizzle the olive oil into the flour/salt mixture by hand or with an electric mixer on low speed, and mix until just incorporated.

Gently stir the yeast mixture. Drizzle it into the flour/oil mixture and mix until the dough forms a ball.

Drizzle a little olive oil into a large, clean bowl. Toss the dough in the bowl to coat it with oil. Cover the bowl with a moist kitchen towel and set in a warm place to rise for 1 to 2 hours, or cover the bowl with plastic wrap and store in the fridge for up to 2 days.

When you are ready to prepare the pizza, preheat the oven to 500°F.

Divide the dough in half and store one half for another use (it can be frozen). Lightly drizzle olive oil on a pizza pan or rimmed baking sheet.

Use your hands to stretch the dough to the desired shape, pressing the dough into the pans with your fingers. The thinner the better!

Spread the pesto over the crust and sprinkle lightly with kosher salt.

Place half of the sliced mozzarella in a layer over the pesto.

Place the sliced tomatoes over the mozzarella.

Top with the remaining mozzarella, then sprinkle generously with the Parmesan.

Bake for 8 to 11 minutes, or until the cheeses are melted and the crust is golden brown.

LASAGNA
8 servings

As meaty and magnificent as it gets.

1 tablespoon olive oil	**Freshly ground black pepper**
Salt	**10 to 12 basil leaves, chopped fine**
10 ounces lasagna noodles	**¼ cup chopped flat-leaf parsley**
1½ pounds ground beef	**3 cups low-fat cottage cheese**
1 pound hot breakfast sausage meat	**2 eggs, beaten**
4 garlic cloves, finely chopped	**1 cup grated Parmesan cheese**
Two 14.5-ounce cans whole tomatoes	**1 pound mozzarella cheese, sliced thin**
Two 6-ounce cans tomato paste	

Bring a large pot of water to a boil. Add the olive oil and a dash of salt. Cook the lasagna noodles according to the package directions until al dente. Drain the noodles and lay them flat on a piece of aluminum foil.

In a large skillet over medium-high heat, sauté the ground beef, sausage, and garlic until brown. Drain off the excess fat.

Add the tomatoes with their juice, tomato paste, ½ teaspoon salt, and freshly ground black pepper to taste. Mix well. Simmer over low heat, uncovered, for 45 minutes, stirring occasionally.

Add half the basil and half the parsley to the meat mixture and stir.

In a medium bowl, combine the cottage cheese, the eggs, ½ cup of the Parmesan, and the remaining herbs. Mix well.

Preheat the oven to 350°F.

To assemble, lay 4 lasagna noodles in the bottom of a deep rectangular baking pan. The noodles should slightly overlap.

Spoon half the cottage cheese mixture onto the noodles. Spread to distribute evenly. Lay half of the mozzarella on top of the cottage cheese mixture.

Spoon just under half of the meat mixture on top of the mozzarella. Spread evenly, being careful not to disrupt the layers below.

Repeat these layers, ending with a thick layer of meat. Top with the remaining Parmesan and bake for 35 to 45 minutes.

Allow to stand 10 minutes before cutting into squares.

CHICKEN SPAGHETTI
8 servings

Soothes the soul . . . and warms a cowboy.

1 cut-up fryer chicken

1 pound spaghetti, broken into 2-inch pieces

2 cans cream of mushroom soup

2½ cups grated cheddar cheese

1 small onion, diced

¼ cup finely diced green bell pepper

One 4-ounce jar diced pimientos, drained

1 teaspoon seasoned salt

Freshly ground black pepper to taste

⅛ to ¼ teaspoon cayenne pepper to taste

Add the chicken to a stockpot. Cover with water and bring to a boil. Reduce the heat to medium and simmer until the chicken is cooked, about 25 minutes.

Remove the chicken pieces from the water using tongs or a slotted spoon and set them aside on a plate to cool.

Remove 2 cups of broth from the pot and set aside.

Bring the remaining broth back to a boil and add the spaghetti. Cook it al dente. Drain the spaghetti, discarding the cooking liquid. Place the spaghetti in a large bowl.

With two forks (or your fingers), remove the bones from the chicken. Shred or cut the meat into bite-size chunks and add it to the bowl.

Preheat the oven to 350°F.

Add to the bowl the cream of mushroom soup, 2 cups of the cheese, the onion, green pepper, pimientos, seasoned salt, black pepper, cayenne pepper, chicken, and reserved broth. Stir well to combine, then taste to check the seasonings.

Pour the mixture into a large baking pan and top with the remaining ½ cup of cheese. Bake for 35 to 45 minutes, or until bubbly.

CHILI
8 servings

Sticks to ribs. Freezes beautifully.

2 pounds ground beef

2 garlic cloves, chopped

One 8-ounce can tomato sauce

1 teaspoon ground oregano

1 tablespoon ground cumin

¼ teaspoon cayenne pepper (optional)

2 tablespoons chili powder

1 teaspoon salt

¼ cup masa (corn flour) or cornmeal

OPTIONAL INGREDIENTS

1 can pinto beans, drained

1 can kidney beans, drained

1 jalapeño, seeded and finely diced

1 can diced tomatoes and chilies (such as Rotel brand)

FOR SERVING

Shredded cheddar cheese

Chopped onion

Corn chips

In a large pot or Dutch oven over medium heat, cook the beef and garlic until the meat is browned, stirring often. Drain off the excess fat.

Pour in the tomato sauce, spices, and salt. Stir, cover, and reduce the heat to low. Simmer for 1 hour, stirring occasionally. (If the chili becomes dry, add ½ cup water at a time as needed.)

After an hour, combine the masa with ½ cup water in a small bowl. Stir together with a fork. Dump the masa mixture into the chili. Stir well, taste to adjust the seasonings, and cook for 10 minutes.

Stir in the optional ingredients, if using, and cook for 10 more minutes.

Serve with shredded cheddar, chopped onion, and corn chips, as desired.

POT ROAST
6 servings

It's the right thing to do.

Salt and black pepper to taste

One 3- to 5-pound chuck roast

2 to 3 tablespoons olive oil

2 onions, peeled and halved

6 carrots, cut into 2-inch chunks

1 cup red wine (optional)

3 to 4 cups beef stock

3 sprigs fresh thyme

3 sprigs fresh rosemary

Preheat the oven to 275°F.

Generously salt and pepper the chuck roast on both sides.

Heat a large pot or Dutch oven over medium-high heat. Add 2 tablespoons of the olive oil. When the oil is very hot, add the onions, browning them on one side and then the other, about 1 minute per side. Remove the onions to a plate.

Throw the carrots into the hot pan and toss them around a bit until slightly browned, about 1 minute. Remove the carrots to the plate.

If needed, add a bit more olive oil to the very hot pan. Place the roast in the pan and sear it on all sides until nice and brown all over, about 2 minutes. Remove the roast to a plate.

With the burner still on high, deglaze the pan by adding the red wine or 1 cup of the stock and scraping the pan with a whisk to loosen all the flavorful bits.

Place the roast back in the pan and add enough stock to cover the meat halfway (about 2 to 3 cups). Add the onions, carrots, thyme, and rosemary.

Cover the pot and roast the meat for approximately 3 hours (for a 3-pound roast) or 4 hours (for a 4- to 5-pound roast). The roast is done when the meat is tender and pulls apart easily with two forks.

Slice and serve with Creamy Mashed Potatoes (page 336).

CREAMY MASHED POTATOES
12 servings

Sinful. In a forgivable way.

5 pounds Yukon Gold or russet potatoes

1½ sticks butter, softened, plus ½ stick for dotting

One 8-ounce package cream cheese, softened

½ cup half-and-half

½ teaspoon seasoned salt

Salt and black pepper to taste

Milk, as needed for thinning

Chopped chives, for garnish

Peel the potatoes and rinse them in cold water. Cut the potatoes in quarters, place them in a large pot, and add water to cover the potatoes. Bring to a boil over medium heat and cook for 20 to 25 minutes, or until fork tender.

Preheat the oven to 350°F.

Drain the potatoes and return them to the pan. With the burner on low heat, mash the potatoes with a potato masher for about 2 minutes to release the steam. Turn off the burner.

Add the butter, cream cheese, half-and-half, seasoned salt, and salt and pepper. Stir to combine, and if the mixture needs thinning, add a little milk. Taste to check the seasoning.

Spread the mashed potatoes in a large casserole pan and dot the surface with the remaining butter. Cover with foil (you can refrigerate it for up to 2 days at this point) and bake for 15 minutes. Remove the foil and bake for 10 more minutes.

Sprinkle with chopped chives and serve immediately.

BEEF STEW WITH MUSHROOMS
6 servings

For long, cold winters on the ranch. Extra wine helps, too.

4 tablespoons flour

**2 pounds cubed beef stew meat
(sirloin)**

4 tablespoons butter

2 tablespoons olive oil

2 shallots, minced

3 garlic cloves, minced

8 ounces white mushrooms

½ cup red wine

**Half a 10½-ounce can beef
consommé**

Salt and pepper to taste

2 fresh thyme sprigs

Cooked egg noodles, for serving

Sprinkle 2 tablespoons of the flour over the meat and toss to coat.

In a heavy pot or Dutch oven, melt the butter in the olive oil over high heat. Working in batches, add the meat and sear it until brown on all sides, taking care not to crowd the meat, a few minutes per batch. Set the meat aside on a plate as it's done.

Reduce heat to medium-low and add the shallots and the garlic. Sauté for 2 minutes. Add the mushrooms and cook for 2 minutes. Pour in the wine, the consommé, and ½ cup water.

Add salt and pepper to taste and stir. Bring to a boil, then add the browned meat and the juices from the plate. Reduce heat to low and add the thyme.

Cover and simmer for 90 minutes, or until the meat is very tender. In a small bowl, mix the remaining 2 tablespoons flour with ¼ cup water and stir it into the stew. Cook the stew for 10 minutes, until thickened. Turn off the heat and allow the stew to sit for 15 to 20 minutes before serving.

Serve with egg noodles.

FRIED ROUND STEAK
6 servings

Lifeblood for hungry cowboys.

½ cup canola oil

1 cup all-purpose flour

1 teaspoon seasoned salt

Ground black pepper

3 pounds cube steak (round steak that's been extra tenderized)

Salt

2 tablespoons butter

Heat the oil in a large skillet over medium heat.

On a plate, combine the flour, the seasoned salt, and 3 teaspoons of black pepper.

Season both sides of the cube steaks with salt and pepper. Dredge each piece in the flour mixture, pressing to coat with as much flour as possible.

Add the butter to the pan right before frying. When the butter is melted, add the steak, working in batches so as not to crowd the meat. Flip when the surface of the meat is deep golden brown and cook about 1 minute on the other side.

Remove to a paper towel–lined plate. Serve immediately.

CHOCOLATE CHIP COOKIES
3 dozen cookies

For a little pick-me-up . . . or a big chocolate fix.

½ cup (1 stick) butter, softened

½ cup (1 stick) margarine

1 cup firmly packed brown sugar

½ cup white sugar

2 eggs

2 teaspoons vanilla extract

2¼ cups plus 2 tablespoons all-purpose flour

1 heaping teaspoon instant coffee granules

1 teaspoon baking soda

1½ teaspoons salt

2 tablespoons flaxseeds, slightly crushed with a rolling pin (optional)

¾ cup semisweet chocolate chips

1 heaping cup milk chocolate chips

Preheat the oven to 375°F.

In a large bowl, stir together the butter, margarine, brown sugar, and white sugar until combined. Add the eggs and vanilla and mix thoroughly.

In a separate bowl, combine the flour, instant coffee, baking soda, and salt. Add the flour mixture to the butter/sugar mixture in batches, stirring gently after each addition.

Stir in the flaxseeds, if using, and the chocolate chips.

Drop balls of the dough onto an ungreased cookie sheet and bake for 11 to 13 minutes, or until golden. Move the cookies to a rack and eat them warm.

CINNAMON ROLLS
Makes 4 dozen rolls (using about 7 pie pans — I often use aluminum ones for easy gift giving)

Guaranteed to heal an aching heart.

DOUGH

1 quart whole milk

1 cup vegetable oil

1 cup sugar

2 packages (4½ teaspoons) active dry yeast

9 cups all-purpose flour

1 heaping teaspoon baking powder

1 scant teaspoon baking soda

1 heaping tablespoon salt

FILLING

2 cups melted butter, plus more as needed

2 cups sugar, plus more as needed

¼ cup ground cinnamon

MAPLE ICING

1 pound powdered sugar

2 teaspoons maple flavoring

½ cup whole milk

¼ cup melted butter

¼ cup strongly brewed coffee

⅛ teaspoon salt

To make the dough, heat the milk, vegetable oil, and sugar in a large saucepan over medium heat; do not allow the mixture to boil. Set aside and cool to a little warmer than lukewarm.

Sprinkle the yeast on top and let it sit on the milk mixture for 1 minute.

Add 8 cups of the flour. Stir until just combined. Cover with a clean kitchen towel and set aside in a relatively warm place for 1 hour.

Remove the towel and add the baking powder, baking soda, salt, and remaining 1 cup of flour. Stir thoroughly to combine. Refrigerate the dough for at least 1 hour, punching it down if it begins to rise too much.

To assemble the rolls, remove half the dough from the pan. On a floured baking surface, roll the dough into a large rectangle, about 30 × 10 inches.

Pour 1 cup of the melted butter over the surface of the dough. Use your fingers to spread the butter evenly.

Sprinkle 1 cup of the sugar over the butter. Sprinkle generously with half of the cinnamon.

Beginning at the end farthest from you, roll the rectangle tightly toward you. Use both hands and work slowly, being careful to keep the roll tight. Don't worry if the filling oozes out as you work!

When you reach the end, pinch the seam together. Cut 1½-inch slices with a sharp knife. Place the sliced rolls onto buttered pie pans, being careful not to overcrowd.

Repeat with the other half of the dough.

Cover the pans with towels and set aside to rise for 20 minutes. Preheat the oven to 375°F.

Bake for 13 to 17 minutes, or until golden brown.

While the rolls are baking, combine all the icing ingredients in a large bowl, adjusting the proportions of sugar and liquid until you have the desired consistency.

Pour icing over warm rolls fresh out of the oven. Allow the icing to settle into the cracks and crevices.

Serve warm. You can also cover and freeze the cinnamon rolls for gift giving.

ACKNOWLEDGMENTS

To my friends and readers of my website, ThePioneerWoman.com, for your love, encouragement, and support over the past several years. I feel it daily. Thank you.

To my editor, Cassie Jones Morgan, for believing in me back when you didn't really have any reason to. You're the first, best, only, and last editor I'll ever have.

To Sharyn Rosenblum, for keeping me on track and making me smile.

To Susanna Einstein, for your help and support.

To my oldest friends, Jenn, Sarah, Jules, Mitch, Kash, Christy, Shaney, Ang, Kristi, Shelley, Susan, and Carrie.

To Mom, Dad, Nan, Chuck, Betsy, Doug, Mike, Missy, Tim, Hyacinth, Connell, Lela, Betty, Becky, Patsy, Edna Mae, Ga-Ga, and everyone who's loved me all my life.

To Bartlesville, for raising me.

To Pawhuska, for being my home.

To my kids, for being wonderful.

To Marlboro Man, for being mine.